KV-512-443

Professional Examinations

Managerial Level

Paper E2

Enterprise Management

EXAM PRACTICE KIT

CIMA
PUBLISHING

WORKING TOGETHER FOR YOU

ELSEVIER

KAPLAN
PUBLISHING

CIMA Publishing is an imprint of Elsevier
The Boulevard, Langford Lane, Kidlington, Oxford, OX5 1GB, UK
225 Wyman Street, Waltham, MA 02451, USA
Kaplan Publishing UK, Unit 2 The Business Centre, Molly Millars Lane, Wokingham, Berkshire RG41 2QZ

Copyright © 2012 Elsevier Limited and Kaplan Publishing Limited. All rights reserved.

No part of this publication may be reproduced, stored in a retrieval system or transmitted in any form or by any means electronic, mechanical, photocopying, recording or otherwise without the prior written permission of the publisher.

Permissions may be sought directly from Elsevier's Science and Technology Rights Department in Oxford, UK: phone: (+44) (0) 1865 843830; fax: (+44) (0) 1865 853333; email: permissions@elsevier.com. You may also complete your request online via the Elsevier homepage (http://elsevier.com), by selecting *Support & Contact* then *Copyright and Permission* and then *Obtaining Permissions*.

Acknowledgements

We are grateful to the Chartered Institute of Management Accountants for permission to reproduce past examination questions. The answers to CIMA Exams have been prepared by Kaplan Publishing, except in the case of the CIMA E2 Specimen paper, November 2010, March 2011, May 2011 and September 2011 answers where the official CIMA answers have been reproduced.

Notice

No responsibility is assumed by the publisher for any injury and/or damage to persons or property as a matter of products liability, negligence or otherwise, or from any use or operation of any methods, products, instructions or ideas contained in the material herein.

British Library Cataloguing in Publication Data
A catalogue record for this book is available from the British Library

ISBN: 978 0 85732 492 4

Printed and bound in Great Britain

11 12 11 10 9 8 7 6 5 4 3 2 1

CONTENTS

	Page
Index to questions and answers	v
Analysis of past papers	ix
Exam Technique	xi
Paper specific information	xiii
Reading and planning time	xv
Approach to revision	xvii

Section

Key features in this edition

In addition to providing a wide ranging bank of real past exam questions, we have also included in this edition:

- Paper specific information and advice on exam technique.

- Guidance to make your revision for this subject as effective as possible.

- Enhanced tutorial answers packed with specific key answer tips, technical tutorial notes and exam technique tips from our experienced tutors.

You will find a wealth of other resources to help you with your studies on the following sites:

www.EN-gage.co.uk

www.cimaglobal.com

INDEX TO QUESTIONS AND ANSWERS

INTRODUCTION

The style of the E2 exam is different to old syllabus Paper 5 questions. Accordingly the questions in this kit have been adapted to reflect the new style of paper.

Note that all questions in the kit are past CIMA exam papers. Papers before May 2010 are past CIMA P5 exam questions. Questions from the E2 exams are from May 2010 onwards.

The E2 specimen paper is included at the end of the kit.

KEY TO THE INDEX

PAPER ENHANCEMENTS

We have added the following enhancements to the answers in this exam practice kit:

Key answer tips

All answers include key answer tips to help your understanding of each question and how to tackle it.

Tutorial note

All answers include tutorial notes to explain some of the technical points in more detail.

Top tutor tips

For selected questions, we "walk through the answer" giving guidance on how to approach the questions with helpful 'tips from a top tutor', together with technical tutor notes.

These answers are indicated with the "footsteps" icon in the index.

Examiner's comments

For exams from November 2010 onwards, some of the examiner's post-exam guidance comments have been included. These have been reproduced with the kind permission of CIMA.

SECTION A STYLE QUESTIONS

SECTION B STYLE QUESTIONS

ANALYSIS OF PAST PAPERS

The table below summarises the key topics that have been tested in the new syllabus examinations to date.

Note that the references are to the number of the question in this edition of the exam practice kit, but the Specimen paper and the November 2011 paper are produced in their original form at the end of the kit and therefore these questions have retained their original numbering in the paper itself.

	Specimen paper	May 10	Nov 10	March 11	May 11	Sept 11
Competitive environments						
PEST analysis and its derivatives						
Stakeholder mapping	Q3					
Corporate appraisal			Q7			
Competitor analysis and competitive strategies		Q4			Q13	Q15
Competitive advantage						
Data for environmental analysis			Q46	Q10		
Porter's Five Forces	Q1				Q11	
Porter's Diamond			Q46			Q14
Value chain						
Discuss developments in strategic management						
Resource based view					Q12	Q16
Transaction cost view						
Ecological perspective						
Approaches to strategy	Q4					
Levels of strategy		Q6		Q9		
Mission/objectives/csf/targets				Q8		
Corporate social responsibility		Q5				
Tools and techniques of project management						
The definition of a programme, a project and project management	Q6				Q57	
Project management methodology models						Q58
Key tools for project managers	Q2	Q25	Q55	Q26/Q56	Q28	
Earned Value Management.						
Feasibility						
PRINCE2						
Production of basic plans for time, cost and quality		Q54		Q56		

	Specimen paper	May 10	Nov 10	March 11	May 11	Sept 11
Risk management						
Scenario planning and buffering						
Organisational structures			Q27			Q29
Teamwork, including the life-cycle of teams						
Control of time, cost and quality						
Project completion						
The use of post-completion audit and review						
The relationship of the project manager to the external environment						
Project stakeholders			Q55			
Role / skills of PM/(sponsor)	Q6	Q54			Q57	Q58
Effective operation of an organisation						
Power, authority, bureaucracy, leadership, responsibility and delegation						
Leadership theories			Q34		Q38	Q39
Organisational culture		Q33		Q37		
Conflict	Q7		Q36	Q64		Q66
Hofstede						
Managing people						
Disciplinary procedures						
Legal issues affecting work and employment						
Communication					Q65	Q66
Negotiation		Q62		Q64		
Managing the finance function		Q62				
Management of relationships with professional advisors						
The principles of corporate governance and the CIMA Code of Ethics for Professional Accountants	Q5					
How to lead and manage a team/ team building	Q7					
The use of systems of control within the organisation					Q65	
The role of a mentor, and the process of mentoring.			Q35			

EXAM TECHNIQUE

- Use the allocated **20 minutes reading and planning time** at the beginning of the exam:
    - read the questions and examination requirements carefully, and
    - begin planning your answers.
- **Divide the time** you spend on questions in proportion to the marks on offer:
    - there are 1.8 minutes available per mark in the examination
    - within that, try to allow time at the end of each question to review your answer and address any obvious issues

    Whatever happens, always keep your eye on the clock and **do not over run on any part of any question!**
- Spend the last **five minutes** of the examination:
    - reading through your answers, and
    - **making any additions or corrections**.
- If you **get completely stuck** with a question:
    - leave space in your answer book, and
    - **return to it later.**
- Stick to the question and **tailor your answer** to what you are asked.
    - pay particular attention to the verbs in the question.
- If you do not understand what a question is asking, **state your assumptions**.

    Even if you do not answer in precisely the way the examiner hoped, you should be given some credit, if your assumptions are reasonable.
- You should do everything you can to make things easy for the marker.

    The marker will find it easier to identify the points you have made if your **answers are legible**.
- **Written questions**:

    Your answer should have:
    - a clear structure
    - a brief introduction, a main section and a conclusion.

    Be concise.

    It is better to write a little about a lot of different points than a great deal about one or two points.
- **Computations**:

    It is essential to include all your workings in your answers.

    Many computational questions require the use of a standard format:

    e.g. income tax computations, corporation tax computations and capital gains.

    Be sure you know these formats thoroughly before the exam and use the layouts that you see in the answers given in this book and in model answers.
- **Reports, memos and other documents**:

    Some questions ask you to present your answer in the form of a report, a memo, a letter or other document.

    Make sure that you use the correct format – there could be easy marks to gain here.

PAPER SPECIFIC INFORMATION

THE EXAM

FORMAT OF THE EXAM

	Number of marks
5 compulsory questions worth 10 marks each	50
1 or 2 compulsory questions worth 50 marks in total	50
	100

Total time allowed: 3 hours plus 20 minutes reading and planning time.

PASS MARK

The pass mark for all CIMA Qualification examination papers is 50%.

READING AND PLANNING TIME

Remember that all three hour paper based examinations have an additional 20 minutes reading and planning time.

CIMA GUIDANCE

CIMA guidance on the use of this time is as follows:

> This additional time is allowed at the beginning of the examination to allow candidates to read the questions and to begin planning their answers before they start to write in their answer books.
>
> This time should be used to ensure that all the information and, in particular, the exam requirements are properly read and understood.
>
> During this time, candidates may only annotate their question paper. They may not write anything in their answer booklets until told to do so by the invigilator.

FURTHER GUIDANCE

As all questions are compulsory, there are no decisions to be made about choice of questions, other than in which order you would like to tackle them.

Therefore, in relation to E2, we recommend that you take the following approach with your reading and planning time:

- **Skim through the whole paper**, assessing the level of difficulty of each question.

- **Write down** on the question paper next to the mark allocation **the amount of time you should spend on each part.** Do this for each part of every question.

- **Decide the order** in which you think you will attempt each question:

    This is a personal choice and you have time on the revision phase to try out different approaches, for example, if you sit mock exams.

    A common approach is to tackle the question you think is the easiest and you are most comfortable with first.

    Others may prefer to tackle the longest questions first, or conversely leave them to the last.

    Psychologists believe that you usually perform at your best on the second and third question you attempt, once you have settled into the exam, so not tackling the bigger Section B questions first may be advisable.

    It is usual however that student tackle their least favourite topic and/or the most difficult question in their opinion last.

    Whatever you approach, you must make sure that you leave enough time to attempt all questions fully and be very strict with yourself in timing each question.

- **For each question:**

    Always read the requirement first as this enables you to focus on the detail of the question with the specific task in mind.

Take notice of **the format required** (e.g. letter, memo, notes) and identify the recipient of the answer. You need to do this to judge the level of depth required in your answer and whether the use of a formal reply or informal bullet points would be satisfactory.

Be **guided by the marks on offer** for each part of the question. This will guide you in terms of the amount you need to write for each part, as a general rule you should write double the amount for a 10 mark question than you would for a 5 mark question.

Consider the **verb** required in the question. The CIMA list of verbs is given in the exam paper. You must ensure that your answer reflects the verb required, e.g. if a level 4 verb is asked for, you will score few marks if you give a level 2 answer. This is especially important for a paper such as E2. Much of the material in E2 will be familiar from E1 studies, but the exam questions for E2 will usually have a higher verb requirement.

Plan your beginning, middle and end and the key areas to be addressed and your use of titles and sub-titles to enhance your answer.

Don't go overboard in terms of planning time on any one question – you need a good measure of the whole paper and a plan for all of the questions at the end of the 15 minutes.

By covering all questions you can often help yourself as you may find that facts in one question may remind you of things you should put into your answer relating to a different question.

- With your plan of attack in mind, **start answering your chosen question** with your plan to hand, as soon as you are allowed to start.

DETAILED SYLLABUS

The detailed syllabus and study guide written by CIMA can be found at:

www.cimaglobal.com

APPROACH TO REVISION

QUESTION PRACTICE IS THE KEY TO SUCCESS

Success in professional examinations relies upon you acquiring a firm grasp of the required knowledge at the tuition phase. In order to be able to do the questions, knowledge is essential.

However, the difference between success and failure often hinges on your exam technique on the day and making the most of the revision phase of your studies.

The **study text** is the starting point, designed to provide the underpinning knowledge to tackle all questions. However, in the revision phase, pouring over text books is not the answer.

The **online fixed tests** help you consolidate your knowledge and understanding and are a useful tool to check whether you can remember key topic areas.

Revision cards are designed to help you quickly revise a topic area, however you then need to practice questions. There is a need to progress to full exam standard questions as soon as possible, and to tie your exam technique and technical knowledge together.

The importance of question practice cannot be over-emphasised.

The recommended approach below is designed by expert tutors in the field, in conjunction with their knowledge of the examiner and their recent real exams.

The approach taken for the operational level is to revise by topic area. However, with the management and strategic papers, a multi topic approach is required to answer the scenario based questions.

You need to practise as many questions as possible in the time you have left.

OUR AIM

Our aim is to get you to the stage where you can attempt exam standard questions confidently, to time, in a closed book environment, with no supplementary help (i.e. to simulate the real examination experience).

Practising your exam technique on real past examination questions, in timed conditions, is also vitally important for you to assess your progress and identify areas of weakness that may need more attention in the final run up to the examination.

In order to achieve this we recognise that initially you may feel the need to practise some questions with open book help and exceed the required time.

The approach below shows you which questions you should use to build up to coping with exam standard question practice, and references to the sources of information available should you need to revisit a topic area in more detail.

Remember that in the real examination, all you have to do is:

- attempt all questions required by the exam

- only spend the allotted time on each question, and

- get them at least 50% right!

Try and practise this approach on every question you attempt from now to the real exam.

EXAMINER'S COMMENTS

General comments made are:

- "misallocation of time"

- "running out of time" and

- showing signs of "spending too much time on an earlier question and clearly rushing the answer to a subsequent question".

Examiner's comments from the May 2011 exam:

- "lack of adequate preparation"

- "lack of care in reading the question set"

- "citing of theory without application"

Good exam technique is vital.

THE E2 REVISION PLAN

Stage 1: Assess areas of strengths and weaknesses

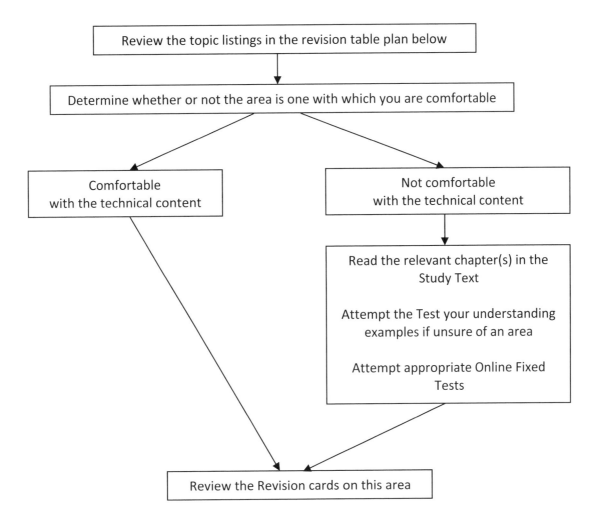

Stage 2: Question practice

Follow the order of revision of topics as recommended in the revision table plan below and attempt the questions in the order suggested.

Try to avoid referring to text books and notes and the model answer until you have completed your attempt.

Try to answer the question in the allotted time.

Review your attempt with the model answer and assess how much of the answer you achieved in the allocated exam time.

Fill in the self-assessment box below and decide on your best course of action.

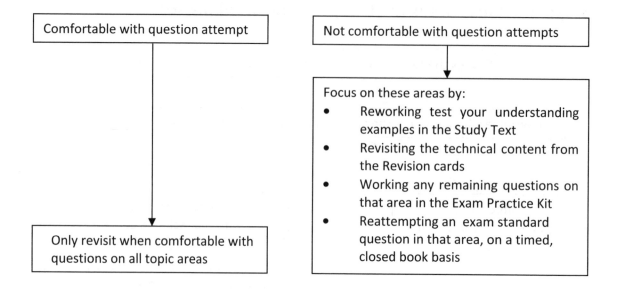

Note that:

 The "footsteps questions" give guidance on exam techniques and how you should have approached the question.

Stage 3: Final pre-exam revision

We recommend that you **attempt at least one three hour mock examination** containing a set of previously unseen exam standard questions.

It is important that you get a feel for the breadth of coverage of a real exam without advanced knowledge of the topic areas covered – just as you will expect to see on the real exam day.

Ideally a mock examination offered by your tuition provider should be sat in timed, closed book, real exam conditions.

THE DETAILED REVISION PLAN

Topic	Study Text Chapter	Question to attempt	Tutor guidance	Date attempted	Self assessment
Verbs	1	–	Before you start practising questions, remind yourself of the meaning of the key verbs you are likely to encounter. This will ensure that your answer always provides the level of detail that the examiner is looking for.		
Levels of strategy	2	6,9	Levels of strategy have been examined twice in E2, once focusing on SBUs and once focusing on the functional level.		
Strategy formulation	2	1, 12,43	Strategy formulation is an important topic. It is important to be able to discuss the different ways of approaching strategy formulation and be prepared to criticise the rational approach.		
Mission, objectives and CSFs.	2	2, 8	These are good questions to make you consider the importance of a mission and the formulation of CSFs.		
Stakeholders	2	40	Stakeholder analysis has been examined a number of times. Students must ensure that they can identify stakeholders, their objectives and discuss how to manage them.		
Competitive advantage	3/5	4, 41, 42, 45, 46	A popular topic, students must ensure they can discuss why competitor analysis is necessary, how to carry it out and the various tools which can be used in assessing competitive advantage.		
Transaction cost view	6	3	Transaction cost view looks at outsourcing of non core activities.		
Corporate governance and ethics	7	Specimen Q5	This question involves students assessing a scenario for corporate governance.		

Topic	Study Text Chapter	Question to attempt	Tutor guidance	Date attempted	Self assessment
Corporate social responsibility	7	5, 44	Good discussion questions on social responsibility. Students must ensure that they can make a good argument for and against social responsibility.		
Culture	8	33, 37	A popular topic. Students must be able to identify cultural types (Handy) and be able to discuss how culture forms and the advantages and disadvantages a strong culture brings.		
Classical management theories	9	34	Students should ensure they are familiar with the main management theories and should be able to apply them to a given scenario.		
Leadership theories	9	38, 39, 60, 61	A popular topic, students should be familiar with a range of leadership theories and should be able to select an appropriate theory to discuss for a particular scenario.		
Teams	10	30, 51	Students must be able to discuss the formulation of teams and their effectiveness.		
Conflict	10	36, 64, 66	Conflict can be questioned in terms of stakeholder conflict or team conflict. Students must ensure they can discuss conflict, its causes and strategies for dealing with it.		
Communication, Meetings, Negotiation, Mentoring	10	21, 35, 65, 62	Students should be able to identify ineffective communication and meetings and suggest ways of making them more effective. They should also be familiar with the negotiation and mentoring processes.		
Management control	11	31, 32, 59, 61	Management control covers a range of topics including appraisals, mentoring, health and safety, diversity and fairness. Students should be familiar with all of these areas.		

Topic	Study Text Chapter	Question to attempt	Tutor guidance	Date attempted	Self assessment
Project management	12	50, 53, 58	Students should be able to define a project from business as usual and must be familiar with the various project management methodologies.		
People and projects	13	47, 51, 58	A number of people are involved in projects, students must be able to discuss each of their roles and responsibilities and potential conflict.		
Project Initiation	14	17, 18, 20	For the initiation stage, students must be able to discuss the types of feasibility and should be familiar with the PID, and its contents and purpose, and be able to discuss the risk management process.		
Project planning	15	48, 54, 56	At the planning stage, students must be able to discuss what happens at the stage of the project and its importance and should be able to draw up a project plan.		
Project Tools	15	24, 25, 28, 55	Project tools are a popular topic. Students must be familiar with all tools used, be able to discuss their effectiveness and in the case of network analysis, be able to produce the diagram.		
Project control and completion	16	22, 23	The final project stages have also been examined a few times. For completion be able to discuss the purpose of the end project review and the post completion audit and suggest activities to be carried out during these reviews.		

The above gives a good selection of questions which cover many areas of the syllabus. Many questions cover a range of syllabus areas; there is significant overlap between some of the management and project management areas. Not all of the questions are referred to in the programme above. The remaining questions are available in the kit for extra practice for those who require more questions on some areas.

Section 1

SECTION A-TYPE QUESTIONS

STRATEGIC MANAGEMENT

1 T (MAY 07 EXAM)

T is the owner manager of a small business that designs and produces high quality garden furniture. The business started out as a hobby using T's creative design and carpentry talents, and he has been surprised by his success. Over the last year the business has experienced unplanned growth and by chance T has just won a contract to supply a local chain of DIY stores.

The local Chamber of Commerce has recently sent him an invitation to attend a number of seminars entitled "Formal Strategic Planning for Small Businesses". However, T is doubtful that the content of the seminars will be of any relevance to him and feels he cannot afford time away from his business. His view is that it is best to let the strategies and developments for his business emerge. *rigit*

5) Bereautic rigit

Required:

Explain the reasons why T is right to be doubtful about the relevance of formal strategic planning for his business. **(10 marks)**

1) not relevent in ever chahy dynmic
2) Logicall follow
3) Time consuming, complicated. environment
4) costly

2 T: CRITICAL SUCCESS FACTORS (MAY 06 EXAM)

T is seeking investment funds for his new venture to open a chain of fast-food restaurants. Despite the competition in this sector, having undertaken market research amongst his target market, T is convinced that he can succeed with his fast-food concept.

He is currently in the process of putting together a business plan which will outline his strategy to enter the marketplace. Having recently attended a seminar on what to include in a business plan, T remembers that he will need to determine what the critical success factors (CSFs) for his business are, but he is confused about how these differ from core competences.

Required:

(a) Explain why T needs to determine the CSFs as part of the development of his strategy and how they differ from core competences. **(6 marks)**

(b) Identify what the CSFs might be for T's chain of fast food restaurants. **(4 marks)**

(Total: 10 marks)

① Speed of service   ⑥ Cleanliness
② value for money   ⑦ Friendly ness of stuff
③ Quality of food
④ Simple / consistent menu
⑤ Location.

3 XTX (MAY 09 EXAM)

XTX Company, established 15 years ago, is in the business of designing, manufacturing and retailing sportswear and training shoes. It currently holds the licence to design the kits for both the national football and rugby teams of H country, where it is based.

Although these licences are potentially highly profitable, the company is currently facing difficult trading times as a result of the economic downturn and rises in manufacturing costs. Its manufacturing overheads are escalating out of control and although D, the Managing Director, has always had a commitment to manufacturing in XTX's home country, he is trying to work through some difficult business decisions about the future strategic development of the company.

He is reflecting on whether it would make business sense to outsource all manufacturing activities and focus on design and retail. He is now considering the possibility of outsourcing all manufacturing activities to country L, where costs are significantly lower. In other words, he is assessing the make or buy decision, which forms the basis of transaction cost theory where organisations choose between hierarchy or market solutions.

Required:

Discuss the factors D will need to consider in making his decision on whether or not to outsource the manufacturing activity. Your answer should make reference to transaction cost theory.   **(10 marks)**

4 FX COMPANY (MAY 10 EXAM)

SM is a consultant who has been asked to work with FX Company, a family owned business, which produces 'home-made' ice cream. Her brief is to undertake an assessment of the company's competitive position. As part of her review she is gathering information from various areas of the business. She has asked the Sales and Marketing Director to provide her with: an overview of the company's competitors; information on whether market growth is high or low; and what FX's market share is. She is surprised by his response that the company does not undertake any competitor analysis and that he has no idea of its market share.

Required

(a)   **Explain why FX Company should undertake competitor analysis.**   **(4 marks)**

(b)   **Discuss why it is important for FX Company to understand the concepts of high/low market growth and market share when undertaking competitor analysis. (6 marks)**

(Total: 10 marks)

5 PW (MAY 10 EXAM)

PW has been asked by her local management accountants' forum to present a paper at the annual conference on the subject of social responsibility. She has been asked to do this as her company has recently won a national award for its socially responsible initiatives including its success in recycling methods, community based projects and reducing its carbon footprint.

PW has decided that her presentation should start by setting out what is meant by the concept of social responsibility since she feels there are often misconceptions surrounding the term. She also wants to emphasise through her presentation the key benefits that companies can gain from developing strategies which are socially responsible. PW is aware that there will be some cynics in the audience who view socially responsible business driven strategies as unrealistic, that they conflict with the achievement of healthy profits and detract from creating shareholder value.

Required:

Discuss the points that PW should include in her presentation on social responsibility.
(10 marks)

6 LEVELS OF STRATEGY – SBU (MAY 10 EXAM)

Required:

Explain why it is important that the strategies of a strategic business unit (SBU) link to both the overall corporate strategy of a company and to the company's functional strategies.
(10 marks)

7 PRC COMPANY (NOV 10 EXAM)

PRC Company, a retailer of baby clothes and toys, has been in existence for 20 years. Its approach to strategy has tended to be informal and emergent rather than planned. However, the company is facing uncertain times and at a recent Board meeting, one of the directors suggested that the company should adopt a more formal approach to how it develops its strategy. He has suggested that the use of strategic management tools and techniques could help and, as a start, has recommended that the company should undertake a corporate appraisal.

Required:

Explain the purpose of corporate appraisal (SWOT), and what would be involved in PRC Company undertaking a corporate appraisal.
(10 marks)

8   PV COMPANY (MAR 11 EXAM)

T has recently been appointed as the new Chief Executive of PV Company which manufactures cosmetics and toiletries. She has spent the first three months meeting with her senior management team, employees and customers of the company to establish how PV is currently perceived by some of its various stakeholders. The discussions with the different groups have revealed that there seems to be a great deal of confusion on what PV Company stands for. It is apparent to T that there are many inconsistencies in the priorities and objectives across the different departments of the company. T has determined that immediate action is needed to establish a clear mission for PV Company.

To start the process, T intends to run a series of events at which the mission will be discussed with different groups of employees. She has asked for your help in preparing for the first workshop session. Specifically, she has asked you to put together a presentation with the aim of helping the various audiences to understand why it would be beneficial for PV Company to have a clear mission.

Required

Discuss the points you would include in the presentation on the benefits of having a clear mission for PV Company.   *ho get clear*   (10 marks)

9   LEVELS OF STRATEGY – FUNCTIONAL (MAR 11 EXAM)

Required:

Discuss the ways in which the strategies of the functional areas of an organisation should support the other levels of strategy   (10 marks)

10   DPW (MAR 11 EXAM)

DPW is a very successful home furniture company operating in P Country. It has a good reputation for being customer focused and providing value for money through its effective operations. Following a systematic analysis of its home/domestic market, it is apparent that the market is reaching maturity and to attain further growth and expansion will involve moving into markets abroad. It has identified F Country as a possible target for its first step into internationalisation.

The company now wants to undertake formal analysis to help it to better understand the external environment of F Country.

Required:

Describe ONE strategic management model/framework and explain how it could be used to help DPW to understand the external environment of F Country   (10 marks)

11 FF (MAY 11 EXAM)

The Board of FF Supermarket is examining the company's current market position. As part of the review, the Board has asked for an analysis of industry competition to be undertaken in order to establish the attractiveness of the industry and sources of competition.

Required:

Discuss the contribution of Porter's Five Forces model in assessing the attractiveness of the industry in which FF currently operates. **(10 marks)**

12 Z COMPANY (MAY 11 EXAM)

Z Company is very successful as market leader in digital media products where it has demonstrated its ability to innovate in new product development and design at a very fast pace, creating new products that its customers had not yet imagined. At a press launch for its latest product, the Chief Executive was asked about the company's impressive performance in recent years. She responded by saying that the company is committed to a resource-based approach to strategic development, with a desire to challenge itself to constantly stretch its capabilities.

Required:

Discuss the main characteristics of the resource-based approach to strategic development that the Chief Executive of Z Company referred to at the press launch. **(10 marks)**

13 K COMPANY (MAY 11 EXAM)

K is a kitchen and bathroom design and installation company which currently has showrooms in one region only of Country T. The company has enjoyed considerable success since it was established five years ago, using high quality products and computer-aided design techniques. This has now encouraged K Company to target other regions of Country T where it hopes to open more showrooms.

Since the company will, as yet, be unknown to potential customers, it recognises that it may be difficult to break into a competitive market in the other regions that are already being served by other well-established local and national companies. In order to help determine whether to pursue the expansion strategy, the owners of K Company have decided to try to collect as much intelligence information as possible on its potential competitors in other regions of Country T.

Required:

Describe what would be involved in K Company gathering competitive intelligence information, making reference to the type of information that is needed and the different sources that could be used. **(10 marks)**

14   PORTER'S DIAMOND (SEPT 11 EXAM)

Porter's Diamond is a useful framework that can help an organisation in identifying the extent to which it can build on home based national advantages to create competitive advantage, when compared with its industry competitors from different countries.

Required:

Discuss the four interacting determinants in Porter's Diamond framework that explain the sources of national competitive advantage.   **(10 marks)**

15   T COMPANY (SEPT 11 EXAM)

S is enrolled on T Company's management development programme. Although S has a financial background, the aim of the management development programme is to help him to gain a better appreciation of the external and competitive environment in which T Company operates. As part of the management development programme, S has been asked to make a presentation to his peers on the importance of undertaking competitive analysis and the types of information that need to be collected for this purpose.

Required:

Explain what S's presentation should include on:

(a)   **Why undertaking competitive analysis is important.**   **(4 marks)**

(b)   **The types of information that should be collected when undertaking competitor analysis.**   **(6 marks)**

                                                                        (Total: 10 marks)

16   COMPETITIVE ADVANTAGE (SEPT 11 EXAM)

There are different views on how an organisation can gain competitive advantage, but contemporary research is placing greater emphasis on the resource-based view.

Required:

Explain the concept of competitive advantage AND what is meant by the resource-based view.   **(10 marks)**

PROJECT MANAGEMENT

17 S COMPANY (NOV 07 EXAM)

S Company operates in the leisure industry and already has a number of different business interests including ice skating rinks and an outdoor artificial ski slope. At the last Board meeting, a suggestion was put forward to convert the 'dry' ski slope into an indoor snow dome to compete with rival companies who have successfully introduced similar facilities in other parts of the country, and which customers of S Company are now travelling to use.

Such a development for S Company would involve using the latest snow-making technology to create real snow in a controlled environment. This would provide a better experience for customers than the 'dry' ski slope, which currently uses plastic matting in place of the snow.

A project team has been set up to develop the idea. Having set out the scope for the snow dome project, the project team is now at the stage of investigating the feasibility.

Required:

Explain the purpose of a project feasibility study, making reference to the different types of feasibility that should be considered for the snow dome project. **(10 marks)**

18 P (MAY 07 EXAM)

A number of volunteers were so moved by news coverage reporting on the difficulties facing earthquake victims in F country that they organised a sponsored walk to raise funds for the appeal. Two of the volunteers visited some of the worst hit areas and this prompted them to set up their own charity. Their first major project is to rebuild and provide equipment for a school in one of the villages that has been devastated by the disaster. They hope to have the school up and running in twelve months' time.

A number of people have been enlisted to help with the project, including some local businesses as well as family and friends. The volunteers realise this will be a more complex project than organising a sponsored walk and therefore will require a much more professional approach to ensure that they achieve their objectives. They have limited experience of managing projects and are trying to determine the purpose of the different phases and activities. P, one of the volunteers, has been given the task of finding out about the first stage, initiating the project, and specifically, how to put together a project initiation document.

Required:

To help P, describe what is involved in the initiation stage of a project and explain what should be included in the project initiation document for the school project. **(10 marks)**

19   R (MAY 05 EXAM)   *Walk in the footsteps of a top tutor*

R has taken on the responsibility for organising the annual conference for the local Society of Management Accountants. Remembering the project management techniques she came across when studying for her professional qualification, R has decided that critical path analysis may be helpful in planning the conference.

As a start, R has drawn up a list of the activities she must complete in preparation for the conference, she has identified the dependency between the different activities and the time she thinks each will take.

Activity		Dependency	Time (weeks)
Determine conference theme	A	–	3
Research alternative venues	B	–	6
Identify and book guest speakers	C	A	4
Book venue	D	B	2
Print conference papers	E	C	8
Print and send out invitations	F	D	4
Confirm final arrangements with venue and deliver documents	G	E, F	2

Required:

Using the information from the scenario, construct a network diagram and explain how information from this could be useful to R in planning the conference.   **(10 marks)**

20   PROJECT MANAGEMENT (NOV 06 EXAM)

It is often claimed that all project management is risk management since risk is an inherent and inevitable characteristic of most projects. The aim of the project manager is to combat the various hazards to which a project may be exposed.

Required:

Explain the concept of risk and the ways in which risk can be managed in a project.
                                                                                    (10 marks)

21   P PROJECT MANAGER (MAY 08 EXAM)

P is the project manager responsible for managing the relocation of H Company's head office to new premises. He thought all was going well with the project and is very surprised when he learns that various project stakeholders are complaining about his poor communication skills.

Some of the complaints made relate to the complex messages he sends and his use of very technical language associated with the project. Whilst he feels he is keeping the project team members up to date, they feel they are overloaded with e-mails covering lots of different issues, not all of which are relevant to them.

Required:

Explain to P what he could do to ensure that his communications with stakeholders about the relocation project are more effective.   **(10 marks)**

22 S (MAY 08 EXAM)

S has been working on a major IT project for his client, X Hotel chain. The project brief was to design and implement a customer reservation system, which would enable customers to book on-line for rooms at any of X's hotels worldwide. When commissioning the project, the hotel chain required that the new system should be ready to coincide with the launch of its new flagship hotel opening in six months' time.

The project is now in the final stage of its lifecycle and the customer reservation system is ready to 'go live'. S is from an IT background and this is his first time in the role of project manager. He is finding the whole process of finishing off the final details of the project tedious, and is keen to get started with the next project that he is due to manage.

Required:

Explain to S why project completion is an important activity and explain what is involved during this stage of the project management lifecycle. **(10 marks)**

23 P WORKS FOR Z CO (NOV 08 EXAM)

P works for ZCo, whose business is commercial interior design. She is managing her first project which involves the refurbishment of a prime site office building. P is due to make her first report to Q, the project sponsor, but things are not going well, causing her to have sleepless nights worrying about the project. The refurbishment is overrunning on both time and budget and P cannot understand how the project has slipped so seriously without her realising. Keen to overcome the problems, P checks a recommended internet site on project management and finds the section on monitoring and control very helpful, particularly the section on progress reports.

Required:

(a) **Describe how the use of progress reports could help P.** **(6 marks)**

(b) **Identify the corrective action P could take to overcome the project slippage on time and budget.** **(4 marks)**

(Total 10 marks)

24 Q COMPANY (MAY 09 EXAM)

Q is a design and engineering company that has developed through the amalgamation of smaller businesses. The majority of the work undertaken by Q Company is project based and involves some complex project work and the coordination of sub-projects. However, the way the company has grown has resulted in a range of different project management practices being used in the various parts of the company. Projects tend not to be managed effectively and efficiently, particularly in terms of consistency of reporting and access to project information. Members of project teams complain that too much time is spent searching for paperwork. In addition, the project teams are often unclear on project progress and consequently there are delays in dealing with problems. All these factors undermine project performance.

T has recently joined Q Company and is surprised by the haphazard approach to project management and the fact that project management software is not used by the company. He has decided to put together a case to persuade the Managing Director to invest in such software and for it to become a requirement for all project teams to use it.

Required:

Describe how project management software could help Q Company to better manage its projects, with reference to the various stages of the project life cycle. **(10 marks)**

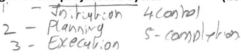

25 V (MAY 10 EXAM)

V has just left her job as a website designer for a large systems design company and is about to start up her own website design business. She will be renting an office which needs to be prepared, and also needs to procure all the necessary equipment before the business can commence operating. She intends to open her business in 12 weeks' time. In her previous role, she often encountered critical path analysis when she was involved in large design projects and she considers that this technique may also be useful to help her to plan the setting up of the new business.

V has devised a list of activities shown below that must be completed before the new business can commence. When drawing up this list she was aware that there was a degree of uncertainty in the timescales for some of the activities. She is concerned that if these uncertainties are not considered at this stage then she may not hit the deadline of opening her new business in 12 weeks' time. (Note: there is no slack shown).

	Activity	Dependency	Time (weeks)
Find rental office	A	–	2
Procure equipment	B	A	1
Prepare office	C	A	3
Recruit staff (2 people)	D	A	4
Delivery and installation of equipment	E	B,C	2
Train staff	F	D,E	2
Design tests on web design system	G	F	1
Test web design system	H	G	1

Required:

(a) **Using the above information, construct a network diagram, clearly identifying the critical path, for setting up V's business.** **(4 marks)**

(b) **Explain to V the difference between 'contingency/scenario plans' and 'buffering' in the context of helping V plan for the uncertainties in setting up the business.**
(6 marks)

(Total: 10 marks)

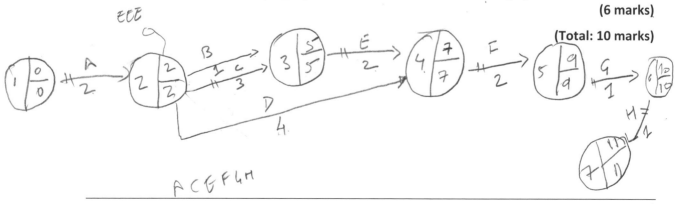

26 F BAKERY (MAR 11 EXAM)

ST is the operations director of F Bakery. He is in the process of putting together a project plan for the introduction of a new production plant that will enable the bakery to expand its product range, moving into high quality cakes and desserts.

ST has identified a number of activities that must be undertaken to set up the new bakery production plant. He now intends to construct a network analysis to assist ST in the planning of the project. This will also enable him to provide an answer for the HR manager who has asked him to provide advice on when she can start the recruitment campaign to select new employees needed to work in the new part of the bakery.

The activities can be broken down as follows:

Activity	Preceding activities	Activity duration In Weeks
A	–	12
B	–	10
C	–	6
D	C	26
E	A	9
F	B	14
G*	E,F	10
H	D,G	6

G* = Recruitment campaign

Required:

(a) Construct a network diagram showing the critical path for the introduction of the new production plant for the bakery and the overall duration of the project.

(4 marks)

(b) Identify the earliest time the recruitment campaign can start.   (2 marks)

(c) Identify the activities where there is float/slack time in the project, and calculate how much float/slack time there is.   (4 marks)

(Total: 10 marks)

27 M (NOV 10 EXAM)

M is a business that sells custom made computer-based information systems. Each customer order is for a unique system, which will involve experts from many functional areas within M. Each customer expects a high level of individual attention. Some systems take only four to six months to design and produce and cost less than €50,000, whereas other systems cost several million Euros and can take up to three years to complete. Projects are continually being completed and started.

A Management Consultant's review of M's organisational effectiveness has concluded that the matrix structure is the most appropriate for M.

Required:

Identify the characteristics of the organisation that make it appropriate for M to have a matrix structure.   **(10 marks)**

28 WBS/GANTT CHART (MAY 11 EXAM)

Due to the complexity of the tasks involved in many projects, communication of responsibility for those tasks is often helped by means of graphical planning techniques.

Required:

(a) Describe the techniques of work breakdown structure (WBS) and Gantt charts.

(4 marks)

(b) Explain the importance of both WBS and Gantt charts in the project communication process.

(6 marks)

(Total: 10 marks)

29 C CONSULTANCY (SEPT 11 EXAM)

C Consultancy Company provides management consultancy to a range of organisations. It employs staff who have different industry backgrounds and who also offer different specialisms, for example, in finance, marketing, IT, leadership, change management and logistics. The Company is currently organised around these specialist areas, with each specialism having a senior manager in charge. However, for some of its project work it is necessary to adopt a matrix structure to meet the client's requirements.

Required:

(a) Describe the key characteristics of a matrix project structure. (4 marks)

(b) Explain the advantages and disadvantages of a matrix project structure for C Consultancy Company's project work.

(6 marks)

(Total: 10 marks)

MANAGEMENT OF RELATIONSHIPS

30 WORKING IN GROUPS (NOV 09 EXAM)

Whilst many organisations emphasise the importance of working in groups, research has revealed that there can be some negative consequences on organisational performance.

Required:

Explain the reasons why working in groups can sometimes have a negative impact on organisational performance.

(10 marks)

31. Z COMPANY (NOV 07 EXAM) *Walk in the footsteps of a top tutor*

Whilst Z Company has a policy and a code of conduct on health and safety, the results from a recent survey suggest that many senior managers are not aware of their responsibilities for health and safety in the workplace.

The Board has nominated H, the Finance Director, to deliver a seminar to help senior managers appreciate the importance of health and safety at work. He is currently considering what he should include in the seminar.

Required:

Explain the key areas that H should cover in the health and safety seminar. **(10 marks)**

32. B COMPANY (MAY 09 EXAM)

B Company produces snack and confectionery products and employs 250 people, most of whom work as factory operatives. A year ago, J was appointed as the day shift manager of the factory. A major part of this role is the responsibility for dealing with human resource issues. In the last year there has been a rise in the number of problems in the factory, including employees constantly arriving late for work, and abusive and aggressive behaviour between employees. This is now impacting on the productivity and performance of the factory.

J is finding that far too much of his time is taken up with trying to resolve the various human resource issues and he has been accused of not treating people fairly. Recently, an employee has taken out a grievance against J regarding how he behaved towards him during a disciplinary interview. The company does have disciplinary and grievance policies set out in the employees' handbook, but J has not been following these procedures.

J has reluctantly decided that he needs advice on how best to handle discipline in the factory and particularly on how to carry out disciplinary interviews

Required:

(a) Distinguish between a disciplinary issue and a grievance. **(4 marks)**

(b) Recommend what J should do when carrying out disciplinary interviews. **(6 marks)**

(Total: 10 marks)

33. KCC (MAY 10 EXAM)

CT established her business, KCC, specialising in making handmade cakes, six years ago. Initially CT worked from her home, developing new recipes and cake designs. The business thrived on the creative talents of CT and her staff. In fact, the business became more successful than CT could have hoped for with a number of upmarket supermarkets now stocking her products.

Six years on, CT is reflecting on her success. She does feel that things have changed significantly since the early days when her business was run from her home kitchen. To satisfy increasing demand, three years ago she bought a factory for the production of her cakes, and in the last year she has opened five shops to sell the company's products.

KCC currently employs over 450 staff and the company has significantly changed compared to when it was first established. It now has a formal functional structure and the culture has more of the feel of a large bureaucratic organisation. CT feels that she has lost the passion and enthusiasm she once had for her business and feels that far too much of her time is spent on management issues rather than creating designs for cakes. She has a senior management team made up of the managers looking after different functional areas of the business. They make decisions about the running of the business, but seem to be focused on achieving efficiencies, control and bottom line performance, and have little interest in the creative side of the business. CT used to be on first name terms with her staff, but this is no longer the case. She was particularly saddened when she overheard an employee comment that he just felt he was a robot on a production line rather than a craft worker and that his ideas for new cake designs do not get heard.

Required:

Distinguish between the characteristics of KCC's culture when it was first set up and the culture the company is likely to have now. **(10 marks)**

34 TS CONSULTANTS (NOV 10 EXAM)

TS Consultants has been asked to investigate the issues underlying the underperformance and low staff morale of the Finance Department in YR Hospital.

The consultants have access to various sources of information such as the recent staff satisfaction survey which shows that staff morale in the department is low. In addition, statistics from the HR Department reveals that both absenteeism and staff turnover are exceptionally high in the Finance Department. There have also been many complaints from other areas of the hospital about both the management and staff working in the department. However, staff enjoy competitive salaries and other excellent working conditions such as free car parking, a subsidised canteen and access to sports facilities.

The consultants have run some focus groups with members of staff working in the department to try to gather more information to help them better understand the causes of underperformance and low staff morale. The findings suggest that there appears to be very much a "them and us" culture between management and staff, with the managers in the department exerting power based on their position and status. Staff say that they are only allowed to undertake the specific activities included in their narrow job descriptions and feel unable to fully contribute as a result of the chain of command in the Finance Department. Staff also say that they are not involved in decisions regarding the department's activities, and many say they have not had any training. They mentioned that there are very few career progression opportunities because of this. They feel their contributions are not recognised by management and that they never receive feedback on their performance. Staff characterise the leadership and management of the department as task-focused, with tight controls and close supervision.

Having undertaken the review, the consultants are preparing the recommendations on how to improve the poor performance and low staff morale.

Required:

With reference to theory, discuss the recommendations TS Consultants could make to help improve performance and staff morale in the Finance Department of YR Hospital. **(10 marks)**

35 P COMPANY (NOV 10 EXAM)

JB has recently joined the Finance Department of P Company as a trainee management accountant. As part of the Company's induction, she has been offered a mentor. However, since JB has not had any previous experience of mentoring, she is unconvinced of the benefits. She has asked LC, the facilitator of the induction session, to explain what is involved in the process of mentoring and how it might be a benefit to her as a new member of staff.

Required:

Explain the points that LC should make concerning the process and the benefits of mentoring for new members of staff   **(10 marks)**

36 LS COMPANY (NOV 10 EXAM)

The data on sales performance in LS Company has shown a significant downward trend over the last year. The Marketing and Sales Department is blaming the Finance Department for the poor performance, since it was the pressure from the Finance Department that led the Marketing and Sales Department to increase the product price. The Marketing and Sales Department staff say that, in current market conditions, this was inappropriate and was the main reason for the loss of market share. They feel that the Finance Department staff are short sighted, too focused on costs in pricing decisions and do not appreciate that there are other factors that should be considered in product price setting. However, the Finance Department thinks that the Marketing and Sales Department has been complacent and has not had an aggressive marketing and sales strategy in place. Perhaps not surprisingly, communications and cooperation between the staff in the two departments is at an all time low and in meetings there is constant in-fighting and disagreements.

To make matters worse, a consequence of the drop in sales has been that the senior management is proposing that there will need to be job losses in the Production Department. The trade union which represents the production workers is now threatening to take industrial action.

Required:

Compare and contrast the different types and sources of conflict occurring in LS Company   **(10 marks)**

37   S COMPANY (MAR 11 EXAM)

S Company has for many years been a long standing household name, designing and manufacturing electrical appliances for use in the kitchen. It has developed a strong culture over the years which can be best typified as a role culture. However, this culture is now acting as a barrier to the company's ability to adapt to become more flexible so that it is able to respond quickly to changes in the environment and initiatives taken by its competitors in product design.

In particular, the company is falling behind its new competitors when it comes to innovations in new product development and design. Effective new product development requires staff to work together across functional boundaries but this is becoming hard to achieve in S Company where people now fiercely protect their functional specialism and will only work on the tasks specified in their job descriptions.

Required:

(a)   Describe the key characteristics of a role culture, explaining why this type of culture is no longer appropriate for S Company.   **(6 marks)**

(b)   Recommend, with reasons, the type of culture to which S Company now needs to change.   **(4 marks)**

                                                                                                        (Total: 10 marks)

38   TR (MAY 11 EXAM)

TR has recently been promoted to his first management position. In the past, he very much enjoyed working as part of a team, but is having some difficulty in adapting to his new role as leader of a team. In his recent appraisal he has acknowledged that his style of management is not effective in all instances. In particular, he feels that he has not been very flexible in dealing with some of the issues that he has faced. He has identified that he would benefit from leadership training to help him better understand the alternative styles of management that he could adopt to help him develop to become more effective in his role.

Required:

Explain to TR, with reference to theory, the different management / leadership styles he could adopt to help him to become more effective in his role.   **(10 marks)**

39 L COMPANY (SEPT 11 EXAM)

When J was promoted to be the new Sales and Marketing Manager for Company L, after working there in different capacities over the last ten years, it was a popular choice among her co-employees. J was always a good team player and enjoyed helping individuals. However, in the six months since her promotion, although staff morale has never been higher, sales have dropped and targets have not been met.

J is now under pressure from senior management to improve the level of performance of the sales and marketing team which she leads. It has been suggested to J, by a senior manager, that her management style has not been as effective as it could be, and that she needs to change her approach to leadership, paying more attention to the task. J disagrees and claims that it is outside factors that are to blame for the poor performance, rather than her leadership style.

Required:

Compare and contrast J's current style of management with the one it is suggested she should adopt. You should support your answer with reference to relevant management style/leadership theories. **(10 marks)**

Section 2

SECTION B-TYPE QUESTIONS

STRATEGIC MANAGEMENT

40   K COMPANY (NOV 04 EXAM)

K Company, a manufacturer of small appliances is facing very difficult times. Many years of steady growth have recently ended with a sharp decline in its sales and a consequent fall in its profits and share price. The CEO has decided in consultation with the Finance Director that urgent action is required and has proposed a plan to turnaround K Company from its current decline.

This plan involves reducing the workforce by 50% to 3,000 and closing six domestic assembly plants, four of which are in the same town. Most of the production is to be moved to other parts of the world where labour costs are lower. K Company's loyal workforce is shocked by the proposals and the trade unions are determined to fight the proposed job cuts with all the means at their disposal.

The plan also involves the sourcing of many components from overseas, a proposal which has shocked its long-established domestic suppliers.

Finally, the board of directors is not entirely united behind the plan and there are rumours that the Production and Marketing Directors are considering resignation.

Required:

(a)   Identify the internal and external stakeholders that are likely to be affected if the proposed plan is implemented. Describe the impact of the proposed changes on each stakeholder group.   **(13 marks)**

(b)   Describe the sources of power available to each stakeholder group. Explain how each group might try to influence the outcome of the proposed plan.   **(12 marks)**

(Total: 25 marks)

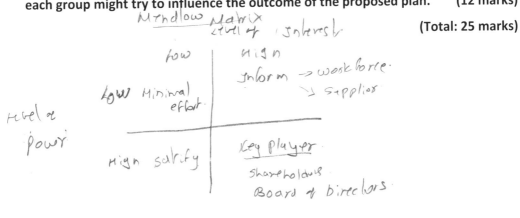

19

41 C CHOCOLATE COMPANY (NOV 07 EXAM)

C Chocolate Company makes and supplies high quality hand-made chocolate products. Since the launch of its internet business, it has experienced huge success and is currently enjoying its position as market leader and has built up a strong brand.

The owner of the business attributes much of the success to a combination of factors, including the unique recipes and the skills of staff associated with hand-made chocolates and the procurement of high quality cocoa beans. The company's marketing capability and use of IT in developing the company's website has enabled it to track and quickly spot trends in changes to consumer buying patterns. It is clear from the company's research information that, to prosper in the industry, constant product innovation is critical in building and maintaining the customer relationship. The flexible approach to new product development allows the company to quickly come up with new chocolate products.

Required:

(a) Explain the extent to which C Chocolate Company is adopting this strategic approach to gain competitive advantage, making reference to the principles of the resource based view. (13 marks)

(b) Demonstrate how the value chain framework would assist C Chocolate Company in understanding its internal position. (12 marks)

(Total: 25 marks)

42 W COMPANY (MAY 08 EXAM)

W Company is a fashion retailer which designs and sells its own brand of women's clothes through its chain of shops in F country. However, it is facing tough operating conditions in its home market where strong competition means there is little opportunity for future growth. The Board has taken the strategic decision that expansion can only be achieved through market development abroad.

Initial research has identified L country as offering the potential to be a possible suitable location for W Company to develop a new market. Further information now needs to be collected on the external environment and competition in L country in order to help evaluate the viability of the strategy being proposed.

If the outcomes from the research are positive, W Company intends to find an existing retail chain in L country that it can acquire, rather than set up a new operation through internal development. A senior management team will be sent from W Company to manage the operations in L country. However, the Board is aware that this could create challenges for the managers if there are cultural differences between the two countries.

Required:

(a) Apply appropriate strategic management models/frameworks to explain the key external environmental and competitive factors on which information should be collected to help W Company evaluate its proposed strategy to move into L country. (13 marks)

(b) Discuss, with reference to appropriate theory, why the management team from W Company will need to take account of cultural differences when managing the new operation in L country. (12 marks)

(Total 25 marks)

43   B BAKERY (NOV 08 EXAM)

B Bakery is a family owned firm with around 250 employees. It has been in business for over 50 years and supplies bread and confectionary products to a number of different businesses, including supermarkets and pub-chains. The firm has experienced mixed fortunes over the years in terms of business performance, but in the last few years has experienced a growth in orders for some of its new healthy product ranges. These products have been developed as a result of the Managing Director's wife's interest in healthy eating. However, the Bakery has recently lost some key accounts as a result of being unable to produce some of its products at a competitive price.

Six months ago, the first non-family Board member, CT, joined the company as Operations Director. CT is surprised to find that the firm does not have a mission statement or any formal planning process in place. He is even more concerned that the Bakery does not have any clear objectives or key performance indicators. In a recent conversation with the Managing Director, CT suggested that the Board should be more proactive and that adopting a more formal approach to planning would help better inform the future development and direction of the Bakery. He suggests that the Board should consider using the rational approach to strategic management.

He was rather surprised by the response from the Managing Director, who said that in his 30 years with the firm, it had grown and been successful despite the absence of formal plans. He commented that planning creates lots of analysis that does not result in action and he prefers strategies to emerge. His view is that planned and intended strategies often turn out to be invalid.

Required:

(a)   **Distinguish between the views of the Managing Director and the Operations Director on how strategy occurs.**   **(17 marks)**

(b)   **State the arguments that the Operations Director could use to persuade the Managing Director of the benefits of having a formal strategic plan.**   **(8 marks)**

(Total 25 marks)

44   C COMPANY (NOV 08 EXAM)

The Chief Executive of C Company, a chemical manufacturing company, has put a number of proposals to the Board on what the company can do to become more socially and environmentally responsible than simply complying with legislation. He wants to introduce a number of social and environmental objectives linked to reducing carbon emissions in production, improving on waste treatment, using more environmentally-friendly methods of waste disposal and recycling. He also wants to support the local community through financial donations and by seconding staff to provide help to local charities.

The proposals will require some investment in clean production technologies, buying environmentally friendly raw materials where possible, and reducing the use of business transport. The Chief Executive is also suggesting the company should have an eco-balance sheet, which includes financial data on environmental costs.

The Chief Executive's interest in socially and environmentally responsible strategies is partly motivated by the media attention on the carbon footprint of companies such as C but is also driven by his personal beliefs. His view is that sustainability should be at the centre of all C Company's activities since it makes good business sense. He sees his proposals as 'win-win', but is facing strong opposition from the Finance Director, who is concerned about the costs and the potential negative impact on financial performance and hence shareholder value.

Required:

(a)   Discuss the different viewpoints of the Chief Executive and the Finance Director on C Company becoming more socially and environmentally responsible.   **(15 marks)**

We have removed part b of this question, as it was no longer valid to E2

45.   **GCU COMPANY (NOV 09 EXAM)** *Walk in the footsteps of a top tutor*

GCU Company is a manufacturer and retailer in the luxury goods market, relying on its brand to retail high design fashion, perfumes, luggage and watches. In the past, little thought was given to the strategy of the organisation because limited competition allowed the company to be successful and profitable without any significant change. However, in the last two years increased competition and other changes have seen the company's fortunes decline, with a significant downturn in sales and profit. A new managing director (MD) has been brought into the company with the key objective of improving the organisation's performance.

The MD is currently considering how the company should best develop in the future. His starting point is to investigate the fundamental basis on which the company should develop its strategy to achieve competitive advantage. He is considering the merits of both the positioning view and the resource based view in achieving competitive advantage.

He feels that analysis needs to be undertaken using strategic management models / frameworks to help determine how the company could best gain competitive advantage.

Required:

(a)   Explain the concept of competitive advantage and distinguish between the positioning view and the resource based view on achieving competitive advantage for GCU.   **(10 marks)**

(b)   Discuss the strategic management models / frameworks that GCU could use analyse information on: → external' So PEST, Porter 5 Forces

      (i))   the *positioning view* to achieve competitive advantage.   **(7 marks)**

      (ii)   the *resource based view* to achieve competitive advantage.   **(8 marks)**

      → Internal Resource Audit & **(Total: 25 marks)**

      Porters value chain

46 S COMPANY (NOV 10 EXAM)

S Company operates in the consumer electronics industry designing and producing component parts, which it assembles into products such as mobile phones, laptops and MP3 players.

To date, it has only sold its products in D Country, its home market, where until recently it was market leader. However, the competitive landscape has changed significantly, as companies from PP Country have entered D Country's market, competing aggressively on product innovation, quality and price. Market intelligence gathered by S Company on the new competitors suggests that they are supported in pursuit of their international strategies by sources of national competitive advantage.

Looking to the future, S Company is evaluating its options on how to respond to the increased competition, including how it could better position itself, and what alternative strategies it could pursue. One option under review is to sell its products in new markets. GR, the Sales and Marketing Director, has identified NN Country as a possible market opportunity. As the first step in understanding whether this is a viable option, he has asked his team to undertake an initial assessment of the external environment in NN Country.

Required:

(a) With reference to Porter's Diamond model, explain the different sources of national competitive advantage that the companies from PP Country may enjoy and which could give them a competitive edge over S Company. **(15 marks)**

(b) Using an appropriate strategic management framework / model, describe the information that GR, the Sales and Marketing Director, would require to help him assess the external environment in NN Country. **(10 marks)**

(Total: 25 marks)

PROJECT MANAGEMENT

47 X (NOV 07 EXAM)

X is the project manager responsible for the implementation of the new customer information database in Y Company. He was selected to take on the role of project manager because of his strong technical capability.

The project represents an important development and financial investment for Y Company. A number of different business areas in the company have interests in the project and are dependent on the new customer information database going live on the due date.

Unfortunately, the project is not going well and the project steering committee wants answers from X. He feels he is under pressure to keep on schedule but lacks the support of his project team, who keep complaining that they do not know what they are supposed to be doing. It would appear that some members of the project team are not completing tasks on time and are not providing the information needed to progress with the system development. At the same time, the project sponsor is pushing X to make short cuts to make sure the system goes live on time.

X feels that many of the problems he faces are due to lack of project controls.

PAPER E2: ENTERPRISE MANAGEMENT

project life cycle stage.

1) time
2) cost
3) quality.
4) Resources
5) Risk
6) scope
7) communication
8) Integration

Required:

7 at every project
1) Initiation
2) planning
3) Execution
4) control
5) complete

(a) Explain the responsibilities of X in his role as project manager. **(12 marks)**

(b) (i) Discuss the purpose of project control. **(4 marks)**

Control steps

1) setting up a standard
2) Measuring actual result
3) comparing Target v/s Actual
4) take corrective measure

(ii) Explain the controls that should be set up for the customer information database project in order to help X manage the various stages of the project. **(9 marks)**

→ Discuss control of each stage of project life cycle

1) Initiating
2) Planning
3) Execution
4) control
5) complete.

(Total: 25 marks)

48 S COMPANY (MAY 05 EXAM)

S Company is a major retailer selling mobile phones. In recent years, the company has opened new outlets and taken on more support staff at the head office. As a result, the company has outgrown its existing headquarters and so the decision has been taken to relocate to a larger purpose-built building.

Although the building work is complete, there are a number of different initiatives associated with the relocation. These include making sure that the premises are ready to move into on time and within budget and setting up a customer service contact team to support the retail outlets dealing with customer enquiries and complaints. In addition, an upgraded office IT support system is to be designed and must be ready for installation in the new premises.

P, the head of facilities management, has decided to establish a project team to ensure that all of the activities associated with the move to the new premises are co-ordinated and within budget. She has the formal role of project sponsor working on behalf of the board and has appointed D to manage the project.

Required;

project obj
scope.st

1 Detailed planning
2 1) Critical path analysis 4 gates.
2) Gantt chart control h s log man.
3) Milestone Resource

(a) Identify and explain the activities that D would need to undertake in the planning phase of the project for re-location.

resource allocation
authorisation of plan. **(15 marks)**

(b) Compare and contrast the roles of P, as the project sponsor, and D, as the project manager.

→ day to day activities of business.
use various stages of Project life   be explain role.

→ get reports on prog **(10 marks)**
→ interested in final results P
(Total: 25 marks)

49 A2D ENGINEERING (NOV 09 EXAM)

Q joined A2D Engineering Company three months ago, taking on the role of project manager responsible for a new product development project. Q feels that he has the ideal qualities to be an effective project manager for the new project, based on his technical knowledge of precision engineering. His style is one of using tight controls and he feels that an autocratic approach is needed to ensure that the project is delivered on time and within budget.

Q is very surprised by the feedback he has recently received from some of the line managers of his project team members. They have told him that the staff they have provided to work on the project are asking to be moved back to their functional areas, since they are very unhappy with the way he manages them.

In addition to this, at the project catch up meeting, the project sponsor suggested that Q might find it helpful to have a mentor. However, Q is very sceptical about the value of mentoring and feels it would be a waste of his time, which would be better used on project activities.

Required:

(a)   Explain to Q why good leadership skills are important if he is to be effective in the role of project manager.   **(4 marks)**

(b)   Describe Q's style of management and, with reference to theory, explain the alternative styles he could use at different stages of the project.   **(15 marks)**

(c)   Explain how mentoring could help Q.   **(6 marks)**

(Total: 25 marks)

50   C HOSPITAL (MAY 06 EXAM) PROJECT MGMT

The main agenda item at the meeting of the Executive Board of C Hospital is to discuss the new pay and reward system. The hospital needs to make changes to the existing pay systems to respond to government requirements to reform reward systems as part of its pay modernisation agenda. The aim is to harmonise the payments systems for different categories of workers in the hospital on to one pay scale. This will mean that there is one pay scale for all employees of the hospital including nurses, physiotherapists, radiographers, technicians and support staff (i.e. cleaners, porters, and kitchen staff). The rationale for the new system is to achieve greater flexibility, to assist in recruitment and retention of staff and to reward people for their contribution to the achievement of hospital targets.

The hospital has 12 months in which to design and implement the new system in order to meet the government target of May 2007. There is a huge amount of work that will need to be undertaken to deliver the new system, and a number of different stakeholders to satisfy.

At the meeting of the Board there was some discussion concerning who should be responsible for undertaking all tasks and activities associated with the development of the new system. The Human Resource (HR) director proposed that a project manager should be appointed and a project team set up. Whilst he would expect some members of his HR team to be part of the team, he is adamant that, although his staff are responsible for administering the current payroll system and dealing with staff enquires about pay and rewards, designing a new pay system should not form part of the 'business as usual' work for the HR department.

Required:

(a)   Describe the attributes of the proposed project in C Hospital that distinguish it from 'business as usual' work.   **(10 marks)**

(b)   Produce an outline of the different stages in the project to design and implement a new pay and reward system for C Hospital.   **(15 marks)**

(Total: 25 marks)

51 T (MAY 08 EXAM)

T works for J Company, which designs and manufactures children's toys. She has recently been appointed as the project manager of a project to design a new range of educational toys for children aged 3 – 6 years. She is currently thinking about the issues that will face her in delivering the objectives of the project. She is confident that she has a good understanding of what needs to happen at the various stages of the project lifecycle and has strong technical skills, which will help her in using some of the project management tools and techniques.

T realises that this will not be enough to ensure successful project outcomes and knows that it will be important to have a good project team. However, she is also concerned that people working in teams can sometimes be problematic, particularly since the project team will be made up of people from different parts of the organisation, who have not worked together before. The team members will come from finance, marketing, production, IT and sales.

[handwritten: 1) Forming 2) Storming 3) Norming 4) performing.]

Required:

(a) Describe the stages of group formation, as suggested by researchers, that T's project team should pass through if it is to become effective in performing the project task. **(10 marks)**

(b) Explain the potential problems that could hinder the effectiveness of T's project team and explain how they might be overcome. **(15 marks)**

[handwritten: 1) Unclear objective. 2) Group conflict 3) Lack of role description 4) Poor leadership & commitment 5) Lack of continuity in group 6) Risky decisions 7) Unproductive meetings]

(Total 25 marks)

52 N (MAY 09 EXAM)

N is the project manager of a major construction project contracted to deliver a new stadium for V city. The stadium will be used for multiple purposes, including sports such as football and rugby matches, as well as for musical events.

The project is a complex one, and N not only has to coordinate the various contractors involved in the building work, but also manage the expectations of the different interested parties to the project. Whilst there are a number of risks and uncertainties associated with the project, meeting the completion date for the stadium is critical since it needs to be ready to host the final of the Rugby World Cup. As with most construction projects, the company that N works for will receive stage payments for construction work. It will also be subject to financial penalties, linked to both the time of completion of the various stages and also quality requirements.

[handwritten: Risk identification, Analysis, Planning, Monitoring → TARA → Mgmt]

Required:

(a) Explain to N the various ways that the risks and uncertainties associated with the construction project can be managed. **(15 marks)**

(b) Explain the different kinds of negotiations N is likely to be involved in as project manager of the construction project. **(10 marks)**

(Total: 25 marks)

53 T HOSPITAL (NOV 09 EXAM)

T Hospital has invested significant funds in a project to develop a patient management IT system which should improve efficiency and patient care. The original project manager has recently resigned and J has been brought in to take over the role of project manager. J has been briefed on the project deliverables and her first job is to assess the progress of the project to date. She is finding this difficult to establish and is appalled by the lack of project documentation available to help her in this task.

It seems the project has been run in a disorganised manner with no formal control systems, and is well over budget and time. J is aware that the project sponsor is complaining about lack of progress and lack of updates on project performance. She is also aware that the representatives of the potential users are dissatisfied with the quality of the development work to date. Given the size and importance of the project to the hospital, J had expected that a formal project management methodology would have been used. She has decided that this is crucial and intends to put a case to the project sponsor that a project management methodology, such as PRINCE2 needs to be used.

At her first project meeting, J was disappointed that the key people she expected to attend did not turn up. Those who did attend wanted to moan about all the problems they were having with the project. When enquiring about why so few people had attended, the response she got was that individuals felt that their time would be better spent working on the project since the meetings they attended in the past never seemed to achieve anything. J's assessment is that members of the project team seem unclear on their roles and responsibilities for the patient management IT system project, and there is no clear project management structure.

Required:

(a) Explain what J should include in her case to support the request to use a project management methodology, such as PRINCE2. [You may use other appropriate methodologies in developing your answer.] **(15 marks)**

(b) Discuss what J should do to ensure that future project team meetings are effective. **(10 marks)**

(Total: 25 marks)

54 COL (MAY 10 EXAM)

COL is a private college offering online tuition and qualifications to candidates all over the world. The Board of Directors of COL has decided to upgrade its computer system in order to enable COL to offer faster, more flexible delivery of courses and examination materials. It feels that this is necessary due to increasing competition in the delivery of online tuition and qualifications from both private and public colleges throughout the world. The Board of Directors and senior managers of COL have spent several months identifying the objectives for the proposed new system and identifying and discussing a range of project proposals. They have identified a clear requirement for the new online system but recognise that they do not possess the internal expertise they need to undertake such a project.

COL has contracted a local systems development company, SYS, to carry out the project. A project manager, D, has been assigned from SYS to lead the COL project. He will be responsible for all of the key stages of the project management process, beginning with the project plan. He will also be responsible for leading the project team, which will be made up of mainly SYS designers and also a number of IT staff and users from COL. He is also responsible for communication of the project's progress and events to Mrs Y, the senior IT manager at COL.

COL has made it clear that no extra money will be available than that presented in the original budget of $3 million and that any cost overruns will be borne by the contracting company. It has also set a deadline for final delivery of the system of 12 months. Again, there is no flexibility on this deadline.

One of the main enhancements to the updated system required by COL is the security of candidates' details. Unauthorised access to these details or candidates' results is the greatest outcome risk to the new system.

Mrs Y has insisted that staff from COL should play an active role in the systems development project and that communications between COL and SYS should be a key feature of the project management process.

Required:

(a) Construct an outline project plan for the upgrade of COL's online system to be presented by D, the project manager, to the key stakeholders of the project.
(15 marks)

(b) Describe the main skills required of the project manager, D, to lead the project team and create customer confidence.
(10 marks)

(Total: 25 marks)

55 V REGIONAL AUTHORITY (NOV 10 EXAM)

V is a regional authority, which is about to invest in a new sporting facility in one of the main towns in the region. The sporting facility will include a large swimming pool, an athletics track and a number of indoor facilities such as a gymnasium and indoor tennis courts. It is hoped that this facility will attract major sporting events to the town and will encourage more local people, particularly schoolchildren, to take part in more sporting activities.

The Finance Director of V has been appointed as the project manager and is in the early stages of setting up the project. This will be a complex project involving the construction of a range of new buildings and facilities involving a large number of specialist building contractors and equipment suppliers. The project is a collaborative venture funded by the regional authority and investment from three large local businesses. The Finance Director has been informed by the Board of V that this is a very high profile project for the regional authority and that overspending on this project is not allowed.

It has recently been reported in the local newspaper that the local residents living near to the proposed site for the new sporting facility are not happy with the proposal. This is largely because the proposed site is in a wealthy area on the edge of the town and local residents feel that it would be more appropriate if the new facility was located more centrally.

The new sporting facility would mean that two other smaller sporting facilities in the town, currently owned and run by the regional authority, would be closed down and staff relocated to the new facility. In the first meeting held by the project manager to communicate the proposals to staff, he was met with a hostile reaction, with many of them being very unhappy about moving to the new site.

The Finance Director is aware that it is a complex project and that the use of project management software will be an important tool in making the project objectives achievable. He is also aware that he must consider the needs of the different stakeholders throughout the duration of the project.

[handwritten: assist 1 Planning → Budgets. 2 Estimating & monitoring 3 monitoring 4 Reporting.]

Required:

(a) Explain how project management software could help the project manager and the project team during the life of the project. **(12 marks)**

(b) Identify the main stakeholders of the project and recommend appropriate strategies that the project manager could use to manage the different stakeholders' expectations. **(13 marks)**

(Total: 25 marks)

[handwritten: 1) project Sponsor – v regional authority 2) Project Manager – Finance director v. 3) Building Contractor & supplier 5) Staff 4) Local residents. 6) End customer]

56 E (MAR 11 EXAM)

Over the years, E has had a number of business successes in the building trade and property development. Her latest venture is to build a hotel in YX town. E has already gained the financial backing, identified a suitable site, had an architect draw up plans and received planning permission. She wants the construction work on the hotel to start without delay.

E has appointed P to be the project manager on the basis of his impressive record of managing successful construction projects. However, conflicts are already emerging as E is interfering in the management of the project. She is frustrated by the time P says he needs for the project planning phase, and is irritated by his insistence on formalising the project management process. E is putting pressure on P to cut corners in the first stages of the project, and to get started on the construction of the hotel.

[handwritten: 1) Difficult to establish control. 2) poor implementation. 3) low morale & demotivated staff. 4) no clarity on work. 5) Time 6) may go over budget. work bou - objective req. confusion.]

Required:

(a) Discuss the potential problems that the hotel project could face without good project planning. **(10 marks)**

(b) Explain the contribution that different project management tools and techniques could make to help P in planning the hotel project. **(15 marks)**

(Total: 25 marks)

[handwritten: 1) Critical path Analysis CPA. 5) PQP. 2) WBS / SOW / PBS & CBS 3) Gantt charts. 4) Milestone & control gates]

57 P COMPANY (MAY 11 EXAM)

P Company manufactures and sells a range of children's clothing through its retail shops and is currently designing a website in order to allow customers to purchase products online. The project is a major investment for P Company and it is seen by the Board of Directors as being a critical strategic development to ensure the continued success of the business in a highly competitive market.

The project team consists of staff from different departments of P Company. This is seen to be important by the Board of Directors, as a number of different business areas in P Company are dependent on the new website going live successfully and on time. The Board of Directors has also appointed G to be the project manager responsible for the development and implementation of this new website. G only joined P Company six months ago as an IT Manager, and she has never previously taken on the role of a project manager. She was chosen by the IT Director to be the project manager on the basis of her strong technical knowledge and experience in website development.

However, G has expressed concerns to the Board of Directors about her appointment as project manager on this strategically important project. She feels that she has a very limited understanding of the roles and responsibilities of a project manager. She is used to the day-to-day operations of the IT Department and is most comfortable with the technical aspects of the project, but feels that she does not have the range of skills necessary to lead such an important project.

Required:

(a) Distinguish the characteristics of the website development project in P Company from the characteristics of 'business as usual' work. **(10 marks)**

(b) Explain to G the role and responsibilities of the project manager for the new website development project. **(15 marks)**

(Total: 25 marks)

58 DG COMPANY (SEPT 11 EXAM)

DG Company has made a significant investment in a project to develop a new client management IT system, which when implemented should help give the company a competitive edge. However, all is not well with the management of the project and B, the project sponsor, is particularly concerned about the progress.

There appear to have been a series of problems throughout the project, which B feels she should have been alerted to. The result has been that the project manager she had appointed has now resigned, complaining that he was unclear on his role in the project, and that B was constantly interfering.

B has now appointed R, an experienced project manager, to get the project back on track, and is keen that, from the start, they are both clear of their roles and responsibilities.

R has reviewed the project and is preparing for his first meeting with B. However, he has found it difficult to establish the status of the project, which seems to have been previously run without adequate controls in place. He is finding it hard to track down the project documentation, and it would seem that the project is running significantly over budget and time. In addition, the project team appears to be de-motivated and is unclear on what each member of the team is doing.

R intends to suggest to B that a formal project methodology such as PRINCE2 should now be used.

Required:

(a) Explain how using a project management methodology, such as PRINCE2, could help minimise the problems that have occurred in the client management IT system project. **(15 marks)**

(b) Distinguish between the roles of B as the project sponsor and R, the project manager. **(10 marks)**

(Total: 25 marks)

MANAGEMENT OF RELATIONSHIPS

59 X COMPANY (NOV 04 EXAM)

Despite the diverse composition of its workforce, the higher grades of management in X Company are dominated by middle-aged males from one ethnic group.

Required:

(a) Discuss the implications for the performance of X Company of promoting only the members of a particular gender/ethnic group. **(10 marks)**

(b) Discuss the various ways in which:

(i) X Company can ensure fair treatment of all its employees

(ii) Governments can assist in the prevention of discrimination in the workplace.

(15 marks)

(Total: 25 marks)

60 J AND T (NOV 07 EXAM)

J has worked for P Accountancy and Consultancy firm for over 15 years. For the last five years she was the team leader for client support. J has a vast amount of experience and her overall outlook to work is positive. She takes a keen interest in the performance of individual members of her team, holding regular team meetings and encouraging her staff to contribute their ideas and to participate in target setting and decision making. The team always achieves its targets.

Six months ago, J gained a well deserved promotion which meant moving to another department. Her replacement is T, who has just completed his professional accountancy qualifications and has recently joined P Accountancy and Consultancy. This is his first leadership role and he is keen to impress his departmental manager. T feels that J's approach had been too soft. His view is that too much time had been spent in meetings and consultation and that staff would have been better just 'getting on with their work' since it is his job to make all the decisions.

T expects people to respect his position and authority without question. All his communications are sent by email or memo and he does not see the point of holding team meetings. He has recently introduced new performance targets without consultation. Most of the team feel the targets set are unreasonable. T has little time for people who need support in performing their role. Morale within the team is at an all time low and absenteeism has increased. Some staff are now looking to move out of the client support department.

T's line manager, F, is aware that T is very ambitious and hopes to progress in the firm. When T was recruited he was identified as having the potential to move quickly up the career ladder within P Accountancy and Consultancy. F feels that T might benefit from the mentoring system operated by the firm. However, F is also aware that there are problems in the client support department since T took over as team leader. He feels that T needs training to help him become more effective in his leadership role.

Required:

(a) Explain the different approaches to leadership demonstrated by J and T, making reference to leadership theories. *(= Adair.)* **(12 marks)**

(b) Describe how the concept of action-centred leadership would help in identifying the training T needs to become a more effective leader. **(7 marks)**

(c) Explain how a mentoring system could help T. **(6 marks)**

1) Task role
2) Individual *Maintenance role &*
3) Group — do

(Total: 25 marks)

61 B LOCAL COUNCIL (MAY 07 EXAM) *Walk in the footsteps of a top tutor*

B Local Council is responsible for providing public services, serving the local community. A new Chief Executive has recently been appointed with the explicit brief of improving the performance of the Council, which is currently in the spotlight for being inefficient and not focused enough on the needs of the local residents.

Over the last three months the Chief Executive has undertaken a review and is not impressed with what he has found. He has identified a number of weaknesses and problem areas which need to be remedied. The culture of the Local Council needs to change radically to become a more performance oriented one.

The initial findings from the review suggest that B Local Council is typified by a very bureaucratic culture, where power is determined by position and status. The managers in the Council defend their territory and are unwilling to share information and cooperate with other departments. Staff are only allowed to undertake the specific activities included in their job description. Many say they have had no training and that opportunities for career progression are limited. They receive no feedback on their performance but work under close supervision in what appears to be a "them and us" culture between management and staff.

The review also identifies that morale is low. Staff feel they are not encouraged to participate in decision making and any ideas they have are stifled as a result of the chain of command. A significant number of staff have told the new Chief Executive that if they could get another job, they would leave the Council. Discussions with the HR Manager reveal that both absenteeism and staff turnover are high, despite competitive salaries and other excellent working conditions and benefits such as free car parking, a subsidised canteen and sports facilities.

The Chief Executive has identified a number of significant changes that need to be made to improve the performance of B Local Council. He is surprised that there is currently no staff performance appraisal in place and is keen that an effective system should be designed and implemented.

[handwritten annotations: → Handy culture theory = Role clture. the culture, Leadership & Lack of motivation. Task clture. Power - people —]

Required:

(a)   Analyse the problems in B Local Council, and discuss what the Chief Executive could do to improve performance. You should include reference to appropriate theories to support your analysis.   (13 marks)

(b)   Explain the key issues that should be considered in the design and the implementation of an effective staff performance appraisal system for B Local Council.   (12 marks)

[handwritten annotations next to (b): ⚹ read agn]

(Total: 25 marks)

62   T4M (MAY 10 EXAM)

T4M is a mobile phone network provider, with its main headquarters based in B country. Whilst there has been significant industry growth in the last decade, more recently there are signs that this growth has begun to level off. At the same time, competition is intensifying.

The Board of T4M is preparing to take on the strategic challenges of the changing operating environment. As well as assessing the external environment, it has started a major review of its internal capability, with a particular focus on examining how efficiency gains can be achieved across the various business functions.

F, the Finance Director, is deliberating on how he can gain efficiency in his department. His initial assessment has identified a number of transaction activities that he feels could be outsourced, such as the work undertaken by the customer bill payment team, including some aspects of customer service on bill queries and payroll. F is very enthusiastic about this and his thinking has been informed by the fact that he was only recently approached by G2O, a company specialising in this type of service, based in H Country.

If the outsourcing strategy goes ahead, along with other efficiencies the Finance Director has planned, then this would mean a substantial reduction in headcount within the Finance Department, with predicted job losses of around 300 staff. The trade union has already heard about the proposal and the possibility of redundancies. It has made it clear that it will put up a fight against redundancies, on behalf of its members, to keep jobs in T4M.

F will need good negotiation skills since it is likely that he will be involved in a number of negotiation scenarios if the outsourcing strategy is implemented.

Required:

(a)   Explain the benefits and drawbacks associated with T4M's proposal to outsource some of the work currently undertaken in the Finance Department.   (12 marks)

(b)   Discuss how F, the Finance Director, should approach negotiations so that they are effective if the outsourcing strategy goes ahead.   (13 marks)

(Total: 25 marks)

63   S CITY POLICE FORCE (MAY 09 EXAM)

P has recently been appointed as the Chief of Police for S City Police Force. She has spent the first six weeks in her new role meeting with employees and representatives from the different communities that her Police Force serves. Many different views and priorities are emerging, but P has observed that her colleagues have no clear direction and have very different views on what the prime purpose of the Police Force should be. There seems to be many inconsistencies in the priorities and objectives of the Police Force.

P feels that it would be beneficial to develop a vision and mission for S City Police Force. She has decided to run a series of events at which the vision and mission will be discussed with different stakeholder groups, including external stakeholders, as well as employees. However, P recognises that these events may be viewed with some cynicism, with some colleagues commenting that these ideas may well be appropriate for profit-making organisations, but not relevant to the Police Force.

P is also concerned that whilst S City Police Force has a strong culture, this is in fact creating barriers to the effectiveness of the way work is done and the willingness of employees to accept the changes she feels are needed. She realises that, in attempting to change the culture, she is likely to meet with resistance and it will not be an easy task. As a first step, she feels that she needs to gain a better understanding of the features of the existing culture.

Required:

(a)   Distinguish between the terms vision and mission.   **(3 marks)**

(b)   Explain the points P could use to convince colleagues of the benefits of developing a mission for S City Police Force.   **(7 marks)**

(c)   Explain why culture is an important concept and discuss a framework model P could use in order to gain a better understanding of the various aspects that contribute to S City Police Force's existing culture.   **(15 marks)**

(Total: 25 marks)

64   ZEZ COMPANY (MAR 11 EXAM)

ZEZ Company is in the business of designing and printing bottle labels for soft drinks distributors. The company is, at present, facing very difficult times as recessionary economic conditions have had a negative impact on the demand for its customers' products, which in turn is having a knock-on effect on the demand for ZEZ Company's labels. As a result, the senior management team has been investigating how the company can become more efficient to ensure its future survival.

Redundancies across the company have recently been announced. In addition, the current operating conditions mean that there will be some significant changes made to the contractual terms and conditions for management and administration staff working in the various functional departments, along with a restructuring of operations.

Of immediate concern to the senior management is the threat made by the trade unions to take industrial action to protect jobs and also the contractual terms and conditions of their members.

Required:

(a) Discuss the different conflict handling strategies that could be used in managing the conflict in ZEZ Company.   **(13 marks)**

(b) Explain the different stages of negotiation that should take place to ensure the negotiation process between senior management and the trade union representatives is effective.   **(12 marks)**

(Total: 25 marks)

65 FPC COMPANY (MAY 11 EXAM)

PR has recently joined FPC Company as the new Finance Director. He is required to work towards getting the finance staff to play a fuller role in the company, becoming more integrated into the strategic and business activities of the organisation. However, PR is aware that this will not be an easy task since his impression is that the Finance Department has a very poor reputation in the company, and current relationships between the finance staff and other departments are not good.

Having discussed the poor perception with other department heads, it is clear that the finance staff are generally viewed as being unhelpful. Many of the complaints surround poor communications. A consistent comment made is that messages received from the Finance Department are too complicated and that too much financial jargon is used. Another common observation is that at inter-department meetings, the finance team use 'financial speak' which other members of staff find hard to understand. The finance staff have an obsession with financial indicators, and do not appreciate that there are other factors which inform decisions. It is also felt that too many emails are sent from the Finance Department, and it is often difficult to find the relevant information on some of the financial spreadsheets circulated which are supposed to help in decision-making.

PR has noted that many of the staff in the Finance Department are de-motivated. None of them appear to have clear targets and objectives, and they have told him that they have had no feedback on their performance and staff development simply has not existed. PR has established that, whilst there is a company-wide staff performance appraisal system in place, none of the staff in his department have had an appraisal in recent years.

PR has identified a number of immediate actions to improve the performance of the Finance Department. He has decided that all staff in the Finance Department need training to improve their communication skills. He also intends to make sure the company's appraisal system is implemented and that all staff in his department will have an appraisal in the next three months.

Required:

(a) Discuss what should be covered in the series of training sessions to help members of staff in the Finance Department improve their communication skills.   **(15 marks)**

(b) Explain how implementing FPC Company's staff appraisal system in the Finance Department could help improve the performance of staff.   **(10 marks)**

(Total: 25 marks)

66   Z COMPANY (SEPT 11 EXAM)

In response to changing customer demands and strong competition, the new product development team of Z Company has been working on a new product range. However, the process has not been easy and conflict between different interest groups is a major problem.   For instance, the Marketing Department staff are complaining that the research and development staff are not working quickly enough in translating their ideas into possible products. Production staff are saying that no consideration has been given to the implications of the new product designs on the production process.

A hastily convened meeting by the Finance Director of Z Company to discuss the financial viability of the new range of products has not helped. This ended in chaos with no agreement being reached as to how to proceed. Members of the Marketing Department returned to their desks complaining that the finance team had not brought along the relevant information on which to base the discussions. They also felt they had not been allowed to voice their views during the meeting, which was dominated by 'financial speak'. Members of the Production Department were unclear on why they had been asked to attend at all and felt they had wasted their time. It is clear that the meeting was poorly run.

Required:

(a)   Explain the sources of conflict between the different groups involved in the new product development process.   **(13 marks)**

(b)   Discuss what the Finance Director should do to ensure that future meetings are effective in achieving satisfactory outcomes for all members.   **(12 marks)**

(Total: 25 marks)

Section 3

ANSWERS TO SECTION A-TYPE QUESTIONS

STRATEGIC MANAGEMENT

1 T (MAY 07 EXAM)

Key answer tips

This question focuses on the disadvantages of the formal approach to strategic planning. You must make sure you do not simply list the disadvantages; you must relate them to the circumstances of T.

Tutorial Note

The formal or rational approach to strategic formulation assumes that organisations will behave logically and will follow a step by step approach. The first step involves defining the mission and objectives of the organisation; this is followed by comprehensive analysis. Following the analysis the steps are: generating strategic options, evaluation of these options and choice of the preferred option, implementation of the chosen strategy and finally monitoring, review and evaluation.

The formal approach assumes a rational planning process and usually results in a deliberately intended strategy. Strategies are determined after detailed analysis of the opportunities and threats facing the organisation and its relative strengths and weaknesses.

Such an approach may not be suitable for T's business for the following reasons:

- T prefers to let his strategy emerge as seen in the recent win of an order from a local chain of DIY stores. This was not a consciously thought out nor a deliberately intended strategy.

- A formal approach can be time consuming, complicated and, hence, expensive for small businesses. T is right to be concerned that time spent attending seminars and then on planning itself would take him away from the main operations of his business.

- In a dynamic environment it could be argued that the key factors on which formally planned strategies are based can become quickly outdated, resulting in the intended strategy failing.

- Formal planning can become very bureaucratic and rigid, thus stifling T's creative talent and undermining T's core competencies.

- In a small business, such as that run by T success is more linked to the ideas of T rather than the effective coordination of different SBUs.

- T may not have the resources to invest in new strategic ventures and may be unwilling to share or delegate control to others. A formal planning approach would thus be a waste of time as T would stick to the narrow product/market options he is already familiar with.

Despite all this, T could still benefit from the seminars. Some of the strategic planning frameworks/models might be helpful in making future decisions about the business. Even performing a regular SWOT analysis may help T become more aware of his business environment.

2   T: CRITICAL SUCCESS FACTORS (MAY 06 EXAM)

Key answer tips

In part (a) you must make the distinction between critical success factors (CSFs) and core competences clear.

In part (b) consider a fast food restaurant and identify the most important things that the restaurant must do right to succeed. Four marks are on offer, so look to suggest four CSFs.

Tutorial Note

Critical success factors are those things which the organisation must get right in order to succeed.

Competencies can either be core or threshold. Core competencies are those things the organisation is good at, which set them apart from the competitors and give them their competitive advantage. Over time core competencies become threshold, so organisations must continually look at developing their core competencies.

(a) Critical success factors (CSFs) are the limited number of areas in which results, if they are satisfactory, will ensure successful competitive performance for the business. They are the vital areas where 'things must go right' for the business to flourish.

CSFs are normally developed by analysing the target market, the demands of customers and the activities of competitors. This should result in five or six key areas, usually customer-driven, where T must out-perform competitors for the strategy to succeed. As such CSFs are crucial elements of a firm's strategy development.

Once CSFs have been identified, each one can be broken down into the key skills, processes and activities needed to ensure success for that CSF. These are the underpinning resources and competences that T must obtain and control. This is usually done through the use of detailed targets or key performance indicators (KPIs).

For example, the CSF of speed of service can be translated into KPIs to measure average and maximum queue length, average wait time, etc. Key resources could include staff flexibility and training so employees can be reallocated tasks when bottlenecks arise.

Core, or distinctive, competences underpin an organisation's ability to outperform competition over the longer term. They must be rare and costly to imitate for competitors, provide value to customers and have to be integrated within the organisation.

For example, analysts have estimated that the McDonalds' brand name is one of the most valuable in the corporate world.

CSFs and core competences are thus closely related. Ideally the firm has core competences in areas that give a competitive advantage for the critical success factors identified. The match between the market-focused CSFs and the internal core competences is a vital part of the resource approach to strategy.

(b) CSFs for a chain of fast-food restaurants could include the following:

- convenience of location as customers are unlikely to travel far for convenience e.g. near to local shopping centres

- speed of service as customers expect a minimal wait in 'fast food' outlets

- while not at the high end of food preparation, the quality of food is still a key concern for customers e.g. taste, ensuring it is still hot when served, consistency between outlets.

- variety of items of the menu is necessary to attract a range of customers e.g. the availability of children's meals

- brand name – customers will visit a chain with which they are familiar

- cleanliness

- friendliness of staff.

3 XTX (MAY 09 EXAM)

Key answer tips

XTX wants to maintain its trading reputation in difficult times. The managing director is considering whether to make or buy the national rugby and football kits, for which they hold the license to design. The key here is to relate your answer to transaction cost theory.

XTX currently produce the kits in-house, so your answer should consider the potential pros and cons of outsourcing the manufacturing process.

Tutorial Note

Transaction cost theory (Coase and Williamson) helps organisations make the decision about which activities to outsource and which to perform in-house. It considers the *hierarchy solution*, which is the in-house solution, and the *market solution*, which involves outsourcing the activity.

XTX is searching for ways to improve efficiency and reduce overhead costs. Transaction cost theory would examine how XTX could achieve this through outsourcing non core activities.

Williamson in 1981 suggested that organisations chose between two mechanisms to control resources and carry out their operations:

- Hierarchy solutions – management decide to own the assets and use policies and procedures of the firm to control their use and performance. XTX currently operates this way as a vertically integrated organisation conducting as much as possible in house. E.g. Design, manufacture and retail.

- Market solutions – when management decide to buy in the use of assets or staff from outside companies under contract such as in an outsourcing arrangement. Whereby a third-party supplier assumes responsibility for the supply of a particular good or service. This supply contract is usually made to an agreed price (lower transaction costs) and the level of quality is arranged over a defined period of time.

By making an agreement to outsource, the Managing Director D would be able to:

Concentrate in-house staff on core activities. XTX would be able to focus on the design and retailing of the sportswear and training shoes. Whilst also reducing management time spent training and motivating staff members who have no clear promotion path or are worried about the economic downturn.

The outsourcer may be able to provide a better quality of service. Failure to achieve the required level of service will lead to the termination of the contract and possible loss of reputation.

The agreement will save costs as it is cheaper to manufacture within L country, which will help in the current climate of economic downturn.

On the other hand if XTX relies on an outside supplier (market solution), in addition to the price for the bought-in input, it will incur the following transaction costs:

- Negotiating and drafting a legal contract with the supplier;

- Monitoring the supplier's compliance with the contract;

- Pursuing legal actions for redress due to non-performance by the supplier;

- Penalty payments and cancellation payments if the firm later finds it needs to change its side of the bargain and draft a new contract with the supplier.

XTX will also need to bear in mind other factors which are less easy to quantify, such as:

- The risk of over reliance on the outsourcer and possible issues with control and security and asset specificity. For example how do they control the manufacture of licensed football and rugby strips and the possibility of counterfeit copies?

- The effect on reputation and customer satisfaction should deadlines not be met or the agreed quality standards not be achieved;

- It is likely that staff involved in the manufacturing process currently would either join the outsourcing company as part of the deal or will leave either through redundancy or of their own accord and, thus, it would be extremely difficult should XTX decide that they want to take the manufacturing process back in house in the future, as the expertise will have been lost.

4 FX COMPANY (MAY 10 EXAM)

Key answer tips

(a) This is a general question looking at why a company would carry out competitor analysis. Try to apply your answer to the scenario where possible.

(b) Part (b) looks specifically at market growth and market share. Explain these concepts then discuss why it is important for FX to understand them.

Tutorial Note

Part (b) uses market growth and market share, which are the elements used in the Boston Consulting Group model (BCG). It is important for companies to know where all of their products fit in the model as this helps them to determine their strategy for that product. Market growth helps companies to assess the potential in their marketplace and market share lets them assess how strong their position in the market place is.

(a) For any company it is important to know about the market they compete in and this includes an understanding of competitor analysis. In order to maintain growth, companies must be aware of changes in their marketplace. If new competitors have entered the market, this will change the dynamics of the market and the potential profit for all companies competing.

Companies must not view undertaking competitor analysis as a one off exercise, but should continually update it to ensure that they are always aware of new developments in their market and to ensure they are not left behind. This is an important step in strategic planning.

If competitor analysis is not undertaken, or is allowed to get out of date, a new competitor could have entered the market and could reduce the sales of FX. In additional, competitors may be offering new products which are proving popular with customers and FX may need to consider updating its product range. Alternatively others may have tried new products which did not prove successful and this would help FX in deciding what new products to try to develop in the future.

(b) Market growth looks at the overall market in which a company competes and how much that market is growing. FX operates in the ice cream industry. FX needs to consider the whole ice cream market and ascertain if it is growing, and if so if it is experiencing a high or a low level of growth. Market growth is usually measured in sales volume or value.

This information lets FX know the potential for them to expand their business in the future. If the market is experiencing high growth then FX has scope to increase their business by trying to gain the new customers who are entering the market. If the market is experiencing low growth then the opportunities are more limited as all companies in the market will be competing for the same customers.

Market share looks at how much of the overall market one company has. Companies aim to have as large a market share as possible and would like this to be growing. A growing market share suggests that a company is gaining a larger % share of the market.

All companies in the market will be competing for as large a share of the overall market as possible. By undertaking this analysis FX will be able to ascertain how strong their position in the market is and if that position is growing stronger or weaker. The analysis will also tell FX how much scope there is to improve their position in the future.

5   PW (MAY 10 EXAM)

Key answer tips

In this question you have to discuss the points that PW would put in her presentation. PW is clearly in favour of social responsibility, but make sure your answer is balanced and recognises the opposing view.

Tutorial Note

Social responsibility can be defined as "taking more than just the immediate interests of the shareholders into account when making business decisions". Social responsibility can cover issues such as the environment, health and safety of the workforce, working conditions and looking after the local community.

There can be a conflict between attempting to be socially responsible and attempting to maximise shareholder wealth.

What is social responsibility?

Social responsibility is where a company looks at the impact it has on its immediate and wider environment.

Elements of social responsibility can include; reducing pollution, looking after local communities and ensuring the wellbeing of employees. In the case of PW's company they have been focusing on recycling, community based projects and reducing their carbon footprint.

Benefits from social responsibility

Companies who are seen to be accepting their responsibility as a member of society and are undertaking elements of social responsibility can attract new customers and investors who want to associate with a company that they believe cares. PW's company is active in community based projects which will bring positive publicity to the company.

Employees who work for socially responsible companies may be better looked after and enjoy better working conditions which may motivate them to work harder for the company.

Within some industries there are strict laws covering their impact on the environment, e.g. oil companies, however, as public opinion changes and concern for environmental factors increases, it is likely that more legislation will follow covering all companies. These new requirements will be easier for companies who have already been acting responsibly. PW's company has been active in reducing their carbon footprint and recycling.

Building up good relationships with local communities and the local authorities may be beneficial to companies, and this goodwill will often come from the company's social responsibility.

Arguments against social responsibility

It is a valid argument that following some of these social responsibility ideas costs additional money and therefore may reduce profits in the short term.

If you consider two similar companies from in the same industry: company A chooses to be socially responsible while company B does not. Company A pays above the minimum wage, ensures that staff conditions are acceptable and monitors and aims to reduce pollution. Company B on the other hand sources cheap goods from abroad with no consideration as to the working conditions of the people making the goods, and it does not actively concern itself with its effect on the local environment. It is true that B will be able to offer its products at a lower price that A, or will be able to gain a higher profit margin. B's shareholders will experience increased wealth compared to A's.

Many may argue that B is doing the right thing by aiming to increase shareholder wealth, as this is normally the main objective of a commercial organisation. It will therefore be left up to the customer to exercise their judgement on which company they want to buy from.

However, companies must realise that their shareholders are not the only groups interested in the way they are run. In the longer term as society's views change and customers demand more social responsibility from the companies they deal with, company A may fare better and show more sustainability than B as customers turn against B and its practices. Being socially responsible will attract new customers who care about these issues and companies who concern themselves with pollution may find ways of improving their processes to reduce waste and actually reduce costs.

6 LEVELS OF STRATEGY – SBU (MAY 10 EXAM)

Key answer tips

This question looks at the three levels of strategy, but focuses on the business strategy. It is important to explain how the business level strategy is supported by the functional strategy below and that how the business level strategies roll up to the overall corporate strategy.

Tutorial Note

Strategy operates at different levels in an organisation. For large organisations, there are three clear levels: corporate, business and functional.

At the corporate level, organisations will decide what industry they want to operate in. At the business level, each strategic business unit (SBU) decides how it will operate in the chosen industry. At the functional level, the functions of the business look at how they can support the business strategies.

Within companies, their strategy is made up of three levels: corporate, business and functional.

The strategic level looks at the organisation's overall goals. At this level the organisation will consider what industry it wants to operate in.

The strategy filters down to the business level, where each individual strategic business unit (SBU) will consider what products to produce and how to compete in their chosen industry. Many large organisations are made up of diverse business units, each act as a separate business and each will require its own strategy.

The strategies of the SBUs are supported by the functional areas underneath them. These functional areas support the strategies on a day to day basis and at this level will consider how to deliver the strategies of the SBU, e.g. staffing levels or training required.

In order for the overall organisation's strategy to be achieved, the SBUs must deliver their strategies, and in turn these will only be achieved if the functional areas deliver their strategies. In this way the strategies of each level roll up to the overall corporate strategy.

The SBUs play a crucial part in this process and they are in the middle of the hierarchy and provide the link between the corporate and functional strategies. The strategies of the SBUs must align with the corporate strategy and to the delivery of these strategies. They have to ensure that the strategies of the functional areas are set in such a way that they facilitate the achievement of the SBU's strategies.

7   PRC COMPANY (NOV 10 EXAM)

Key answer tips

There are two parts to the requirement, ensure you answer each part as marks will be available for each.

Firstly the purpose of SWOT must be addressed, and then an explanation of what would be involved.

This is a 10 mark question and SWOT analysis clearly has 4 sections which need to be addressed. Allowing 2 marks for explaining what would be involved in each aspect of SWOT will give the bulk of the marks. You then need to ensure you provide at least 2 marks worth for the purpose of SWOT. (The marking guide allowed up to 3 marks for this).

By tackling the question in this way, you will provide a balanced answer, avoid duplication and should secure a good mark.

Tutorial Note

Corporate appraisal, or SWOT, is carried out as part of the analysis phase of strategy formulation. It brings together the internal analysis which considers the company's internal strengths and weaknesses, and the external analysis which considers the opportunities and threats within the industry.

In carrying out internal analysis, the company will use tools such as resources audits or Porter's value chain analysis. In external analysis, models such as PEST and Porter's five forces can be used.

Examiner's comments

The answer should start by explaining the purpose of undertaking a corporate appraisal and then develop to explain what is involved in undertaking a corporate appraisal, with references to strengths, weaknesses, opportunities or threats.

Weak answers will simply describe a SWOT but without making any connection between the different elements. Good answers will be explicit in explaining the purpose of corporate appraisal as part of the rational strategy decision making process, and will make reference to the information needed to inform the corporate appraisal.

Corporate appraisal, sometimes referred to as SWOT, involves the quantitative and qualitative review of a company's internal strengths and weaknesses and its relationship with external opportunities and threats. In essence, it could be used to summarise the key issues from PRC's business environment and its strategic capability, that are most likely to impact on its future strategic development.

Conducting a corporate appraisal brings together information derived from an analysis of the trends in the external and competitive environments and internal developments that may be of significance to PRC Company. The outcomes from the corporate appraisal could then be used to determine the company's current position and inform whether it should continue with its existing strategy or formulate a new strategy that will enable it to operate more effectively.

The process of conducting a corporate appraisal will require PRC to draw on two sets of data:

- Information on the current performance and resource position of the company to establish internal capability. Data will need to be captured from performing an analysis of the internal position of PRC Company, its resources and competences, and conclusions from value chain analysis.

- Information on the business environment and how this is likely to change, identifying key trends. This information will need to be collected through the process of external environment analysis (for example using the PESTEL framework and competitor analysis using Porter's five forces framework).

The internal appraisal for PRC Company should highlight:

- *Strengths*, which are the particular skills or distinctive/core competences which the company possesses and which will give it an advantage over its competitors. These are the things the company should seek to exploit. In identifying strengths, it is important that it highlights not just what PRC Company is good at, but how it is better, relative to the competition.

- *Weaknesses*, which are the shortcomings in the company and which can hinder it in achieving its strategic aims. For example, lack of resources, expertise or skill.

Strengths and weaknesses should relate to industry key factors for success and help PRC Company to assess how capable it is in dealing with changes in its business environment.

- *Opportunities* relate to the events or changes outside the company, i.e. trends in its external business environment which are favourable to the company. For example, what opportunities exist in the business environment, what is the capability profile of the competitors, are they better placed to exploit these opportunities? The events or changes identified will provide some strategic focus to the decision-making for managers in the company.

- *Threats* relate to events or changes outside the company, i.e. trends in its business environment which are unfavourable and that must be defended against. The company will need to introduce strategies to overcome these threats in some way or it may start to lose market share to its competitors.

The external appraisal will assist PRC Company in identifying opportunities which can be exploited by the company's strengths and also to anticipate environmental threats against which the company must protect itself. In other words, strategies should be developed to minimise weaknesses, or develop strengths, taking advantage of opportunities or counteracting problems from environmental changes.

Using the SWOT analysis should help PRC Company to focus on future choices and gain a better understanding of the extent to which it has the internal capability to support the changes. It will also facilitate the identification and generation of possible future strategic options for PRC.

8 PV COMPANY (MAR 11 EXAM)

Key answer tips

Start by explaining what is meant by the term mission. Then go on to develop the specific benefits for PV Company of having a clear mission. Ensure you use the scenario in your answer. Plan your answer well; ensuring that you are clear about the points you are making and ensuring that each point you make is clear and well developed.

Tutorial Note

A mission is a broad statement of the overall purpose of the organisation and should reflect the core values of the organisation. It should seek to answer questions such as: what is our business? what is valued by our customers?, what should our business be?

Examiner's comments

There were few really good answers to this question.

Common errors

Many candidates confused the broad nature of mission statements with the more specific nature of objectives. Rather than confining discussion to the justifiable claim that a mission statement is useful because objectives can be derived from such statements, some candidates went on to argue that the mission/objectives should be specific, time bound and measurable. There was a similar tendency for candidates to claim too much for mission statements when they came to discuss the relationship between mission statements, values, culture and strategic planning.

The mission essentially provides a broad statement of the overriding purpose of PV Company in terms of the products and services it provides. It is also concerned with the scope and boundaries of the company's operations in product/market terms. The mission should, therefore, be used to guide the company's current strategic decision making, articulating what PV Company does and who the organisation is for; in other words its raison d'être. It should reflect the company's core values in line with the values and expectations of the various stakeholders.

The development of a mission is an important element in the strategic planning process, in that PV Company's objectives should be set to support the mission. The benefits of this would help to provide a basis for consistent strategic and operational planning. It could assist in translating PV Company's purpose and direction into objectives suitable for assessment and control.

The mission is an essential element in the definition of what constitutes the strengths and weaknesses of PV Company and could act as a benchmark by which plans are judged against and it should help to ensure consistency in both future decisions and evaluation of possible strategies across the organisation.

Since a mission is concerned with why an organisation exists, a key benefit is that it will convey the scope and boundaries of PV Company's activities. This should help in providing clarity on purpose which currently appears to be problematic with different parts for the company having different priorities and objectives.

The mission can be powerful in communicating the intentions of PV Company and inspiring a common vision of the future. It provides everyone with unanimity of company purpose and a sense of shared values. The ideal is that everyone in the company will buy into the mission which should then provide a common source of direction for all employees, focusing on the company's strengths and competitive advantage.

It would also help in establishing clarity on PV Company's values. The values incorporated in the mission should relate to the culture and should capture the basic, perhaps often unstated, beliefs of the people who work for PV Company.

The mission could be embodied in a mission statement which could be reproduced and used on different media to reinforce the key elements of the mission as a communication vehicle not only for employees but also other stakeholder groups.

9   LEVELS OF STRATEGY – FUNCTIONAL (MAR 11 EXAM)

Key answer tips

Start by explaining the different levels of strategy. Then focus on the functional strategy. Ensure that you explain the nature of the functional strategy and discuss the links between the functional strategies and the business and corporate strategies.

Tutorial Note

Strategy operates at different levels in an organisation. For large organisations, there are three clear levels: corporate, business and functional (operational).

At the corporate level, organisations will decide what industry they want to operate in. At the business level, each strategic business unit (SBU) decides how it will operate in the chosen industry. At the functional level, the functions of the business look at how they can support the business strategies.

Examiner's comments

This question seemed to cause difficulty for candidates.

Common errors

Many candidates appeared not to have an understanding of the 'other layers of strategy' referred to in the question and a significant number of candidates confused operational strategy and functional strategy even suggesting they operated at different levels. As a result, they were unable to offer a coherent answer to the question.

Weak answers just describe the different levels of strategy. Good answers make clear the relationships explicitly in terms of how functional level strategies support the organisation's corporate strategy

In explaining how the functional strategies support the overall corporate strategy of an organisation it is helpful to think about the different levels as a hierarchy, whereby activities at the lowest level (functional) are guided by decisions at the higher level. In making the distinctions between the different levels, Hofer and Schendel distinguish between the corporate strategy (what business to be in), business strategy (what market segments to serve and how) and functional strategy (the detailed strategies of departments such as HRM, Finance, Marketing, Sales, Production etc).

Functional strategies, which are sometimes referred to as operational, are the longer term management policies that are intended to ensure that the functional areas of the company play their part in helping the organisation to achieve its overall goals. They are important since this is the level at which corporate and business level strategies are implemented in detail. This means translating the objectives of the organisation and SBUs into digestible elements.

Functional strategies within operating companies do accumulate upwards, like building blocks into business unit development and hence into overall organisation's strategy. Steps taken by the functional departments need to be tied into the business unit strategies because otherwise departmental actions can thwart or counter the thrust of the overall business, or add too little to the value within the overall value of the business.

It is essential that the various functions of the organisation contribute to the achievement of higher level strategies, working in a supportive sense rather than conflicting with the corporate and SBU strategies since it is the accumulated effect of the strategic steps taken in each function of a business (HRM, Finance, Marketing, Sales and Production etc) that determines the strategic development of the business. For example, the recruitment strategies developed by HRM need to be designed to ensure that new staff are recruited with the skills needed for the future development of the organisation.

In developing functional strategies there is both a top down and bottom up communications exchange. This helps to ensure that the right strategic decisions are taken, that the detail will work and that everyone is aware of the plan and personally engaged in it to ensure its achievement.

10   DPW (MAR 11 EXAM)

Key answer tips

The question asks for one strategic management model or framework. Given that the question asks about analysing the external environment of F country, this suggests a model which looks at the macro environment. The most obvious model to select would be PEST. Porter's Diamond could also be used if carefully applied. Porter's five forces focuses on the industry level, therefore is not going to score well.

Start by explaining the model selected and the component parts of the model, then apply the model to the scenario given.

Tutorial Note

PEST is a useful approach to use when analysing an organisation's wider environment. It highlights the various aspects of the external environment which should be considered: namely political, economic, social, technological, environmental and legal. By considering each of these aspects in turn, the organisation should be able to determine a clear picture of their external environment and this will assist them in developing a suitable strategy.

Note: other variations of PEST are available and would score equally well.

Examiner's comments

This question was generally well answered, especially by those candidates who chose to use the PEST framework for their answer. Those applying Porter's Diamond model also tended to score well.

Common errors

Candidates choosing Porter's Five Forces model did less well because this model only covers the more immediate competitive environment and neglects the influence of the broader macro environmental factors.

There are a number of strategic management frameworks that could be used to assess the external environment in F Country to decide whether to move into F Country. These include PEST, Porter's five forces, and Porter's Diamond. This answer will explain PEST.

The PEST framework is a useful way of organising information on the macro-environmental influences that can be used to assess the external factors that might impact on DPW's development in F country. This would involve an analysis of the political/legal, economic, socio-cultural and technological factors. The headings can be used as a checklist to assess the relative importance of the different influences on DPW Company's proposed strategy.

With regard to the information that should be gathered on the general environment in F Country it will be important to assess the nature of the political and economic environment. This would include exploring the legislative and government policies and attitudes to competition that could impact on DPW Company's development. For example, is the government of F Country encouraging inward investment by offering grants to companies or does it have policies in place to protect its own industries? DPW Company would also want to consider the political stability in F Country. If there is political instability and unrest, it may not be a positive step to enter the market. It would also be interested in any current or future legislation relating to the home furnishings retail industry.

Information should be collected on the nature of the economic climate such as the rate of economic growth, level of tax rates, interest rates, exchange rates, and levels of consumer disposable income and the percentage of household income spent on home furniture. All of these factors could impact on the demand for DPW Company's home furniture products.

Research should be undertaken to determine whether the social factors are encouraging for DPW Company, for instance in terms of the customer attitudes, values and beliefs of people in F Country and the extent to which there is a market for home furniture and whether people would be willing to buy home furniture from a foreign retailer. Information on factors such as home ownership, current trends and buyer behaviour for home furniture would be useful. Information on social factors would also help in determining the cultural context of F Country, in order to gain an understanding of any potential cultural differences, not only of customers, but also future employees.

Technological factors that would need to be explored relate to the communications infrastructure and any technological issues that might impact on the way the retailers operate. This could relate to computer tracking of stock, as well as ordering and payment systems. Also, the state of the transport systems needed to move stock around the country would need to be assessed.

The PEST framework can be expanded to consider environmental/ethical factors. Interest here will centre on the sustainability in the use of materials/resources and the cost of packaging and disposal of waste associated with home furniture products. It also is about ethical conduct in the management of employees.

Examiner's comment: Candidates could legitimately develop their answers using Porter's Diamond.

11 FF (MAY 11 EXAM)

Key answer tips

Start by explaining Porter's five forces model and its components. Then apply the aspects of the model to the supermarket industry. Few marks will be gained without adequate application to the supermarket industry.

Tutorial Note

Porter's five forces is a model used as part of external analysis. While models such as PEST focus on the macro environmental factors, Porter's five forces considers the attractiveness of the industry the organisation operates in. The model is useful in determining whether to enter a new industry, or whether to remain and expand operations in an existing industry. It can also be used to determine what competitive strategy should be adopted within the industry.

Examiner's comments

A mixed response as far as the whole cohort of candidates was concerned. A small number of candidates gained maximum marks for the question and many others gained good marks ranging from 7 to 9 of the 10 marks available.

Common errors

These fell into two main categories; candidates who lacked an understanding of the Five Forces model and those who demonstrated an understanding of the model but did not apply it adequately to the supermarket industry.

Porter's Five Forces model is a useful framework that FF Supermarket could use to help it assess the attractiveness of the supermarket industry. Industry attractiveness refers to the potential for profitability that derives from competing in that industry. Each industry's attractiveness, or profitability potential, is a direct result of interaction of different environment and industry forces that affect the nature of competition.

The model brings together the following five competitive forces:

- Threat of new entrants/barriers to entry
- Bargaining power of suppliers
- Bargaining power of buyers
- Threat of substitute products/services
- Competitive rivalry

It is the collective strength of these forces that will determine the profit potential of the supermarket industry. For example:

- Barriers to entry are those factors which will need to be overcome by new entrants if they are to compete successfully in the supermarket industry. Barriers for the supermarket industry might include, high capital requirement to entry, access to supply channels, customer or supplier loyalty, experience, expected retaliation by existing players. Understanding whether the barriers to entry are high or low would help FF Supermarket appreciate the likelihood of new entrants moving into its industry and how it could increase barriers.

- The bargaining power of suppliers is primarily related to the power suppliers have to raise their prices. If the suppliers have high power then this could influence the margins of FF Supermarket in an unfavourable way and hence have direct consequences for the profitability of the supermarket. Power of suppliers will be higher where the supply is dominated by a few firms, which is an unlikely scenario for the supermarket industry. Power will also be higher where there are significant switching costs associated with moving to another supplier.

- The bargaining power of buyers is gained through their ability to force prices down, or get improved product quality. It also depends on the size and number of buyers. Power will be greater when buyer power is concentrated in a few hands and when the offering is undifferentiated. In terms of the supermarket sector, there are low switching costs for buyers, so supermarkets have tried to differentiate on bases other than range of products to reduce buyer power.

- Pressure from substitutes is where there are other products that satisfy the same need. For the supermarket general substitution is prevalent. FF Supermarket will need to understand how to retain customers, perhaps for example through the use of a loyalty card.

- Rivalry amongst existing competitors refers to direct competition between an organisation and its immediate rivals, i.e. those organisations offering similar products/services. It will be influenced by the number of firms operating in the industry, and industry growth rates. If there are numerous organisations, particularly with strong brands, and there is low industry growth then this will not be an attractive industry. FF supermarket will need to develop aggressive strategies to compete in such industry conditions.

The outcomes from the analysis can be used to derive conclusions about the potential opportunities and threats facing the supermarket sector. The information from the analysis would also help in identifying the factors driving profitability and inform the competitive strategy needed.

12   Z COMPANY (MAY 11 EXAM)

Key answer tips

Start with an explanation of the resource-based view (RBV), its principles and characteristics. This aspect of the answer needs to be developed in some detail. The scenario does not offer many examples, but where possible these should be used.

Tutorial Note

The resource-based view of strategy sees competitive advantage stemming from some unique asset or competence possessed by the organisation. It is often referred to as an 'inside-out' view as the focus is on what the organisation has (its resources) and what it is good at (its competences). In order to gain competitive advantage, the resources should be **unique** and difficult for competitors to gain, and the competencies should be **core** and difficult for competitors to imitate.

Barney identified four criteria for unique resources: valuable, rare, imperfectly imitable and difficult to substitute. Prahalad and Hamel identified three characteristics of core competencies: provides potential access to a wide variety of markets, increases perceived customer benefits and hard for competitors to imitate.

Examiner's comments

Generally poorly answered but with a few very good answers from well prepared candidates.

Common errors

The main reason for poor performance in the answers to this question was lack of knowledge about the resource based approach to strategy development.

The Chief Executive puts the impressive performance of Z Company down to adopting the Resource-Based View (RBV) to strategy development.

The RBV is based on the fundamental principle that competitive advantage is derived from some unique assets or competences possessed by a company. This takes an inside-out approach to strategy since it is based on harnessing the internal capabilities of the company to achieve sustainable competitive advantage. This is in contrast to the more traditional positioning approach which views the external environment as the critical factor in determining an organisation's strategy. The strategic choices when adopting the RBV are not dictated by the constraints of the external environment but influenced more by examining how the organisation can best stretch its core competences relative to the opportunities in the external environment.

The RBV posits that it is the resources and capabilities that reside within an organisation which help an organisation to develop to achieve competitive advantage. It has developed from the work of Prahalad and Hamel's work on core competences which focuses on the strategic intent of an organisation to leverage its internal capabilities and core competences to confront competition. Adopting the RBV would mean that superior performance and profitability is dependent on the possession of a set of unique resources or abilities that cannot be easily imitated by its rivals.

The resources of the organisation are essentially the inputs that enable it to carry out its activities and can be categorised into two types: tangible and intangible resources. Tangible resources are essentially the physical inputs into an organisation that can be seen, for example plant and equipment, raw materials, finance, employees. Intangible resources range from intellectual property rights such as patents, trademarks and copyrights, technological resources, brand and reputation.

It is suggested that intangible resources are the most likely source to achieve competitive advantage, as is probably the case for Z Company. This, it could be argued, is because intangible resources are more difficult to imitate than tangible resources and therefore, more likely to be a source of sustainable competitive advantage. For resources to be unique, Barney (1991) suggests that they must add value, be rare, difficult to imitate and cannot be easily substituted.

Resources alone, however, are not a basis for competitive advantage. Differential performance is based on how an organisation utilises its resources. For example, one of the most important resources for an organisation is the skill and knowledge possessed by the organisation's employees. It is this skill and knowledge acquired over time and embedded in the organisation's culture that influences how it operates and determines its success.

Competences become core competences if they are difficult for the competition to acquire. When competences are rare, difficult to imitate, non-substitutable, and allow opportunities to be exploited or threats neutralised, then they can be considered core competences and serve as the basis of an organisation's sustained competitive advantage.

Z Company's capabilities appear to be its ability to innovate at a fast pace, its design capability and ability for fast product development. Capacity for innovation is not something that can easily be acquired so could be viewed as providing sustainable competitive advantage.

13   K COMPANY (MAY 11 EXAM)

Key answer tips

The key to success in this question is to ensure that you have read the question requirements carefully. The question asks for two main things: the **type** of information required, and the **sources** of information. It would be reasonable to assume that each part of the requirement is worth five marks; therefore it should be relatively easy to see where the marks will come from. Use the scenario where possible and consider what type of information would be useful in the case of a company considering operating in another region. Then consider where this information may come from.

Tutorial Note

In terms of the type of information required, consider what information would be useful for a company considering moving to a new region. They would require information about the companies who currently operate in that region, the types of products offered by these companies, customer preferences in that new region etc. Any relevant point will gain marks in your answer.

In terms of sources of information, again any relevant source quoted will gain marks. Consider publically available sources first, such as the internet and published accounts. These will be available to all so will rarely offer all the information required. Then consider more specific sources of information, such as market research. This will offer better, more relevant information but will be costly to gather.

Examiner's comments

For candidates who interpreted this question correctly, it was a straightforward question which resulted in some high scoring marks.

Common errors

A surprising number of candidates interpreted this question very broadly to mean not only the types of competitive intelligence information as the question intended but also to the broader environmental context , and so spent much unproductive time applying PEST and Five Forces analysis in a discussion of the general environmental context. Another weakness was that some candidates only described the types of information or the sources, but not both as required by the question.

The overriding purpose of gathering competitor intelligence is to identify the specific competitive advantage of rival organisations. This would help K Company in developing a better understanding of the strengths and weaknesses of its potential competitors and to help predict competitor behaviour were it to follow through with its plans to open up showrooms in other parts of the country.

Having identified which part of the country to concentrate on, the first step would require K Company to make a choice on which competitors it should collect information about. This could be based on which of its competitors it perceives as posing the greatest threat. This is likely to include both local businesses and other larger "chains" like K Company itself.

K Company would need to collect intelligence to help it understand the strategic resources of its main competitors. In other words, those resources which set competitors apart from other players in the industry. It would involve undertaking competitor profiling. This is the basic analysis of key competitors investigating, for example, their objectives, resources, market strength, products and services and current strategies. In terms of the types of intelligence that would be helpful, this might include:

- *Information on current products and services.* It is important to collect information not only about the competitors' products/services, but also their segmentation strategies, branding and image, and customer segments targeted.

- *Understanding of the present strategies of key competitors.* This could be identified from what the company actually does. Information on explicit statements of intent could be gained from annual reports and presentations to financial analysts.

- *Indentifying competitors' objectives.* For example, is a particular competitor seeking sales growth or market share growth in an aggressive manner? Is it investing in new premises?

- *Identifying the competitors' resources and capabilities.* This will therefore involve gathering information on their management profiles, organisational structure, financial strength and technologies to understand not only what they are doing now, but also what they are capable of doing in the future. The scale and size of the company's resources are both important indicators of the competitor's threat.

To find out the above information will involve collecting both qualitative and quantitative information. The gathering of information should be viewed as a continual process, hence competitor rivals should be continuously monitored for signs of activity and the industry scanned for the emergence of potential new rivals.

There are a range of different sources available to K Company which could be accessed to gain information about its potential competitors, for example:

- Web based Home pages of competitors

- Annual report and accounts

- Newspaper articles and on-line data sources on company information using, for example, LexisNexis

- Magazines and journals including trade media, business management and technical journals

- On-line data services such as FAME to collect financial and statistical information

- Directories and yearbooks covering particular industries

- Market research reports and reviews produced by specialist firms such as Mintel, Economist Intelligence Unit, which might provide information on market share and marketing activity.

- Customer market research could be independently commissioned to establish consumer attitudes and awareness towards K Company's potential competitors in the various regions.

14   PORTER'S DIAMOND (SEPT 11 EXAM)

Key answer tips

The requirements of this question were clear; discuss the four determinants in Porter's Diamond model. It was important to ensure that your answer for each part explained how the aspects of the model helped in establishing national competitive advantage. Simply describing each of the four aspects would not have scored well.

Tutorial Note

Porter's Diamond attempts to explain why some nations tend to produce firms with sustained competitive advantage in some industry more than others. There are four aspects to the model: factor conditions, demand conditions, related and supporting industries and firm strategy, structure and rivalry. When discussing the model, it is important to be able to explain how these factors contribute to national competitive advantage.

Within the factor conditions, Porter suggested that there were two sorts: basic factors and advanced factors. Basic factors were factors such as raw materials, availability of labour and capital. These are largely 'natural' and not created by policy or strategy. Advanced factors were factors such as infrastructure, training and skills, R&D etc. These factors were deliberately developed and Porter argues that it is only these advanced factors which contribute to competitive advantage.

Examiner's comments

Many answers provided the correct labels for the four interacting determinants of Porter's Diamond model but in many cases were unable to explain how they contributed to national competitive advantage

Common errors

Many candidates did not differentiate between basic and advanced factors and so were unable to indicate how competitive advantage could be achieved; similarly many specified home demand conditions but were unable to say how the existence of demanding domestic consumers contributed to efficient firms that could go on to compete successfully in a global economy and so on.

Porter's Diamond is based on four interacting determinants that assist the country, and hence individual organisations operating in that country, to be more competitive in international markets. These are factor conditions; home demand conditions; related and supporting industries; firm strategy, structure and rivalry.

Taking each determinant in turn:

- *Factor conditions* refer to the factors of production that go into making a product or service. Different nations have different stocks of factors which can be categorised as human resources; physical resources; knowledge; capital; infrastructure. It is not sufficient to have an abundance of the factors; rather it is the efficiency with which they are deployed that is important.

  Porter also distinguished between basic factors, which he claims are unsustainable as a source of competitive advantage, and advanced factors.

- *Home demand conditions* refer to the nature of the domestic customer becoming a source of competitive advantage. Dealing with sophisticated and demanding customers with high expectations in an organisation's home market will help drive innovation and quality, which in turn will help an organisation to be effective in other countries.

  Although economies of scale are relevant, it is not necessarily about the quantity of home demand but the information that the home market gives organisations and the impetus to innovate. If the customer needs are understood in the home market earlier than in the world market, the firms benefit from the experience.

- *Related and Supporting Industries.* Porter proposes that a nation's competitive industries are clustered, where a cluster is a linking of industries through relationships which are either vertical (buyer-supplier) or horizontal (common customers, technology, skills).

  Related and supporting industries of local clusters of related and mutually supportive industries can be a source of competitive advantage. In other words, competitive success in one industry is linked to the success in related industries. Having a domestic supplier industry can be preferable to a good foreign supplier as proximity to managerial and technical people along with cultural similarity can facilitate free and open information flows.

- *Firm strategy, industry structure and rivalry* are related to the fact that nations are likely to secure competitive advantage in industries that are more culturally suited to their normal management practices and industrial structures. For example, industries in different countries have different time horizons, funding needs and infrastructures. Fierce domestic rivalry and competition will drive innovation, force down costs and develop new methods of competing. This can enhance global competitive advantage.

15   T COMPANY (SEPT 11 EXAM)

Key answer tips

This is a general question about the importance of competitor analysis and the types of information which would be required. The scenario does not give any information about the situation of the company; therefore your answer will be general.

Ensure you answer the two parts of the question in enough detail. The reasons for carrying out competitor analysis should come straight from the text book. In terms of the types of information required, ensure that you develop this part of the answer well. It is worth six marks, so a brief list will not earn many marks.

Tutorial Note

According to Wilson and Gilligan, competitor analysis has three main roles:

–   To help management understand their competitive advantages and disadvantages relative to competitors;

–   To generate insights into competitors' past, present and potential strategies;

–   To give an informed basis for developing future strategies to sustain or establish advantages over competitors

Examiner's comments

This was generally well answered but some candidates mistakenly concentrated on sources in part (b) of the question suggesting that they had not read the question carefully enough.

Common errors

As indicated, neglecting to specify a good range of types of information as asked for in the question.

(a)   In explaining why undertaking competitor analysis is important, the presentation should include points on the following:

- The overriding purpose of gathering competitor intelligence is to identify the specific competitive advantage of rival organisations. This would help the company in developing a better understanding of strengths and weaknesses of its potential competitors and to help predict competitor behaviour.

- It should also help management in understanding the competitive advantage (or indeed disadvantage) of the organisation relative to competitors.

- It can help in generating insights into the past, present and potential strategies of its competitors and how they have reacted. This in turn will provide an informed basis for developing future strategies to sustain and establish advantage over competitors and to assist with the forecasting of the returns on strategic investments when deciding between alternative strategies.

(b)   The second part of the presentation should include points to highlight the types of information that should be collected on competitors.

The first point would be to identify the competitors for which information should be collected. This could be based on which competitors it perceives as posing the greatest threat.

Other types of information that should be collected as part of competitor analysis include:

- The present strategies of key competitors, for example; how is the firm competing and where the firm is competing.

- Identifying competitors' current goals and objectives. For example, is a particular competitor seeking sales growth or market share growth in an aggressive manner? Is it investing in new premises?

- Information on competitors' current products and services. Also their segmentation strategies, branding and image, and the customer segments targeted.

- Identifying the competitors' resources and capabilities. This will therefore involve gathering information on their management profiles, organisational structure, financial strength and technologies to understand not only what they are doing now, but also what they are capable of doing in the future. The scale and size of the company's resources are both important indicators of the competitor's threat.

16   COMPETITIVE ADVANTAGE (SEPT 11 EXAM)

Key answer tips

There are two requirements in this question, ensure that both are answered. The bulk of the marks will come from the explanation of the resource-based view (RBV). Start with an explanation of competitive advantage and then go on to discuss RBV. Ensure that the concept of competitive advantage is fully developed, and where possible include examples of how competitive advantage can be gained.

When discussing RBV, ensure you fully cover resources and competencies, and explain how these contribute to competitive advantage.

Tutorial Note

The resource-based view of strategy sees competitive advantage stemming from some unique asset or competence possessed by the organisation. It is often referred to as an 'inside-out' view as the focus is on what the organisation has (its resources) and what it is good at (its competences). In order to gain competitive advantage, the resources should be **unique** and difficult for competitors to gain, and the competencies should be **core** and difficult for competitors to imitate.

Barney identified four criteria for unique resources: valuable, rare, imperfectly imitable and difficult to substitute. Prahalad and Hamel identified three characteristics of core competencies: provides potential access to a wide variety of markets, increases perceived customer benefits and hard for competitors to imitate.

Examiner's comments

Most were able to define 'competitive advantage' but the resource based view was in many cases reduced to a number of well drilled bullet points. There were however, a few good answers.

Common errors

Many answers did not provide even the basic ingredients of the resource-based view and thus scored no more than three or four marks.

Competitive advantage refers to the significant advantages that an organisation has over its competitors. It can be gained on the basis of price or through some form of differentiation, such as quality of service, product design or branding which allows an organisation to charge higher prices for its products/services.

The resource based view (RBV) to achieving competitive advantage is a more recent paradigm of strategic management. This is an inside-out-view where competitive advantage is gained from the exploitation of an organisation's resources, competences and capabilities. In other words, it refers to the distinctive groups of skill that would allow an organisation to provide particular benefits and deliver competitor advantage and is not dictated by the constraints of the external environment.

The RBV approach emphasises the development of strategy based on internal capability, hence an organisation would need to use strategic management frameworks that would help it in understanding the internal aspects of the organisation. In other words, to determine what it is good at, what its strengths are and what its weaknesses are.

Adopting the RBV means that superior profitability would depend on its possession of unique resources or abilities that cannot be easily imitated by its rivals. The assumption here is that an organisation is a collection of resources, capabilities and competences that are relatively unique. These can provide the basis for an organisation's strategic development and its ability to compete better than those of competitors.

The RBV has developed from the work of Prahalad and Hamel's work on core competences which focuses on the strategic intent of an organisation to leverage its internal capabilities and core competences to confront competition. This is sometimes referred to as strategic stretch.

Resources can be tangible, such as plant and equipment, access to raw materials and finance, trained/skilled workforce or intangible such as brand and intellectual property. However, it is the way the resources are used which provides the capability to compete. For resources to be unique, Barney (1991) suggests that they must add value, be rare, difficult to imitate and cannot be easily substituted.

Intangible resources are often the most likely to create sources of competitive advantage, as it is argued that they are more difficult for competitors to understand and imitate. In addition, it is the way resources are integrated with each other to perform a task or activity that provides the capability or competence for an organisation to compete. Therefore, one of the most important resources for an organisation is the skill and knowledge possessed by the organisation's employees, which is acquired over time and embedded in its culture.

PROJECT MANAGEMENT

17   S COMPANY (NOV 07 EXAM)

Key answer tips

This is a straightforward question on feasibility studies. Start your answer by explaining the purpose of project feasibility for example to establish if the proposed project will meet its objectives and help to decide between alternative project strategies. Next you need to explain the different types of feasibility that should be considered and relate your answer to specific issues within the Snow Dome project.

Tutorial Note

There are four main types of feasibility which should be considered when assessing a project's feasibility.

Technical feasibility considers whether the technical capability exists to undertake the suggested project. It asks the question: "can it be done?"

Social (operational) feasibility considers social factors associated with the project, such as staffing levels required before and after and skills required. It asks the question: "does it fit with the organisation's goals and values?"

Ecological (environmental) feasibility considers the impact the project will have on the local community and on the wider environment. It asks the question: "how will it impact on the environment?"

Economic (financial) feasibility considers what benefit the organisation will gain from the project compared to the costs of the project. It asks the question: "is it financially worth it?"

Feasibility studies are carried out as part of the initiation stage of a project. Their main purpose is to make the decision whether or not to proceed with the project. As part of this there may be a number of alternative strategies to meet identified needs and the feasibility study can help decide on which proposal best meets the needs.

The study should address the following types of feasibility:

Technical

- The technology exists as other competitors are using it.

- S should investigate which models of real snow makers competitors are using and if newer technology available.

- Presumably the snow makers were developed in ski resorts so should have high standards of reliability but S should try to discover what problems may arise with the different technologies on offer and to what extent the technology has been tried and tested.

- Different snow making machines may make snow at a wider range of temperatures, some snow may last longer, some may resist clumping better and some may give a more authentic skiing experience. What performance does S require of the technology?

Social (Operational)

- The new venture may result in higher staffing levels than at present. Operational feasibility could involve examining the number and skills of people required and whether this can be met through recruitment and training.

- Operational feasibility should also consider timescales and whether the snow dome could be built to meet targeted dates.

Ecological (Environmental)

- S needs to consider the impact of the snow dome on the local community and what that might do to the company image. Higher usage might lead to greater traffic congestion, for example.

- The impact on the environment should also be considered. For example, the snow dome would presumably use a great deal of energy to make the snow in the first place and then keep the whole indoor area cold enough to prevent thawing.

Economic (Financial)

- A financial feasibility study would need to analyse the costs of the project (for example, decommissioning the existing dry slope, building new facilities, acquiring snow machines, ongoing maintenance costs, ongoing energy and water costs and finance costs) and the expected impact on revenue (for example, looking at the numbers of customers and whether or not prices can be raised).

- Evaluating these figures could involve payback calculations and/or discounted cash flows.

18   P (MAY 07 EXAM)

Key answer tips

There are two requirements in this question: what is involved in the initiation stage of a project and explain the contents of a project initiation document (PID). Ensure that you answer both requirements fully.

Use the scenario as much as possible to illustrate your answer.

Tutorial Note

Initiation is the first phase in the project lifecycle and commences when a need or objective is defined. A number of activities take place at the initiation stage which aim to assess the need and the possible ways of meeting it. By the end of this stage a project initiation document (PID) will be produced which will outline what the project is aiming to achieve and how it will achieve its objectives. This document can be used to obtain authorisation to take the project forward to detailed planning and acts as a base document against which the success of the project can ultimately be measured.

The main sections contained in a PID are listed in the textbook; you should ensure you are familiar with this list as it will provide a good structure for the second part of this question.

Project initiation is the first stage of the project planning process and usually involves the identification of a need, opportunity or problem. In this case the need for a new school has been identified with the opportunity for the charity to build the school.

At this stage a feasibility study will be undertaken and a decision made whether or not to proceed. This will be based on forecasts funds to be raised, cost and availability of manpower (both locally and in terms of volunteers willing to travel to F), suitable skills and building materials.

If the project is to be undertaken, then the project team will be brought together and a project initiation document (PID) prepared.

This is a formal document listing the goals, constraints and success criteria for a project. When all the stakeholders in a project have agreed the document, it will be referred to as a means of resolving disagreements about the project as it progresses.

A PID should contain at least the following sections:

Purpose statement. This explains why the project is being undertaken and could include justification for rebuilding and equipping of the school as opposed to some other project in the earthquake zone

Scope statement. This puts boundaries to the project by outlining the major activities. For example, does the project involve just the school or local water supplies and infrastructure as well? It is important to include this section in order to prevent 'scope creep', as the volunteers think up other things they might want to do to help the disaster area.

Deliverables. What are the main outcomes expected from the project? Deliverables tend to be tangible elements of the project, such as reports, assets and other outputs. In this case the desired outcomes are the construction and equipping of a new school building in twelve months. Any constraints should also be acknowledged such as budget or available resources (that is people, money and equipment needed). More specifically this section could also consider, for example, whether the school is to be built to its former design or new classrooms and facilities added, whether equipment refers to desks or IT resources.

Cost and time estimates. Even at this early stage, it is a good idea for the project team to have some feel for the organisation's expectations in terms of the project budget. These estimates will necessarily be modified later in the project, but are necessary to give a starting point for planning. Since fundraising is part of the project, the amount of funds that must be raised to fund the school project should be estimated.

Objectives. A clear statement of the mission, critical success factors and milestones of the project. The objectives can be defined in terms of the triple constraints of the time they should take, what they should cost and the quality that should be delivered.

Stakeholders. A list of the major stakeholders in the project and their interest in the project. This will include the charity, local pupils, local government in F and possible suppliers.

Chain of command. A statement (and diagram) of the project organisation structure. Here the project team is made up of volunteers but the PID should still set out the roles, responsibilities and signatory powers of the different members during the project, along with other issues associated with control. The communications, types of meetings and reports should also be explained in the document.

19   R (MAY 05 EXAM) *Walk in the footsteps of a top tutor*

Key answer tips

This question has two requirements. The first is to construct a network diagram. Make sure you are able to construct a network diagram and can calculate the earliest and latest start times. The question then asks for you to explain the usefulness of this diagram to planning within R. Ensure you answer both parts of the question.

Tutor's top tips

The first step in constructing the network diagram is to try to draw he basic shape of the network. Remember that the diagram is made up of activity lines and nodes and that each activity line must start and end with a node.

Step 1: go through the list of activities given and highlight those which can start straight away (these will be shown as having no dependency). In this case, activities A and B can start straight away.

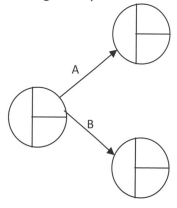

Tutor's top tips

Step 2: Now go through and add in all the other activities. C, D, E and F are straightforward:

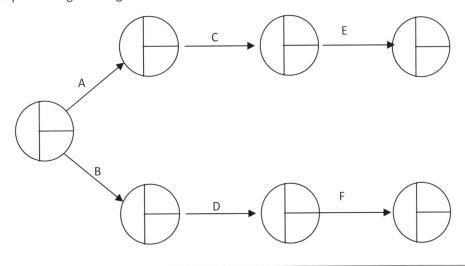

Tutor's top tips

Step 3: Activity G is more difficult as it comes after both E and F. There are two ways this can be drawn.

(a)   Use a dummy line to join the nodes after E and F. A dummy line is shown as a dotted line and has a duration of zero. Activity G can then be drawn coming from the combined node:

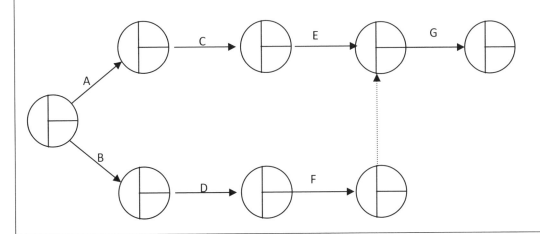

(b)   Draw E and F going to the same node and draw activity G coming from that node:

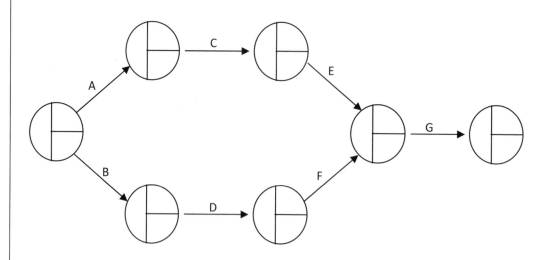

Both of these diagrams are correct and will give exactly the same answer. We will use (b) for the remainder of the answer.

Tutor's top tips

Step 4: Now the basic shape has been drawn, the durations for each activity can be added:

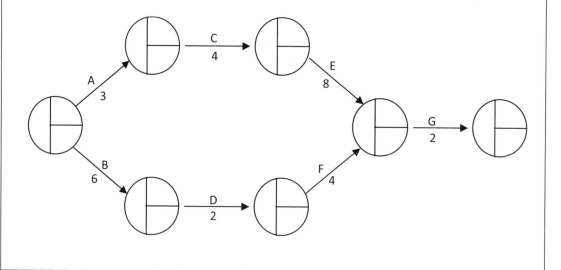

Tutor's top tips

Step 5: Working left to right, calculate the earliest event times (EETs). The first node always has an EET of zero. Take the EET of the node at the beginning of the activity line and add on the duration of the activity to get the EET for the node at the end of the activity line. Where there is a choice of EETs, always select the highest:

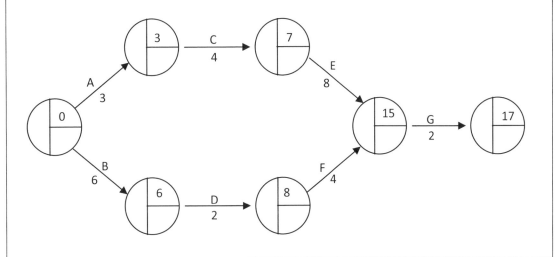

Tutor's top tips

Step 6: Working right to left, calculate the latest event times (LETs). On the end node, the EET and LET are the same, so start with a LET of 17.

Take the LET of the node at the end the activity line and deduct the duration of the activity to get the LET for the node at the beginning of the activity line. Where there is a choice of LETs, always select the lowest:

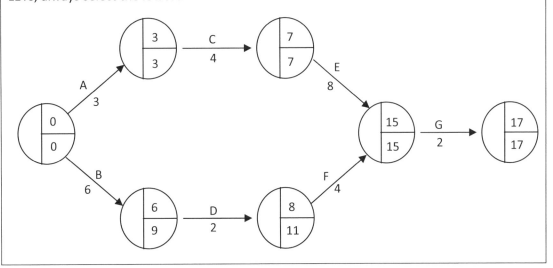

Tutor's top tips

Step 7: The references for the nodes can now be added and the critical path can be shown. The critical path is a continuous path from the first to the last node showing those activities which must be done on time or the overall duration of the project will be extended.

The activities on the critical path can be found by looking at the nodes. If the EET and LET are the same on the node at the beginning and the end of the activity line then that activity is on the critical path. In this example, the activities on the critical path are A, C, E and G. These are normally denoted by two lines drawn on the activity line. In this example, we have shown the critical activity lines in bold.

As well as the activities on the critical path, the diagram also shows the overall duration of the project. This can be read from the end node. In this case the overall duration of the project is 17 weeks.

Float or slack in activities can also be ascertained from the network diagram. Where a node shows a different EET and LET, the difference between them shows the slack for the activity. From our diagram we can see that there are 3 weeks of slack for activities B, D or F.

The network diagram for planning the conference is as follows:

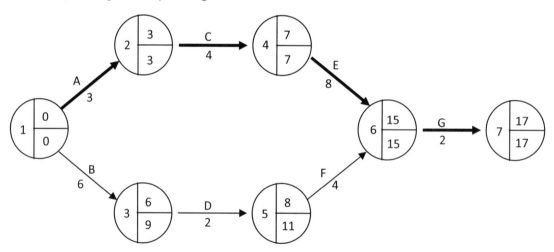

This can help in planning the conference as follows:

Information	How useful
Project duration is 17 days	• R can plan her own time to ensure that enough time is allocated to planning before the conference starts.
Critical path is ACEG	• R can put more time into ensuring that these activities are not delayed otherwise this will increase the overall duration of the planning phase. • R could look into alternatives – for example considering different printers to produce the conference papers. Time saved here would reduce the overall duration of the planning.
Latest finish times	• R can make a diary note emphasising when activities must be finished by, e.g. book speakers by day 7 and venue by day 11 at the latest.
Slack	• Activities B, D and F have 3 weeks of slack. This would help R in managing resources as these activities could be rescheduled if required. As long as activity F is complete by week 15, the project will be on time.

20 PROJECT MANAGEMENT (NOV 06 EXAM)

Key answer tips

There are two requirements in this question, ensure you answer both. Firstly you have to explain the concept of risk and then go on to explain how risks can be managed. In answering the second part of the question, you should use the risk management process. This will give your answer structure and ensure completeness.

Tutorial Note

Risk and uncertainty are always present in projects. It is important to assess the risks in a project and manage the risks appropriately as this will have an impact on the likelihood of success of the project.

The risk management process has four main stages:

– Risk identification, where a list of potential risks should be drawn up

– Risk analysis, where the potential probability (likelihood) and impact (magnitude) of each risk is assessed and from this the risks can be prioritised

> – Risk planning, where the management of each risk is considered. The management methods are often summarised as TARA – transfer, avoid, reduce, accept
> – Risk monitoring, where the progress of managing the risks is tracked. It is important to continually reassess risks as new risks could have emerged, or existing risks could have changed in their likelihood or potential magnitude.

The concept of risk

Risk can be defined as the probability of an undesirable event occurring. Within project management there will always be the chance of hazards or problems occurring that can threaten the project manager's ability to achieve the objectives of the project within the constraints of cost, time and quality set by the sponsor. Risk management means taking deliberate actions whilst planning and executing a project so as to increase the likelihood of the project being successful.

Ways in which risk can be managed in a project

Risk management is one of the nine knowledge areas of the Project Management Institute, covering risk identification, risk quantification, risk response development and risk response control. Each of these shall be considered in turn.

Risk identification

Risk identification means recognising that a hazard exists, and then attempting to define its characteristics.

Risk quantification

Risk quantification means making an estimate as to the relative likelihood and impact of each particular risk, relative to other identified risks of the project. 'Likelihood' refers to the statistical chance of a particular risk occurring, whilst 'impact' refers to the scale of the adverse effect on the project resulting from the occurrence of that risk. This then enables the project manager to prioritise the risks identified, so as to decide the order in which the risks shall have responses planned for them.

Risk response development

Risk response development means deciding how to address each risk identified, by means of contingency plans. The purpose of such plans is to speed up the response to the risk if the hazard occurs. Having such plans is intended to minimise the adverse effect on the project from identified hazards.

Possible approaches to risk management include the following: risk avoidance, where both the impact and likelihood of the risk are high; risk transference, where the risk has a high impact but low likelihood; and risk reduction, where the risk has a high likelihood but low impact. Avoidance usually requires fundamental replanning, whereas transference means transferring the risk to a subcontractor or insurer. Risk reduction can be achieved via training team members or enhancing internal controls.

Risk response control

Risk response control means ensuring that the responses required by contingency plans to hazards are fully implemented, and that remaining stages of the project are adequately replanned so as to take account of the changes made as a result of the contingency plan. This will ensure that the plans for the remainder of the project remain valid.

Risk response control also means measuring the effectiveness with which risks are managed, so as to allow continuous improvement in managing risk in future projects. This can form part of the formal closure stage of the project.

21 P PROJECT MANAGER (MAY 08 EXAM)

Key answer tips

The best way to tackle this question would be to read through the scenario carefully and look for the communication issues given. For each of the issues, suggest what P could do to improve his communication.

You are asked to consider all communication with stakeholders with regards to the project, consider how the improvements you suggest would improve the stakeholders' understanding of the project status.

Tutorial Note

This question concerns barriers to communication. Many of the problems listed are common problems, which are detailed in the textbook:

- Unclear message
- Information omitted/too much information
- Use of technical jargon
- Inappropriate medium
- Sending mixed messages

A number of these problems can be clearly seen in the scenario.

The success of H Company's relocation project will depend upon good planning, control and communication.

The problem

The process of communication between P and the other members of the project team is causing misunderstandings. The main problems highlighted are:

- Information overload – team members feel that they receive too many e-mails and that the e-mail cover too many different issues. This is leading to confusion.

- P is sending complex messages which the team members do not always understand. It is difficult to ensure that all team members are performing the tasks required if the communication from the project manager is not clear.

- P uses technical jargon which not all team members will understand. Project teams are often multi-disciplinary as members are recruited from a variety of areas. Not all team members will have, or require the same technical knowledge.

- P gives too much detail, which is not relevant to each team member. It would appear that P issues blanket e-mails to all members. This can result in team members ignoring the messages as they feel they do not need them.

The solution

P needs to think about the following:

- Who does the message need to be communicated to?
- Which is the best method of communication to this person?
- The style, tone and language of the message

Specific recommendations

When P communicates he must make it very clear what the message is. He needs to think about how he can make his communications less complex. For example by removing jargon or not sending all information to all recipients, only what is necessary.

P needs to make it clear to the recipient(s), whether the communication is to keep them informed of the project progress or does he require them to feedback information.

If P uses various mediums of communication such as emails, presentations or phone calls, it is very important that the words and gestures do not mislead or contradict. Perhaps he could look for or ask for confirmation of understanding.

When he communicates P needs to select the best method, by considering any bias or possible reactions from the receivers. Especially when conveying any bad news about H Company's relocation project, he must clarify that they have fully understood and not made their own assumptions.

P also needs to be aware of other distractions that can occur. By telephone the message could get distorted by background noise. Overloading recipients with emails may lead to people ignoring them. P could consider indicating how important emails are using a flag system and/or could group issues together within fewer emails.

22   S (MAY 08 EXAM)

Key answer tips

This question has two separate requirements, ensure that you answer each of them. The first requirement is to explain why project completion is an important activity, and then move on to explain what activities would be carried out during this stage. Your answer should clearly explain to S the reason for this stage with the X Hotel chain.

Weak answers will explain the various stages of the project lifecycle rather than focusing on project completion.

Tutorial Note

Project completion is the final stage of the project life cycle. At this stage the project is delivered to the users, the project team is disbanded, the success of the project is evaluated and lessons are learned to improve future projects.

Evaluation meetings usually take place at the end of the project, both internally with the project team members and externally with the customer. A final meeting is then held to formally sign-off the project and hand over the deliverables to the customer.

A further review (post completion audit) is normally held a few months after the project is completed. This audit reviews the success of the project as a whole and how well the expected benefits have been achieved. It also reviews the project management skills used in the project and carries forward any lessons learned to future projects.

Why the completion stage is important

S must realise that project completion is a very important part of the project lifecycle as it is an assessment as to whether the project has met the requirements of the X Hotel chain.

More specifically, the project completion stage is important for the following reasons:

- It will show whether the design and implementation of the reservation system has achieved the project deliverables of X Hotel chain. If not, then the project cannot be said to have been completed successfully.

- It will ensure a formal acceptance by and handover of the project to the users/client

- Once loose ends have been tidied up the project team and steering committee can be formally disbanded.

- A number of reviews should be carried out during this stage and these can be used to highlight key lessons that can be learned from the project which can be carried forward to improve other projects which may be carried out in the future.

What completion involves

S will produce a completed report for the customer reservation system that will summarise the following:

- Achievement of the project deliverables to X Hotel chain. This can be assessed by comparing actual deliverables to the requirements laid out in the project initiation document (PID).

- The time taken compared to what was agreed, with an explanation of any variances given

- The actual expenditure on the customer reservation system compared to the budget

S must test the customer reservation system before customer sign off, and make it clear who is responsible for any problems that may occur once the system has gone live. A post completion audit should also be undertaken a short time after the project has been completed to check if the project was managed correctly and whether the reservation system benefits have been achieved within budgeted time and cost.

The information will be presented in a report which should contain the following:

- A summary showing areas that benefited from the project planning and tools used and those that did not.

- A review of the end results compared with expectations. Any discrepancies will be identified, investigated and explained. With suggestions on how they may be avoided in the future.

- A cost-benefit review comparing the feasibility study to actual cost and benefits.

- Final recommendations on how future project management procedures by S can be improved.

23   P WORKS FOR Z CO (NOV 08 EXAM)

Key answer tips

This question tests candidate's ability to explain the use of progress reports within a refurbishment project. The scenario provides some examples of the problems within the project, namely overruns on both time and budget. You must ensure that you address these issues in your answer. The second part of the question asks you what kind of corrective action should be taken to overcome the project slippages. State the obvious answers first.

(a)   The progress report is an extremely important control mechanism within a project. It is a formal and regular report which notes what has happened in the report period and the project status to date. It serves to report progress on two levels:

- Communicate with the team

- Report to Management and sponsor

Between the project manager and the team, it provides an opportunity to acknowledge effort, motivate individuals, and demonstrate the importance for team participation. It also serves to identify emerging problems, propose solutions and make adjustments in the schedule for conflicts.

The report to management and the sponsor is likely to be more formal but less detailed than the team briefings. Here we are looking at a broad overview of the overall schedule, budget and any problems.

The report is used to:

- Describe the project and its deadline briefly.

- Describe the current status of schedule and budget.

- Explain any variances and their causes, or speculate and schedule delays.

- Detail any changes in project definitions and objectives.

- Summarise the expectations with regards to completion and deadlines.

- Detail the expected date of the next report.

- Current status of risks and issues.

(b)

Tutorial note

When discussing slippage, consider the 'project triangle' of cost, time and quality. In this project time and cost have slipped. To correct one of these aspects will often impact on the other and correction of both of these slippages will often have an adverse effect on the quality of the project.

Slippage refers to a movement away from the plan. This movement may occur for a variety of reasons:

Time slippage: Delays in completion of tasks.

Cost slippage: Excessive costs possibly due to delays.

Quality slippage: Failure to adhere to standards set.

The refurbishment within Z Co is overrunning on both time and budget. P who is about to produce her first report to the project sponsor is struggling to understand why.

The reasons for slippage may relate to poor planning or poor quality of staff or work, or could be due to lack of commitment to ensure that resources are available when required.

This is an important project and it is important that P controls and monitors the project on a more regular basis. Producing the highest possible quality report, implemented procedure and if necessary project extension.

P could improve monitoring by using techniques such as Gantt charts and network analysis and maybe project software such as Microsoft Project.

P's team will have to make up lost time somewhere along the way, which may mean cutting down on quality and thoroughness of the refurbishment. It may be possible, or essential to offer overtime to get the project back on track, although this could further effect budget overspend. P may also look at rescheduling of tasks, for example looking for tasks that could be run in parallel to save time. She may also consider rescheduling of resources to perhaps redeploy under-utilised staff onto the project?

P must ensure that she does not blame team members or outside forces for delays when explaining the missed deadlines, but does need to take action if problems are self-inflicted.

She needs to check supplier invoices to ensure that all charges are as agreed at the start of the project. She must also start carefully monitoring all spend on the project to avoid against any unnecessary spending. She may have to look at the remaining budget for the project and looks for areas of saving which may help to bring the project expenditure back to the budgeted level.

To reduce costs on a project, often the quality has to be considered. It may be possible for P to change the quality of some aspects of the refurbishment in order to save cost. Any such changes would have to get the approval of the project sponsor.

24   Q COMPANY (MAY 09 EXAM)

Key answer tips

The various stages of the lifecycle of a project need to be related to the use of project software in this complex project. Using the stages of the lifecycle will give your answer a good structure. Ensure you consider the issues within the scenario and think about how software would avoid or minimise them whilst supporting the role of the project manager.

Tutorial note

All projects can be split into stages; this is known as the project lifecycle. There are a number of models showing the stages in the project lifecycle. It will not matter which model you use in your answer. Gido and Clements identified four phases in a large project:

Need/ Solution/ Implementation/ Completion

Alternatively, the Project Management Institute uses a five stage model:

Initiation/ Planning/ Execution/ Controlling/ Completion

A project management software package is a software product designed to assist in planning a project. It also allows the project manager to record and report project progress. Examples of such packages are PMW (Project Manager Workbench) and Microsoft Project. Such packages allow managers to construct network diagrams (with the Critical Path highlighted), Gantt charts and Resource histograms showing which resources are working on which days. Adding values to activities can easily produce project costs, including the costs of the project resources. The products have flexible reporting systems allowing the user to print out a variety of progress reports.

Project management software can support the project manager in planning, estimating, maintaining and reporting throughout the project life cycle. It can handle vast amounts of complex data and can help improve accuracy by helping to reduce human error assuming, of course, that the data is input correctly in the first place.

Stages in the project life cycle

Gido and Clements identified four phases of large projects

Phase 1

Identification of a need – this involves undertaking of a feasibility study to decide whether to go ahead with the project. This will consider all alternative solutions for satisfying the need identified.

Here implementation of project management software is very important, as the software compiles a number of project tasks into the Feasibility Study of Project Management and Project Planning. This project involves some very complex work and will require good coordination.

Phase 2

Development of a Proposed Solution – the most appropriate solution to satisfy the need should be chosen, with identification of the best possible course of action to be taken.

The projects need to be managed effectively, with consistency of reporting and access to project information. The software will automatically produce the critical path of the project and a Gantt chart for resource planning. If the project manager enters the duration and precedence of project activities then the software can automatically produce the project network and define the critical path of the project. This will identify the critical activities for the project manager, the activities that need to be delivered on time to achieve the required overall duration of the project. The project manager will need to carefully allocate and closely monitor these critical activities.

The software allows for multiple versions of the network diagrams and project plans to be easily produced. Any changes can quickly be reflected with little effort on the part of the Project Manager. E.g. "what if" analysis.

Phase 3

Implementation – this will include setting plans/standards for everything that needs to be delivered. Actual performance can then be measured against standard. Timely appropriate action can then be taken if any slippage has occurred.

The actual duration of project activities may be entered by the project manager. This may lead to updates in the project plan, which can be reprinted by the project manager and distributed to the project team and the sponsor. Such reports are quick and easy to produce, thereby freeing time for other management tasks. The software also has the facility to tailor standard reports if required.

When the project manager enters resource costs then the software produces a projected cost for the whole project based on the estimated activity durations. If actual durations are entered then the software can calculate actual costs and compare these with the projections. This allows the project manager to monitor actual and projected costs and to communicate these to the project sponsor. The software facilitates resource planning which will visually display the usage and availability of resources. Thus identifying where there are surpluses or too few resources.

This will reduce the time that has been previously been spent searching for paperwork and also give a clear indication to all project teams of the project progress.

Phase 4

Completion – Evaluation through selected review and audit of project performance. Continuous improvement through feedback (Total Quality Management) should be undertaken in order to improve performance on future projects. The software may be used to produce the completion report detailing the costs and resources entered throughout the project life.

25   V (MAY 10 EXAM)

Key answer tips

(a)   This is a reasonably straightforward critical path diagram. It is only worth 4 marks, so must be able to be completed within 7.2 minutes. Ensure you clearly show the critical path.

(b)   This part looks at uncertainty in project planning and asks you to explain two of the methods used to assist with this; scenario planning and buffering.

(a)

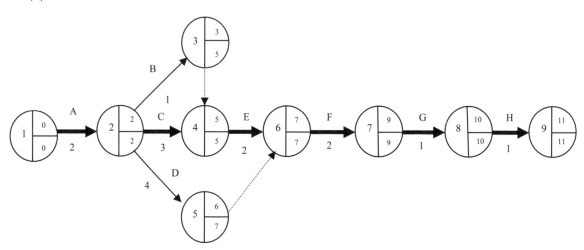

The critical path for the project is ACEFGH. The overall duration of the project is 11 weeks.

(b)

Tutorial note

All projects involve some uncertainty. At the planning stage estimates are made for duration and costs, but unforeseen events can impact on these estimates. Project managers need to take account of uncertainty in their planning by using techniques such as PERT, scenario planning and buffering.

Uncertainty is an inevitable feature of any project. At the outset of the project, many estimates will need to be made about the element   making up the project and none of these will be known with absolute certainty. Contingency/scenario planning and buffering can help in the following ways.

Contingency planning involves changing the assumptions surrounding elements of the project and looking at how changes to these assumptions would affect the overall outcome of the project. If we look at testing, V may consider what would be the outcome if testing took three weeks instead of one. In this case, the overall duration of the project would increase to 13 weeks and V would not meet the deadline of 12 weeks. In this case, V would have to have a contingency plan drawn up for what could be done in this instance to keep the project on track.

Buffering is a technique that can be used along with critical path analysis. It involves adding extra durations to the more risky activities in the project. This adds padding to the original estimate and allows for the fact that it can be very difficult to ensure that all stages and activities are carried out exactly as planned.

As it stands, the critical path analysis gives the project an overall duration of 11 weeks. The deadline for the project is 12 weeks so V has one week of contingency added into the project. V will have to consider if one week is enough, if some contingency plans should also be set up to ensure overall success of the project.

26   F BAKERY (MAR 11 EXAM)

Key answer tips

This is a reasonably straightforward critical path diagram. Part (a) asks you to draw the network diagram for 4 marks. Ensure you clearly show the critical path and highlight the overall duration.

Parts (b) and (c) can relatively easily be determined from the diagram drawn in part (a). As long as your answers to part (b) and (c) are consistent with your diagram in part (a), you will obtain the marks.

Tutorial Note

Follow the step by step approach to preparing a network diagram.

–   Draw the basic shape of the network, starting with the activities which can start straight away

–   Add the other activities

–   Be especially careful with the activities which follow more than one activity. For this you can use a dummy activity line, or have more than one activity share the same end node.

–   Once the basic shape is complete you can add the activity durations

–   Calculate the EET working left to right

–   Calculate the LET working right to left

–   Add in the node references and highlight the critical path.

Be careful with part (b). The earliest time G can start is shown by the node at the beginning of the activity line.

Examiner's comments

There was a marked difference between candidates who had prepared well for this question and those who had missed the necessary preparation. A large proportion of well prepared candidates gained full marks for their answer while the less well prepared scored only a handful of marks or even zero marks.

Common errors

Some candidates omitted to calculate float/slack, others claimed the earliest start time for recruitment was week 34 rather than week 24 as required and some made minor mistakes in their completion of the network diagram.

(a)

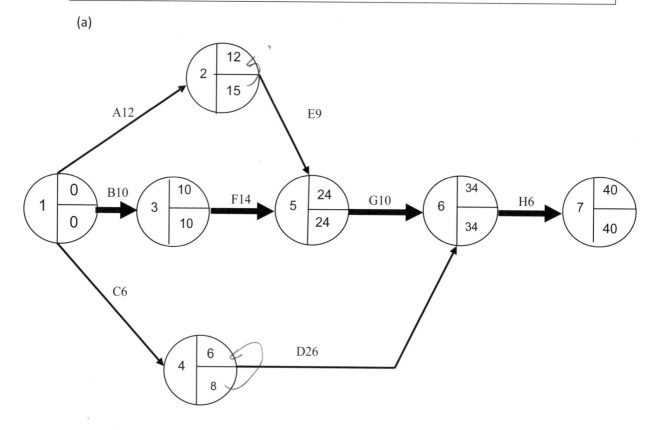

- Critical Path = B,F,G,H
- Duration = 40 Weeks

(b)   The recruitment campaign can start in week 24.

(c)   Activities A and E have 3 weeks float time. 15−12 =3

Activities C and D have 2 weeks float time. 6−6 =2

27   M (NOV 10 EXAM)

Key answer tips

This question requires the identification of the characteristics which make a matrix structure appropriate.

There are 5 key characteristics associated with matrix structure which students should be aware of from the text book. Identifying the characteristic would earn 1 mark each and the additional 5 marks would be given for showing how M demonstrates each characteristic.

Tutor's top tips

Many students may find it hard to see that they have earned enough marks in this question. There are 2 marks available for each element, one for the identification of the characteristic and one for the evidence from the scenario showing how this applies to M.

The 5 characteristics can be taken straight from the text book:

1   The business of the organisation consists of a series of projects, each requiring staff and resources from a number of technical functions.

     Evidence from M: M undertakes a number of custom-made projects, which are complex and involve experts from many functional areas.

2   The projects have different start and end dates, so the organisation is continually reassigning resources from project to project

     Evidence from M: Projects are continually being completed and started.

3   The projects are complex, so staff benefit from being assigned to a technical function where they can share knowledge with colleagues.

     Evidence from M: They make custom made systems to the unique specifications of the customer. Some projects can take up to three years. These facts suggest that the projects are complex.

4   The projects are expensive, so having resources controlled by functional heads should lead to improved utilisation and reduced duplication across projects.

     Evidence from M: Some projects cost several million Euros.

5   The projects are customer-facing, so the customer requires a single point of contact to deal with their needs and problems.

     Evidence from M: Each customer expects a high level of individual attention.

Examiner's comments

Generally low scoring answers. A pass standard answer would identify at least three characteristics applied to M that are appropriate to adopting a matrix structure.

Common errors

Many candidates were unable to identify the characteristics in terms of developing to say why a matrix structure is appropriate.

The characteristics of M that are appropriate to it adopting a matrix organisational structure are as follows:

- The business of M consists of a series of projects which are custom made, which are complex and require staff from a number of different functional areas;

- The projects undertaken by M have different start and end dates, so the organisation is continually reassigning resources from project to project as one ends and another begins;

- The projects undertaken by M are complex so the staff benefit from also being assigned to a technical function (such as finance or procurement) where they can share knowledge and experience with colleagues in their functional teams;

- The projects undertaken by M are often expensive, so having resources controlled by functional heads should lead to improved utilisation and reduced duplication across the different projects;

- The projects undertaken by M are customer facing and customers expect a high level of customer focus. Therefore, the customer will require a single point of contact (the project manager) to deal with customer requests and problems.

28 WBS/GANTT CHART (MAY 11 EXAM)

Key answer tips

This question focuses on two common project management tools; WBS and Gantt charts. You are asked to describe the techniques in part (a) and then explain their importance in project communication. In part (b) remember to concentrate on issues of communication within projects.

Tutorial Note

Work breakdown structures (WBSs) and Gantt charts are commonly used tools in the planning stage of projects. The WBS is usually the starting point when planning a project. It involves breaking the project tasks down into manageable pieces and setting out the logical sequence of events.

The WBS allows work packages (WPs) and statements of work (SOW) to be produced which specify the work to be carried out within each package described in the WBS, and indicates the required timing of each piece of work and who is responsible.

From this, product breakdown structures (PBS) can be developed which specify the products and materials required to complete each activity. This can lead on to the cost breakdown structure (CBS) which will consider the cost of all resources required for the project. The completed CBS will form the budget for the project.

Gantt charts are used to help plan and present the timing of activities within a project. Activities are represented by horizontal bars on the chart. The length of the bar represents the duration of the activity. The Gantt chart usually shows two bars, one showing the planned duration and the other showing the actual duration of the activity.

Examiner's comments

Generally answers to this question were done well.

Common errors

The most common error was to repeat in part (b) what had been covered in part (a) but without explaining explicitly the importance of the techniques in the communication process as the question required.

(a)   A Work Breakdown Structure (WBS) is a hierarchical way of organising the project work to be done into manageable units referred to as work packages. It is a technique used in project management to divide a project into packages of work which have defined deliverables and responsibilities. The work packages can then be used to construct a comprehensive list of activities, set out into a logical sequence of project events.

A Gantt chart can use the information from the WBS process to construct a graphical representation of the activities of a project shown as a bar chart. Each bar in the graph represents the period over which a particular activity is scheduled to be performed. It illustrates the start and finishing time of the various tasks and the resources required for each activity at a particular point in time of the project.

(b)   Both WBS and Gantt charts have a role in the project communication project process. For example:

- The WBS process enables work packages to be put into the project plan as a comprehensive list of tasks and activities that must be undertaken in the project lifecycle. This can assist the project manager in communicating to the project team specific responsibilities and work elements that need to be undertaken. It can be used by the project team to identify and understand project priorities. WBS also provides a framework for monitoring and control of resources and costs as part of project progress reporting.

- Gantt charts can be used in project communication as a reporting tool in the monitoring of actual progress of the project against projections/forecasts, for example, on a week-by-week or day-by-day basis. Gantt charts provide visual representation of activities and provide an overview of responsibilities of the progress of the project for the project team, assisting in project coordination.

29   C CONSULTANCY (SEPT 11 EXAM)

Key answer tips

Part (a) of the question requires you to describe the key characteristics of a matrix structure for 4 marks. You could include a quick diagram in you answer to demonstrate these characteristics. Part (b) asks for the advantages and disadvantages of this structure for C Consultancy for 6 marks. Ensure that you balance your answer between the advantages and disadvantages.

Tutorial Note

A matrix structure aims to combine the benefits of a functional structure and a project based structure.

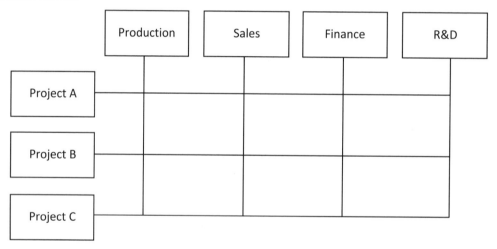

Project teams are made up from members drawn from a variety of different functions. Each individual has a dual role as they maintain their functional responsibilities as well as membership of the project team. Both vertical and horizontal relationships are emphasised.

Examiner's comments

Many answers did not make clear the project matrix structure but were well drilled into providing a good list of advantages and disadvantages of such a structure.

Common errors

Omitting to describe the nature of a project management matrix structure in the first part of the question.

(a)   A matrix structure is based on a dual chain of command and is often used as a structure in project management. In the case of C Consultancy Company, it would involve establishing cross specialist teams, as necessary, to work on particular consultancy projects.

Since the consultancy projects will be time bound, a matrix structure provides a way of resourcing and organising work, bringing people together to work on a particular client project and then returning to their specialist area.

Consultants would have a dual role in terms of belonging to their specialist area as well as being a member of a project team. This would mean reporting to both the senior manager of the specialist area and the project manager for their work on a particular consultancy project.

(b)   The matrix structure could bring a number of advantages to consultancy project work. For instance, it would bring together a wide range of expertise cutting across specialisms to work on a client project. This would also enable the company to offer a broader portfolio of consultancy interventions. From an employee perspective, it can facilitate the development of new skills and adaptation to unexpected problems, broadening a specialist's outlook by working with others.

Whilst there are benefits, there can be disadvantages to the matrix project structure. One of the main problems is associated with the lack of clear responsibilities and potential clashes and tensions between the different priorities of the project tasks and the specialist area.

Employees may end up being confused by having to report to two bosses and deciding whose work should take precedence. Conflicts may arise due to the differences in the backgrounds and interests of staff from different specialist areas working together, and some attention will be required to assist team development in the early stages of the project.

The project manager may be reluctant to impose authority as they may be subordinates in later projects.

MANAGEMENT OF RELATIONSHIPS

30   WORKING IN GROUPS (NOV 09 EXAM)

Key answer tips

The question was worth 10 marks for a discussion on why working in groups can have a negative influence on performance. There are many points which can be made here, ensure that you make enough points and discuss fully why performance may be adversely affected.

Tutorial Note

Groups are commonly used within organisations and have many benefits, but this question focuses on the problems with group working. These are widely recognised to include:

–   Conformity, where conforming to the group culture and norms becomes the most important thing to members. In this case group goals are given precedence over company goals.

> - Abeline paradox, where a decision can be made by a group which it turns out was no one's choice of outcome.
>
> - Groupthink, where the group becomes so close knit that the members stop challenging each other.
>
> - Risky shift, where the group takes decisions which are riskier than those which the individual members would take.

Groups are widely used within organisations; however group working can have negative consequences on organisational performance.

According to Belbin, an effective group needs a number of key roles fulfilled. Groups which are not correctly balanced in terms of the roles can be ineffective and can cause dysfunctional behaviour which can lead to conflict. In this situation the group would negatively affect the performance of the organisation.

Very effective and cohesive groups can bring their own problems. It can sometimes be the case that membership of the group becomes the most important thing to a worker and that they put the needs of the group before the needs of the organisation. This can lead to dysfunctional decision making as each group starts to care more about the results of the group than the overall impact they are having on the organisation.

Groups develop their own norms of behaviour and these become the guiding principles to the members. Where the group's norms differ from the organisation's norms, members are more likely to conform to the group norms. This can become a problem if the group norms are sufficiently different to the norm of the organisation. It can be very difficult to change the attitudes within a group as the group has effectively set up its own culture and culture can be very difficult to change. It can also be the case that the group becomes insular and tries to exclude outsiders. This would have a serious impact on the productivity of the organisation as a whole.

Strong groups can also suffer from "group think" where the group members know each other so well that they stop challenging the consensus of the group. Decisions are no longer discussed fully as all members are aware of the others' points of view so see no need for discussion. In this case all members go straight to the decision which they know all the member of the group will agree with. The organisation can miss out in this case as alternatives are rarely explored.

Lack of discussion can lead to decisions which none of the members of the group would have selected on their own. The Abilene paradox shows this problem clearly. All members of a family assumed that all the others wanted to drive to Abilene, Texas. In reality none of them did. No one wanted to upset the consensus so all went along with it. After a 100 mile drive they arrived at Abilene and realised that none of them had actually wanted to go there.

Group decision making can also lead to more risky decisions being taken. Where individuals may be more reluctant to take risks on their own and take full responsibility for the outcome, in a group the responsibility for the decision shared so riskier decisions can be made more easily. Groups can be influenced by a few strong personalities who can shape the whole group. Where this is the case, the weaker members of the group may feel that it is easier to "go along" with the majority view rather than challenge it.

Another problem which can occur within groups is that some members of the group do not fully contribute, leaving some of the harder working members of the group to do a disproportionate amount of work. It is possible for an individual to be underperforming but for this to go unnoticed as they are operating as part of a group.

31 **Z COMPANY (NOV 07 EXAM)** *Walk in the footsteps of a top tutor*

Key answer tips

Make sure you learn at least the main issues covered in the health and safety parts of the syllabus. This question was very easy if you had learnt the material.

Tutorial Note

In the UK, the issue of health and safety at work is governed by the Health and Safety at Work Act 1974. This act applies to all organisation employing five or more people and sets out the responsibilities of management with regard to health and safety in the workplace.

A senior member of the organisation should be responsible for implementing the health and safety policy, which should include:

– Provision of risk-free plant and systems of work

– Provision of information, training, instruction and supervision

– Maintenance of a safe workplace

– Adequate facilities

– The safe handling, storage and transportation of articles and substances

– Means of entry and exit

Employees also have basic responsibilities in this regard.

A health and safety seminar should aim to address the following areas:

Introduction

- Health and safety should be introduced as part of the wider issue of risk management.

- Senior managers may be unaware of the typical hazards faced by their employees so a useful starting point would be to outline specific risk areas in Z Company, giving examples.

- Within this context it should be pointed out that health and safety is about taking practical actions to control real risks, not about trying to eliminate risk altogether.

Relevant legislation

- Senior managers should be told that health and safety is not just a good idea for progressive companies but that many of the recommendations are set in statute.

- Relevant legislation could then be discussed. The main piece of legislation covering health and safety in the workplace in the UK is the Health and Safety at Work Act 1974, for example.

- The legislation in many countries puts the responsibility for health and safety on BOTH the employer and employee. These two areas can then be discussed in more detail.

Employer's responsibilities

Typically the law states that the employer has a duty to provide the following:

- Safe ways in and out of the place of work;

- A safe working environment

- Safe equipment and procedures

- Arrangements for the safe use, handling, storage and transport of articles and substances;

- Adequate information, instruction, training and supervision, for example in reporting accidents, injuries and illness.

- Adequate investigation of accidents

Each of these should be related to Z Company's specific circumstances, practices and policies.

Employee's responsibilities

The employee typically has a duty to:

- Be responsible for his or her own health and safety;

- Consider the health and safety of other people who may be affected by his or her actions;

- Co-operate with anyone carrying out duties under relevant legislation (this includes his or her employer)

Consequences and available courses of action should health and safety provisions be breached

- Employers must ensure safe and healthy working conditions for their employees. If they do not do so they may be in breach of a common law or statutory duty enabling the employee to make a civil claim against them.

- Alternatively, they may be guilty of a criminal offence and be open to prosecution by the Health and Safety Executive (or equivalent).

- If employees have been injured at work they may have an action against their employer for damages.

Z Company's policy and code of conduct

- Either by reference at each of the above stages or at the end, Z Company's policies and code of conduct should be examined to link it to legislation or best practice, so managers are more aware of what is expected of them and their employees.

32   B COMPANY (MAY 09 EXAM)

Key answer tips

Start by explaining the facts about disciplinary and grievance. Ensure you clearly explain the differences between them. One is employer to employee and the other from an employee to a representative of the employer, such as a manager. In part (b) explain the process involved in a disciplinary interview relating it to the scenario given.

Tutorial Note

Discipline is action taken by the employer against the employee. The important point to make about discipline is that its purpose is to achieve change in the behaviour of employees. Grievance, on the other hand is an action taken by an employee where they feel that they have been unfairly treated by superiors or colleagues.

(a)   Discipline is a code of acceptable conduct or a system of rules establishing behaviour patterns.

An important part of any employee relations policy to be followed by management is to provide a clear statement of what behaviour is expected of an employee and the procedures to be followed in controlling behaviour.

Disciplinary action requires a manager to use authority to deal with situations whereby an employee has committed an offence.

This may be due to:

Internal issues

Excessive lateness in arriving at work, poor work performance, violation of safety rules, insubordinate attitude, absence for no good reason or without warning or general non-compliance with the rules.

External issues

Involvement with competition or undertaking private work to the detriment of the employer, it may be due to personal abuse of alcohol/drugs, or law-breaking activities.

The aim of a disciplinary procedure is to correct unsatisfactory behaviour rather than punish it.

A grievance occurs when an individual feels that they are being wrongly treated by colleagues or those in authority such as managers.

Grievances can be genuine and well founded, others may be imaginary. But they must all be treated seriously because if they are left unresolved they can grow until they become a grievance of the whole workforce and a subject of dispute.

On an individual level the grievance may be due to a dislike of something that a superior has said or done, e.g. being unfairly appraised in the annual report, unfairly blocked for promotion or discriminated against on the grounds of sex or race. Within B Company an employee has taken out a grievance against J as they feel that J behaved unfairly in a disciplinary interview.

A group grievance is often about pay, e.g. where one person feels they are getting less pay for doing the same job as another or there is felt to be some inequity in a piecework system.

(b)   Disciplinary interviews are very formal affairs where managers control the proceedings and can plan in advance how they will deal with the guilty party and future consequences. J will need to gather all the facts and qualify the reasons for the interview and the direction in which it will proceed.

J should follow these guidelines when carrying out a disciplinary interview.

J should seek to **establish the facts** and, assuming the complaint is valid, confirm that a company rule has been broken to the offending employee. J must ensure that the employee is not intimidated by the interview, but that the employee fully understands the seriousness of the situation.

J needs to **present the case against the employee**, specifying transgressions, along with dates and times. For example J needed to be clear to the employee during the interview the reasons for the disciplinary action, whether it was due to continued lateness or abusive behaviour and explain B Company's position with regards to the issues raised.

The **employee should then be allowed to present their case**. If new information comes to light, the interview may need to be re-scheduled. The employee has the right to bring a friend or colleague as a witness to the details of the interview. J may have failed to inform the employee about a colleague or friend being allowed to be present or maybe he didn't give the employee a chance to state their case.

Once the evidence has been heard, the interview will be concluded **by summarising the main points**. It is usual to then **deliberate the points** and **decide what action**, if any, needs to be taken.

The employee will then be informed that a penalty is, or will be, enforced either now or in the event of further misconduct. The seriousness of the offence and the consequences of further offences must be discussed. **A record of the interview should be kept** in the employee's file for review at a later date. J will hope that this will prevent further misconduct and so ensure the future efficiency and appropriate conduct of the employee.

J should **involve the HR department at all stages of a disciplinary process**, including the interview itself, as they are seen as the experts in this field and will be able to ensure that J is always working in line with the correct procedures, as failure to do so could have far reaching consequences both for J and the company.

33   KCC (MAY 10 EXAM)

Key answer tips

This question focused on the change of culture which KCC has experienced due to its growth. You have to explain the characteristics of KCC's original culture and the culture it currently has. Ensure that you apply your answer to the scenario.

Tutorial Note

Handy's cultural types could have been used in your answer:

– Power culture – this culture is based on one or a few powerful central individuals who control all activities and make all decisions

– Role culture – This culture tends to rely on formalised rules and procedures to guide decision-making. It is the most common culture in large bureaucratic organisations

– Task culture – this is typified by teamwork, flexibility and commitment to achieving objectives.

– People culture – in this culture the individuals fulfil personal goals and objectives, whether or not they are congruent with those of the organisation.

Initially KCC was a small, home run company which, according to Handy, demonstrated a power culture. The culture came from the founder of the company CT and from her creativity and enthusiasm. This is common in an entrepreneurial structure where the culture emanates from the key person at the centre of the organisation.

Now, as it has grown, KCC is a large, structured company employing hundreds of members of staff. The company is now operating in a more bureaucratic manner with a clear functional structure and several layers of management. This type of organisational structure is characterised by formal rules and procedures which control all aspects of the work carried out by the employees.

CT is no longer able to run the company as she used to, there is now a separation between her and the workforce. Relationships in the new organisation are more formal. CT does not know all the names of all the employees and has effectively lost the personal touch which she used to enjoy in running the company.

The creativity of the company has also been lost in the new structure. Tasks are clearly defined and workers are expected to simply complete their assigned tasks. Workers are not expected, or encouraged, to show initiative and are allowed little freedom to make any suggestions about the process. Some workers have complained that they feel like robots.

The focus of the business has moved away from its previous creativity and is now more focused on cost control and profit. The new company exhibits more of a role culture where each person focuses on their own roles. This is typical in a bureaucratic, hierarchical structure.

34 TS CONSULTANTS (NOV 10 EXAM)

Key answer tips

The answer should start with an explanation of relevant theory on motivation and leadership. Using the theories as frameworks, the answer should develop to discuss recommendations of how performance and staff morale could be improved in YR Hospital.

The examiner's answer uses Herzberg, but states that alternative theories could be used. Given the details in the scenario, Herzberg is the most obvious theory to use and in many ways is the easiest to apply in this case. Other models discussing styles of leadership can also be used in the answer.

The problems with the Finance Department are clearly given in the scenario so few marks will be earned by simply restating the problems. Few marks will be earned by simply explaining the theory.

Stick to the focus of the question, which is to discuss recommendations to improve the performance and morale of the department. Ensure that the recommendations made are backed up by the scenario and by the theory you have chosen to use.

Tutorial Note

Herzberg's theory followed on from the work of Mayo and emphasised the motivational needs of individuals. His theory has two factors: hygiene factors which do not motivate, but the absence of which would cause dissatisfaction and demotivation, and motivating factors which will actively motivate staff.

The importance of this theory is that managers must understand that if the hygiene factors are not in place, then no amount of motivating factors will encourage staff to work harder or improve morale.

Examiner's comments

Overall good performance.

Common errors

Features of weak answers included too much time explaining problems or repeating material directly from the scenario rather than discussing the recommendations. Also, no explicit use of theory or just a description of theory without application (e.g. describing the range of leadership styles without application).

In making their recommendations TS Consultants could refer to Hertzberg's theory on motivation. Essentially, the two factor theory proposed by Herzberg suggests that there are hygiene factors which need to be in place in order to reduce staff dissatisfaction. If they are absent this can lead to dissatisfaction and consequently impact on performance. For example, factors surrounding the job context such as pay, working environment, company policy and interpersonal relationships. These factors tend to be extrinsic to the job itself and whilst they are unlikely to motivate staff, if they are not right can cause dissatisfaction and de-motivation. The other set of factors are those, which if present, can motivate individuals to superior effort and performance. They tend to be related to the job itself, in other words are intrinsic factors and are referred to as motivators or growth factors.

Applying this theory to the Finance Department based on the Consultants findings, it is apparent that the hygiene factors such as competitive salaries and good physical working conditions are in place. However, there are some hygiene factors that need attention, specifically the nature of supervision. The consultants should recommend that action is needed to address the nature of supervision by management and the poor relationships suggested by the 'them and us' culture, which would involve a shift in the approach to leadership in the department.

Another set of recommendations should be made which relate to the potential motivating factors, such as those relating to recognition, challenging work, responsibility and advancement. This could include reviewing job design to determine possibilities for job enlargement and job enrichment. This would involve exploring the design of job roles in the Finance Department to widen the scope of jobs, providing more interesting and challenging work for staff. The benefit to employees would be the development of new skills and being given greater responsibility through empowerment. This would, however, require the managers to adopt a more participative leadership style, with junior staff given greater responsibility for their own areas of work and encouraged to participate in decision making, but with managers providing constructive feedback.

Another recommendation would be to look at how improved prospects for career development could be achieved. This might mean providing opportunities for lateral moves to enable staff to gain new experiences and competencies.

A recommendation could be made to introduce some kind of recognition scheme since recognition is an important motivator. This could be achieved, at one level, by simply encouraging managers to thank members of staff for their contribution, acknowledging extra effort and performance. More formal recognition systems could also be considered.

TS Consultants should make a recommendation which highlights the training and development needs of managers in the Finance Department. To resolve some of the difficulties, it is likely that the managers will need to adapt their leadership style to a more democratic approach. Reference to the Blake and Mouton managerial grid would help identify the focus on the training needs for the managers. It would seem from the scenario that currently they have the characteristics of authority-compliance management with a high concern for the task, but low concern for people. Leadership training and development should be designed to help the managers to understand the need to balance concern for the task with the concern for people. Development interventions should focus on helping them to develop better working relationships with their teams, perhaps using team building techniques.

(Answers could develop with reference to alternative theories on motivation and management/leadership styles).

35   P COMPANY (NOV 10 EXAM)

Key answer tips

This question has two requirements; the process of mentoring and the benefits of mentoring. Ensure you answer both parts fully.

Weak answers will simply identify a limited number of benefits of mentoring. Good answers will develop to explain the process of mentoring with a fuller consideration of the benefits, in the context of a new member of staff.

Tutorial Note

Mentoring is viewed as a useful technique for helping people develop. Mentoring is a relationship where one person helps another to improve their knowledge, work or thinking. It can be a very valuable development tool for both the mentor and the mentee.

A mentor should stimulate, guide, council, support, tutor and nurture learning.

Examiner's comments

Mixed performance but with some good answers.

Common errors

Weak answers tended to discuss what happens as part of induction and general training and hence did not evidence appreciation of the concept of mentoring.

LC could start by explaining to JB that the purpose of a mentoring system is to provide new employees with a forum to discuss development issues in a relaxed and supportive environment. A mentoring system would be useful to JB, as a new member of staff, in helping her socialise into the culture of the organisation and facilitate quicker learning about the way the organisation works. LC could go on to say that the mentoring relationship is not based on authority but, rather, a genuine wish by a mentor to share knowledge, advice and experience with junior members of staff.

LC should explain that the mentor would be in a senior position within P Company, and the purpose would be to guide and support JB, as a less experienced employee. LC should also explain that whilst JB's mentor will hopefully be from the finance function that she has joined, the person acting as mentor would not be her direct line manager. The reason for this is to ensure that the mentor can act as an independent arbiter, and avoid the danger of conflict given the developmental nature of mentoring versus line management. The mentor would normally be a role model, having already achieved a status to which JB might aspire.

LC could then explain the different functions of mentoring, for example differentiating between career-enhancing and psychological functions.

In terms of career enhancing, a mentor could help JB in her career with P Company through exposure, visibility and sponsorship. Having a mentor could also help JB in expanding her network of contacts and in gaining greater exposure in the organisation.

The psychological function of mentoring could help JB enhance her competence and effectiveness in her role. LC could point out that the role of the mentor would be to encourage and assist JB in analysing her performance and identifying her strengths and weaknesses. The mentor would provide JB with honest but supportive feedback and guidance on how she could work on her weaknesses. The mentor would also provide feedback and encourage JB to reflect on her behaviour and experiences as she develops into her new role. LC could explain that JB could ask her mentor questions and learn from her mentor's experience, using the mentor as a safe sounding board. So having a mentor should help JB in her new job through encouragement and nurturing her learning and development.

LC should also explain that mentoring would work alongside some of the more formal control mechanisms such as appraisal. The mentor would be able discuss with JB her training needs, advise on qualifications and provide a forum for her to discuss any interpersonal problems and career goals.

36   LS COMPANY (NOV 10 EXAM)

Key answer tips

This question required you to discuss the types and sources of conflict within LS Company.

The answer should start by providing a brief explanation of the concept of conflict. It should then develop to compare and contrast the different types of conflict and, for each type, explain the possible sources of conflict.

Weak answers will simply describe the different types of conflict, or the different sources without making the connections between the two, nor provide examples from the scenario. Good answers will make reference to the scenario information to illustrate both the types and sources of conflict, and will make explicit the examples of sources of conflict with each particular type of conflict.

Tutorial Note

There are two main types of conflict; horizontal and vertical. Horizontal conflict occurs between groups and departments at the same level in the hierarchy, while vertical conflict occurs among individuals and groups at different levels.

For each type, there are a number of sources of conflict.

Examiner's comments

Some good answers evidencing appreciation of the different types and sources of conflict.

Common errors

Weaker answers explained how to manage conflict rather than comparing and contrasting the sources. Other weaker answers repeated information directly from the scenario and did not develop to discuss the different sources of conflict.

Conflict is essentially a disagreement and is when one party is perceived as preventing or interfering with the goals and actions of another. It can occur in a variety of forms and at different levels in an organisation. Whist conflict can be considered as an inevitable feature of organisation life; in the case of LS Company it is having negative outcomes.

In LS Company, the poor communications and cooperation between the staff in the Marketing and Sales Department and the Finance Department is an example of horizontal conflict. This type of conflict occurs between groups of staff or between departments at the same level in the organisation hierarchy.

The sources of the conflict may be due to the fact that the priorities and goals of the departments are different. The staff in each of the two departments will want to focus on their own goals, which they may view as being mutually exclusive. This is illustrated by the fact that both departments are blaming each other for the poor sales performance. The Finance Department is seen by the marketing and sales staff as controlling and only taking a short term and cost based view. At the same time, the Finance Department staff think that the poor sales performance is because the marketing and sales strategy is ineffective, and that the marketing and sales staff have been complacent.

It is likely that another possible source of conflict is due to the difference in the perceptual differences (cognitive and emotional) of staff working in the different functional departments. The staff in the two departments will probably have different skills and attitudes, and perhaps the consequence of this is a lack of understanding of the nature and challenges of each other's work, and suspicion and lack of trust between staff.

In contrast, the threat of industrial action from the trade union is an example of vertical conflict. This type of conflict occurs between individuals or groups who are at different levels in the organisation hierarchy, and can often arise because of status and power. The grounds for handling vertical conflict is normally formalised by rules and regulations.

The source of conflict is because senior management will be looking to reduce costs in the Production Department, as a result of diminishing sales orders, whilst the employees and the union want to protect workers' jobs. The workers in the Production Department, may, individually feel powerless, with little say in the decisions about their future and job security. Standing together in a union will provide them with strength that equalises their power with senior management in this conflict. The union will exert pressure through the threat of industrial action to try to make senior management reconsider the proposal to cut jobs in the Production Department.

Both types of conflict in LS Company are dysfunctional and destructive since both management and staff time and effort will be wasted in addressing the conflicts. The lack of communication and cooperation between the Finance Department and Marketing and Sales Department, and the threat of industrial action will both impact negatively on the performance of staff, and hence on the company.

37   S COMPANY (MAR 11 EXAM)

Key answer tips

Be careful in answering this question to ensure that you have answered all parts fully. Part (a) asks about the characteristics of a role culture and an explanation as why is it not appropriate for S Company. This part is worth six marks. Part (b) goes on to ask for a recommendation for the type of culture which would be more appropriate. In part (b) you are asked to give reasons for your answer. Part (b) is worth four marks.

Tutorial Note

This question discusses Handy's four cultural types:

–   Power culture – this culture is based on one or a few powerful central individuals who control all activities and make all decisions

–   Role culture – This culture tends to rely on formalised rules and procedures to guide decision-making. It is the most common culture in large bureaucratic organisations

–   Task culture – this is typified by teamwork, flexibility and commitment to achieving objectives.

–   People culture – in this culture the individuals fulfil personal goals and objectives, whether or not they are congruent with those of the organisation.

Examiner's comments

This question was generally well answered. Some answers were very good indeed.

Common errors

There was a tendency amongst some candidates to repeat bits of the scenario as part of their answer and for others to repeat points made in part (a) again in part (b), thus taking up examination time and yet gaining no additional marks.

(a)   The concept of organisational culture is an important one for S Company because it can exert a strong influence on business performance. It can shape the behaviours and actions of individuals in the workplace and is often referred to as the 'glue' that holds the organisation together.

There are different types of culture which are determined by an organisation's structures, processes and management methods. Currently, S Company is typified as having a role culture which can be very efficient and successful in a stable environment when work is predictable and the organisation can control its own environment. However, this type of culture appears to be having an adverse effect on S Company's performance as the company now faces very different operating conditions and needs to become more flexible to respond to the quickly changing environment. The reasons for this can be explained by examining the characteristics of a role culture.

Role culture is usually associated with a formal structure, comprising well established rules and procedures. Job descriptions are clearly defined, tightly describing the tasks of an individual's job. This leads to a strict division of labour with people often reluctant to take on wider responsibilities, as in the case of S Company. Staff tend to be obsessed by fulfilling their narrow job duties, with a preoccupation on day to day administrative activities rather than longer term issues. These characteristics would make it difficult for the organisation to be flexible and adapt to the more competitive operating environment, acting as a barrier to new product development needed by S Company to compete.

Within a role culture, the organisation will be dependent upon various functions, each of which has its own areas of strength and influence, with an emphasis on internal processes rather than external focus. This type of culture is also impersonal, relying on formalised rules and procedures for work routines and communication and for guiding decision making in a standardised and bureaucratic way.

Relations between staff are dominated by hierarchy and authority with formal and rigid control systems. Individuals are selected for particular roles on the basis of their ability to complete a particular task to the required level and over achievement is not actively pursued. These characteristics of a role culture can mean that it is more resistant or very slow to adapt to change and getting people to work together across boundaries can be difficult.

Innovation is often stifled, since the culture is one which insists people go through layers in the hierarchy to gain approval. Decisions are made at senior level with little involvement from other members of the organisation. In fact, new ideas from below may be regarded with suspicion from above. Individuals are required to perform their job and not to overstep the boundaries of authority. This is occurring in the case of S Company, and would seem to be partly responsible for the lack of flexibility, responsiveness and ability to be effective in new product development.

(b)   It is apparent that the culture of S Company needs to change and it is recommended that a task culture would be more appropriate given the changes in business conditions. This type of culture is typified by teamwork, flexibility and commitment to achieving objectives rather than emphasising a formal hierarchy of authority.

The task culture is often reflected in a matrix structure or project teams, where the focus is on completing a job or project. A task culture tends to encourage greater flexibility, with people working together across functional boundaries to achieve organisational objectives, and people are not hindered in terms of their contribution by tight job descriptions. This would better suit new product development activities where people need to work effectively across boundaries.

Staff become loyal towards the work rather than towards formal rules. The principal concern is to get the job done, breaking down rigid hierarchies and functions. Therefore, the individuals who are important are those with the skills and ability to accomplish a particular task. Skill and expertise are more important than length of service and position in the organisation.

Team work is fundamental to a task culture, rather than the achievement of individuals. By nature a task culture fosters creativity and is adaptable, responsive and able to change very quickly and well suited to new product development activities.

38   TR (MAY 11 EXAM)

Key answer tips

The answer should start with an explanation of the basic principles of management styles theory. It should then develop to explain the various styles that TR could adopt.

The examiner's answer uses the Tannenbaum and Schmidt's continuum of leadership but marks can be awarded where candidates have used alternative but appropriate theoretical frameworks to answer the question. Other suitable models would be Blake and Mouton's managerial grid; Lewin's leadership styles or Likert's four systems of management. Each of these models gives a number of different styles of leadership which could be adopted.

Tutorial Note

There are a number of leadership style theories which could be used to answer this question, the main ones are:

– Lewin's leadership styles

– Likert's four systems of management

– Tannenbaum and Schmidt's continuum of leadership styles

– Blake and Mouton's managerial grid

All of these models have a number of styles of leadership within them. Any of them would be useful in this answer.

Examiner's comments

Overall, not very well answered. However, there were some very good answers which demonstrate what can be done with adequate preparation.

Common errors

Three types of errors occurred:

•   Some candidates had insufficient knowledge of relevant theory

•   A number of candidates mixed up management style theories with motivation theories

•   Some candidates simply described theory without relating it to the scenario or explaining how it could help TR become more effective in his role

A number of researchers have contributed to theories which have been developed to help explain the different leadership styles that managers can adopt. One such theory which could help TR in understanding the alternative styles he could use is Tannenbaum and Schmidt's continuum of leadership behaviours. The continuum is based on the degree of authority used by a manager and the degree of freedom for the subordinates in decision making. Tannenbaum and Schmidt identified a range of various styles along the continuum ranging from boss-centred to employee-centred. Boss-centred tends to be associated with an authoritarian approach whereas employee-centred is associated with a more democratic or participative approach.

This theory identifies four different styles labelled, 'tells', 'sells', 'consults' and 'joins' which reflect the degree of authority used by a manager and the degree of freedom for the subordinates in decision making. Taking each style in turn:

- 'Tells' is where TR would make all the decisions and tells the subordinates what to do. The advantage of this style is that decisions can be made comparatively quickly. The downside is that staff may resent simply being told of the decision by TR and this could result in getting compliance rather than commitment from his staff.

- 'Sells' is where TR would make the decision, but rather than just announcing it or telling his staff, he would try to persuade them to accept it. As with 'tells', this style means that decisions can be made quickly by TR, who would have to use his skills of persuasion in selling the decision. However, staff may feel they have been manipulated and controlled.

- 'Consults' is when TR does not make the decisions himself until he has presented the problems to his staff, hears their views and suggestions and then adopts the solutions suggested. This approach should mean that staff feel that they have been involved in the decision making process and hence are more likely to support TR. However, consulting can be time consuming. TR will need to be willing to take on board the suggestions made, otherwise staff may feel that they have not really been listened to and this can be damaging.

- 'Joins' is where TR would define the problem but then delegates the decision-making power to his staff. He would indicate the limits within which the decision must be made. Staff should feel empowered in the decision making process. However, they may disregard the limits and TR could find a decision made which is unacceptable to the organisation. Depending on how it is handled, staff may feel that TR is not taking on responsibility as their leader.

(*Marks can be awarded where candidates have used alternative but appropriate theoretical frameworks to answer the question, for example Blake and Mouton's grid; Lewin's leadership styles; Likert's four systems of management*)

39   COMPANY L (SEPT 11 EXAM)

Key answer tips

In this question you have to discuss J's current style of leadership and then compare this to an alternative style of leadership which would be more effective. You are asked to back your answer up using appropriate management/leadership theories.

A number of models could have been used here, but Blake and Mouton's managerial grid, or Adair's action-centred leadership would be the most obvious choices.

Tutorial Note

Blake and Mouton's managerial grid charts people-orientated versus task-orientated leadership styles. Managers can score between 1 and 9 for each orientation and these are plotted on the grid.

The two extremes are: task-centred leadership, where the main concern is getting the job done, and group-centred leadership, where the prime interest of the leader is to maintain the group, trust, friendship and relationships.

Adair's action-centred leadership adds a third dimension, by suggesting that effective leadership is concerned with not only the task and the group needs, but also with the needs of the individuals within the group.

Examiner's comments

Candidates often had knowledge of leadership/management style theory but made poor use of it in trying to answer the question set.

Common errors

A significant number of candidates repeated bits of the scenario rather than comparing and contrasting J's existing leadership style with the task orientated style advocated by a senior manager. Other candidates provided an outline of two or three leadership/management style theories but did not then apply them to answer the question set.

There are a number of different management styles and leadership theories which could be used to compare and contrast J's approach and the approach senior management thinks she should adopt.

It would seem from the scenario information that J's approach is more people centred than task centred. Adair's action centred leadership model is based on the premise that effective leadership requires the bringing together of task, team and individual needs. In J's case, senior management is suggesting that J has a focus on the needs of the individual and the group, but has not paid sufficient attention to the task achievement.

The Blake and Mouton managerial grid provides a useful framework for understanding and applying effective management. The grid was developed from the precept that management is essentially concerned with production and people. The grid suggests that any combination of concern for production and concern for people may be present in an organisation.

Using the Blake and Mouton grid, perhaps J could be viewed as adopting the country club approach to management where the emphasis is on people. People are encouraged and supported and any inadequacies are overlooked on the basis that they are doing their best and that coercion or a more authoritative/directive approach would not improve things.

It could be argued that senior management wants J to adopt a task oriented style where the emphasis is on achieving the task, without concern for people. J would be responsible for planning, directing and controlling the work of her subordinates, treating people as commodities or machines.

In fact the most effective approach would bring together both J's current approach and the approach her senior management team suggests. This is a team style, and whilst it might be viewed as idealistic it advocates a high degree of concern for both production and people. It endeavours to discover the best and most effective solutions aimed at the highest attainable level of production to which all involved contribute and in which everyone finds a sense of achievement. In adopting this approach J would assume that employees are committed to the organisation, and that any conflict which occurs can be successfully managed.

(Note from examiner: Although this answer has been based on Adair's action centred leadership, and Blake and Mouton Managerial Grid, alternative management style and leadership theories could be used to develop the answer).

Section 4

ANSWERS TO SECTION B-TYPE QUESTIONS

STRATEGIC MANAGEMENT

40 K COMPANY (NOV 04 EXAM)

Key answer tips

Part (a) of the question asks for examples of stakeholders that would be affected by the proposed change given in the scenario. Note that you asked for both internal and external stakeholders. For each stakeholder group identified, you have to describe the impact the proposal would have on them.

Part (b) asks you to identify the sources of power each stakeholder group has and to identify how they may influence the proposal.

Carefully consider how many stakeholders you need to identify and discuss. There are many groups available in the scenario but it would not be necessary to discuss them all. It is better to select fewer and discuss them more fully than to try to discuss them all.

Tutorial Note

A stakeholder is a person, or a group of people, who have views on the strategic development of an organisation and who can affect, or be affected by the activities of the organisation.

There are a number of classifications of stakeholders. Internal stakeholders are those groups within the organisation, such as employees and management. External shareholders are external to the organisation and would include shareholders, governments, local communities, suppliers, customers and pressure groups.

That this distinction is complicated by the fact that those holding shares may well include many of the internal stakeholders noted above as well as stakeholders external to the business.

(a) **Stakeholders**

Stakeholders are those individuals or groups that have an interest or 'stake' in the organisation. The plan will affect both internal and external stakeholders as follows:

Stakeholder	How affected
Internal stakeholders	
Directors, senior and junior managers	Some will lose their jobs.
	For those that remain, the future prospects for promotion will be much reduced as the number of senior posts will be reduced.
Assembly line workers	Will lose their jobs in the plants that are to be closed.
Employees in the countries to which production is being moved	New employment and prospects in the Company.
External stakeholders	
Suppliers	Existing domestic suppliers will lose contracts; new suppliers in new countries will gain contracts.
Customers	Should see lower prices. A key concern for the firm will be whether they see a reduction in quality as well.
Trade unions	Very affected, as they must work to save jobs and/or obtain the best severance package for the employees they represent.
Local communities	Local shops and services in the locality of the plants closing will lose business and may close.
	The local economy in those towns to which production has been moved will benefit from the extra income that the new jobs will bring.
Local and national governments	The move will affect local regeneration plans in both countries concerned.
Shareholders	If the plan is successful they will benefit from an increase in dividends and capital growth, if it fails they will lose wealth.

(b) **Stakeholder power**

When assessing the power of stakeholders the following factors are usually considered:

- status of the stakeholders

- control of resources

- formal representation in decision-making processes

- possession of key knowledge and skills.

These can be applied to K Company as follows:

Existing employees / trade unions

In the case of K Company, the power of existing employees derives from their skills and expertise. Their power will be limited as K Company has every right to move its operations overseas if it wishes to do so and, as the company can obtain a workforce in the other countries at lower cost, it is not dependent on its existing workforce.

Threatened with job losses, employees will use industrial action and try to attract the interest of the local media to gain public sympathy.

Directors

The production and marketing directors are against the plan. They possess not only skills and experience but can vote against plans. However, the board of directors as a whole has agreed the policy, so the production and marketing directors have limited power to change things.

If they do resign, K Company should be able to recruit people with similar experience, so is not dependent on them.

The CEO and directors supporting the plan will use company resources to implement the plan and they will counter negative publicity by explaining the economic necessity for the plans.

Suppliers

The power of existing suppliers comes from being able to disrupt supplies to K Company. They may also have power if there are long-term contracts that they can enforce. Such power is limited in its effectiveness, however.

Government

The local government has the power to influence K Company by persuasion but ultimately has little power to interfere in the international operation of companies.

On the other hand, government officials in the countries to which K Company intends to relocate will welcome the plans and may offer tax concessions to make the move more attractive.

Shareholders

Shareholders could vote to support the plan or vote against it at the company's Annual General Meeting. If they did not support the plan, they could remove the CEO and appoint someone who would pursue an alternative policy.

Shareholders thus have high power if they choose to use it. For most companies the shareholders rarely unite to act against the directors.

41   C CHOCOLATE COMPANY (NOV 07 EXAM)

Key answer tips

Some students struggled with the wording of the requirement in part (a) ("**this** strategic approach") as no strategic approach has been mentioned in the question up to this point. You could have chosen a range of approaches to use here but the simplest approach is to assume that you are being asked to discuss the resource-based view of strategy, mentioned later in the requirement.

Part (b) is more straightforward provided you apply the value chain model to C's specific activities.

Tutorial Note

There are two opposing views on strategy formulation that consider how the organisation attempts to gain competitive advantage. **The positioning view** sees competitive advantage stemming from the organisation's position in relation to its competitors, customers and stakeholders. It is referred to as an 'outside-in' view as it is concerned with adapting the organisation to fit its environment.

The **resource-based view** sees competitive advantage stemming from some unique asset or competence possessed by the organisation. It is often referred to as an 'inside-out' view as the focus is on what the organisation has (its resources) and what it is good at (its competences). In order to gain competitive advantage, the resources should be **unique** and difficult for competitors to gain, and the competencies should be **core** and difficult for competitors to imitate.

Barney identified four criteria for unique resources: valuable, rare, imperfectly imitable and difficult to substitute. Prahalad and Hamel identified three characteristics of core competencies: provides potential access to a wide variety of markets, increases perceived customer benefits and hard for competitors to imitate.

(a)   There are two main approaches to understanding and, hence, developing competitive advantage:

- The positioning view sees competitive advantage arising from a firm's position in relation to its competitors, customers and suppliers. The emphasis is on adapting the firm to fit its environment and is often described as an "outside-in" approach.

- The resource based view, on the other hand, sees competitive advantage as stemming from the possession of unique assets and/or competences. The key emphasis is on finding markets where the firm can exploit its internal competences and is thus an "inside-out" approach.

Looking at the approach taken by C Chocolate Company ("C"), we can make the following observations:

- The owner has highlighted recipes, staff skills and procurement as the key factors driving C's success. These are all internal competences suggesting that the owner is viewing strategy from a resource-based view.

- C's marketing and IT emphasis seems to be on identifying market trends and responding quickly to them through product innovation. This would reflect more of a positioning approach than a resource based view. However, from a resource-based view, it could be argued that C has developed the core competence of rapid product innovation and is simply exploiting that competence within the high-quality chocolate market.

- To create superior performance based on resources, those resources must be valuable, rare, imperfectly imitable and difficult to substitute. These criteria can be applied to C as follows:

    - Unique recipes can help C defend against competitive rivalry through creating customer loyalty. However, rivals will also have their own secret recipes so such assets are not "rare" unless C's recipes are much better than those of rivals. Furthermore, modern advances in chemistry technology mean that rivals should be able to analyse and hence imitate C's recipes.

    - Similarly, staff skills can be copied and may even be able to be substituted using advanced technology.

    - Procurement of high quality cocoa beans is also relatively straightforward for rivals to imitate.

    - Thus, C does not have any unique competences that satisfy all of Barney's criteria and hence, it could be argued, C is not basing its competitive advantage on a resource-based view, or is doing so inadequately.

In conclusion, there are arguments supporting the view that C is adopting the resource-based view but that it needs to improve its development of core competences, especially in the area of limitability.

Tutorial Note

Porter's value chain is a model used for internal analysis. It suggests that the internal position of an organisation can be analysed by looking at how the various activities performed by the organisation add or do not add value, in the view of the customer.

The value chain model splits activities into primary and support activities. The primary activities are involved in the physical creation of the product or service, sales and distribution to the customer, and after sales service. These should all add value to the product or service.

Support activities such as infrastructure, IT, HR and procurement help the primary activities run more smoothly.

(b)   The value chain was developed by Porter to help firms analyse their activities in order to understand the basis of their competitive advantage. In particular, the value chain looks at identifying whether activities are giving a cost advantage over competitors (consistent with a generic strategy of cost-leadership) or quality advantages (consistent with a generic strategy of differentiation).

C's competitive strategy fits closest to Porter's idea of differentiation so the value chain could be used to identify where quality advantages arise and where, if at all, quality is being compromised. Furthermore, linkages between activities can then be considered to ensure that the bigger picture is consistently supporting the chosen strategy.

More specifically, a value chain analysis would reveal the following:

Inbound logistics

- C has managed to find a supplier of high quality cocoa beans. Whether or not this constitutes a value driver depends on whether or not competitors also have access to similarly high quality beans.

- If one particular plantation is known to grow the very best beans, then C could consider trying to get an exclusive supply arrangement to block rivals.

- Given variations in the quality of harvests, C would need to ensure that it employs expert buyers to guarantee that C only buys beans of the required quality.

Operations

- Key value drivers in operations are unique recipes, skilled staff and product innovation.

- To ensure that C's competitive strategy is sustainable C would have to ensure that it has the resources to develop new product recipes but, as stated in part (a), many rivals will also have their own secret recipes, so recipes are unlikely to be a sustainable source of advantage.

- Staff skills need to be enhanced and developed through appropriate training, particularly to ensure that the benefits of high quality cocoa beans are not compromised in operations. The value chain approach would also mean that C should seek to ascertain the skills base of rivals to see if they have a relative advantage.

Outbound logistics

- There is little information given in the question regarding outbound logistics but C would need to ensure that packaging and delivery methods maintain the quality of the chocolates. Any attempts to cut costs here could compromise the overall customer experience.

Marketing

- C appears to have a strong market research facility, which, when coupled with a flexible production model, allows C to meet market demands quickly and efficiently.

- Looking at the linkages within the value chain, C would have to ensure that the marketing of products communicates the quality of beans procured and skilled staff used in operations.

Service

- No information is given in the question concerning after-sales service. Another advantage of the value chain is that it forces the management of C to consider activities beyond just operations. Under the primary activity "service" C should compare its guarantees and after sales service with rivals. For example, if goods are damaged in shipping, does C offer a no-quibble money back guarantee to customers, commensurate with its high quality image?

Support activities

- C's relationship with its supplier could also have been discussed under the "procurement" heading.

In conclusion, value chain analysis will enable C to have a deeper understanding of the basis of its relative competitive advantage and which areas give room for improvement.

42   W COMPANY (MAY 08 EXAM)

Key answer tips

In part (a) candidates need to be able to apply models to the scenario to help assess the competitive and external factors. The most appropriate models will be Porters five forces for an analysis of the competitive forces within the industry, and PEST for analysis of the macro-environment.

Part (b) requires candidates to justify why management within W must consider the cultural differences whilst operating in a different country with reference to an appropriate management theory. The obvious theory to use in this answer is Hofstede.

Tutorial Note

External analysis can be carried out at different levels. PEST can be used to analyse the macro-environment and Porter's five forces can be used to analyse the industry or competitive environment.

PEST analysis forces the company to consider various issues concerning the external environment. These are Political, Economic, Social and Technological. Other variations of PEST also include Environmental and Legal considerations.

Porter's five forces looks at the company's competitive environment by analysing five forces: threat of entry, competition/rivalry, substitutes, the power of buyers and the power of suppliers. These forces determine the profit potential of the industry.

(a)   PEST and Porter's five forces model are two strategic models that could be used to assess the external environmental and competitive forces that face W Company, whilst they are looking at the possibility of developing a new market in L country.

The PEST framework looks at the Political, Economic, Social and Technological factors that may influence W Company and Porter's five forces model assists in analysing the competitive environment within L country's fashion sector. W company needs to understand the environment within L country.

PEST Framework

Political

Information needs to be collated on the political stability within L country as well as its government or legislative policies.

- For example, does L country have strict legal guidelines for company's (especially foreign ones) operating within their country?

- Are there any political difficulties currently within L country, such as the risk of civil war, as this can have a detrimental effect on the success of W Company?

Economic

For W Company to succeed in L country, they need to obtain a variety of different economic data such as:

- Levels of consumer disposable income – If disposable income is low then fashion and luxuries are usually stopped by most households

- Approximate spend per head/household on fashion

- Tax and Interest rates within L country – If tax rates are high people have less income to spend and if interest rates are high, it encourages people to save not spend.

- Levels of economic growth achieved in L country

Social

W Company must also understand its potential market and any difficulties that it may encounter. Looking at the following:

- The number of women within certain age groups and locations

- The importance and acceptance of fashion to different age groups

- Potential cultural issues and the importance of these to W Company's acceptance within L country – E.g. the wearing of head dresses in certain countries.

- The working day of its potential employees and the temperatures that they may be exposed to – E.g. some countries have siestas during the day

Technological

Information needs to be collected on the levels of technological advancements within L country and the acceptance of this to potential customers and employees.

- They need to assess the current availability as well as future potential developments in the communications and transport infrastructure – E.g. the use and acceptance of supplier chain integration

- W Company could also incorporate environmental issues such as the level of acceptable omissions within L country and how waste is disposed of.

Porter's five forces model

Porter's five forces model will allow W Company to assess the potential of setting up with L country by focusing in particular on the level of competition.

The model involves W Company looking at not only the existing competition but new entrants into the market as well.

If existing competition is high with strong established companies and brands, there may be legal or bureaucratic factors restricting the success of W Company. They need to ascertain the number of retailers, market shares and industry growth rates.

Further information on potential substitutes as well as the power of buyers and suppliers within L country would be very useful. To help W company understand the price and availability of materials and the potential market opportunities and therefore the potential selling price.

Tutorial Note

Hofstede developed a model to explain national differences by identifying five key dimensions along which national culture seems to vary:

- power distance – how much society accepts the unequal distribution of power.

- uncertainty avoidance – the degree to which individuals feel uncomfortable with risk

- individualism/collectivism – the extent to which individuals prefer loose or tight knit social groups.

- masculinity/femininity – the degree to which masculine or feminine values predominate.

- long/short term orientation – how much society values long or short-term values and traditions.

Hofstede's model can be used to influence business behaviour and management styles.

(b) The management team of W Company must focus their attention on the cultural differences when operating within a different country. Many companies fail to do this and therefore do not gain acceptance in the new country.

W Company needs to look at the culture within L country and how it may influence its strategy and the way businesses operate within L country compared to that within F country.

The type of management structure, employees and working relationships may be very different within L country, due to the difference in culture.

W company could use Hofstede's research to help them establish the differences between F country and L country and how that will influence the management style and relationship with employees.

Hofstede's research looked at different cultural characteristics by identifying key dimensions of common culture:

- Power distance

- Individualism/collectivism

- Masculinity/femininity

- Uncertainty avoidance

- Time orientation

Countries can be classified against these dimensions from high to low and therefore have different scores.

Power distance

How a society accepts the unequal distribution of power within organisations. (Acceptance of an inferior position).

F country may have high distance power, where managers may make autocratic decisions and managers are respected. In L country, it may be that employees challenge management decisions. W Company may need to modify how subordinates are managed.

Individualism/collectivism

This looks at the extent to which people work independently taking care of themselves (individualistic) or closely working and dependent on others (collectivism).

In certain countries, they have collectivist cultures such as Japan. W Company needs to find the best way to manage the employees with L country. Knowledge of whether the country favours individualism or collectivism can help W company decide on the structure for their new venture in L country.

Masculinity versus femininity

Hofstede's study suggested that men's goals were significantly different from women's goals. Women focus on relationships with colleagues and the mix of work and family life, whilst men value job opportunities and rewards offered.

W Company needs to establish if the masculine or feminine index is high. What is important to employees – to live in a desirable area for their families' or to have the opportunity of high earnings? This can influence the reward structure in the new venture.

Uncertainty avoidance

When uncertainty avoidance is strong, a culture tends to perceive unknown situations as threatening so that people tend to avoid them. Organisations will rely heavily on rules and regulations to create certainty.

In certain countries, uncertainty avoidance is weak as people feel less threatened by unknown situations and thus are more open to ideas and innovations.

If L country tends towards high uncertainty avoidance, the potential employees are likely to be unwilling to take risks, so there may be problems if new work practices, for example, are to be introduced. In countries with high uncertainty avoidance, more formal rules and regulations should be out in place.

Time orientation

W company will need to assess the time orientation in L country in order to determine whether the existing management approach will work.

Time orientation is concerned with the extent to which people expect rapid feedback. A long-term orientation is characterised by respect for hierarchy whilst short-term orientation is marked a protection of one's own reputation.

There are many other factors that W Company may need to consider before setting up operations within L country such as:

- Language barriers

- Religious beliefs

- Levels of education (potential employees).

43   B BAKERY (NOV 08 EXAM)

Key answer tips

Part (a) asks you to distinguish between the views of the Managing Director and the Operations Director on how strategy occurs. The first step is to identify which view each of the directors hold. The Managing Director favours an emergent approach and the Operations Director favours a formal/rational approach. There are 17 marks available for part (a) so you will have to discuss both models fully, and use the scenario to back up the points you are making.

Part (b) asks for the advantages of the formal/rational model of strategy formulation. The benefits of the rational model should be well known, but use the scenario as much as possible in your answer.

Planning your answer is important in this question, as you need to ensure that you have not dealt with the advantages of the formal approach in part (a).

(a)   Strategy formulation is a continuous process of refinement based on past trends, current conditions and estimates of the future, resulting in a clear expression of strategic direction, the implementation of which is also planned in terms of resource allocation and structure.

The term 'emergent strategy' was developed by Mintzberg based on the idea that most of what organisations intend to happen, does not happen and is eventually rejected along the way. He argues that strategies can emerge, perhaps as a result of the processes of negotiation, bargaining and compromise, rather than be due to a deliberate planning process.

Emergent strategies result from a number of ad hoc choices that may have been made lower down in the hierarchy. They develop from patterns of behaviour; one idea leads to another, until a new pattern is formed and a new strategy has emerged. For example, the new healthy eating product range emerges, developed as a result of the Managing Director's (MD) wife's interest in healthy eating. This eventually opens up a new market. B Bakery has changed strategic course.

Emergent strategies develop progressively over time. They are reactive, evolving, unpredictable and they capitalise on luck/unintended results.

A rational process is considered to be one 'based on reasoning', one that is not subjective but objective, and one that is logical and sensible. Using rational behaviour, policy is formed by firstly defining the goal and then selecting the means to achieve the goal by rational analysis.

In many problem-solving situations, an assumption is made that the goals or objectives can be measured or assessed in quantitative terms. Rationality in this sense is based on the choice the decision-maker makes with reference to clear-cut alternatives. The following areas are present:

Complete knowledge of environmental factors

Although there has been growth, B Bakery is unable to produce some of its products at competitive prices. This needs to be investigated.

Ability to choose the alternative that returns the best outcome

Loss of key accounts shows that B Bakery is unable to adapt to produce the desired product at the right price for some of its customers.

Ability to order the preferences using some yardstick of utility. (Money as the common denominator).

If the decision-makers preference was for health, then the rational approach would be to choose the option that is the lowest in salt and fat, not the cheapest.

The rational approach to strategy formulation is when an organisation takes a systematic and structured approach to its development. Internal and external information is collected, and decisions are integrated into a comprehensive strategy. Managers ascertain, review and evaluate every option available, and they are then able to choose what appears to be the best option in the light of rational criteria.

The rational approach involves:

- setting a mission

- establishing long-term objectives;

- carrying out analysis (SWOT analysis, stakeholder analysis)

- generating strategic options

- analysis of strategic options:

  - is it feasible given resources?

  - is it suitable to the firm's existing position?

  - is it acceptable to stakeholders?

- implement chosen strategy

This approach to strategy evolves from top down. First, we have the corporate strategy. With this, we can then discuss the business unit strategy, which will then allow us to develop the organisational and functional strategy, (marketing, finance, HRM, etc). Actual performance is compared with plans and assessed in the review and control process.

(b)

Tutorial note

The benefits of formal strategic planning are listed in the textbook. Not all of the points will be relevant to this scenario, for example, security for stakeholders is not relevant as this is a family owned firm. Use the textbook list, but ensure you apply each to the scenario as far as possible:

– long term view – avoids a focus on short term results

– goal congruence – ensures the whole organisation is working towards the same goals

– communicates responsibility – everyone is aware of what is expected from them

– co-ordination – ensures all areas of the business work together

– security for stakeholders – demonstrates that the organisation has a velar view of where it is going

– basis for strategic control – a formal strategy provides clear targets, which enables the success of the strategy to be reviewed.

B Bakery is a family owned firm, which has been in business for over 50 years.

The MD feels that the business has had some growth in the form of its healthy eating range and that a formal process may be too static, time consuming and costly due to level of analysis required.

A formal rational model as suggested by the Operations Director (OD), considers the missions and objectives of B Bakery's (BB) business. This would give the business a vision and purpose.

The OD needs to show the MD that the rational approach suits B Bakery. This is an organisation that operates in a stable environment and which have the resources to undertake strategic planning.

The MD needs to be persuaded of the following benefits of strategic planning to B Bakery:

It will help BB to take a long-term view and avoid short-termism while at the same time providing a sensible approach towards the uncertainty in the future. Especially since BB has lost some key accounts.

It will help co-ordinate the activities within BB, ensuring that operational decisions fit with the overall plan and longer term goals. This will also allow careful allocation of resources.

The plan will give the bakery standards by which actual performance can be measured and controlled. It may be that in the last few months, too much time and effort has been spent sourcing healthy ingredients rather than cheaper ones.

The OD could explain that the process of forming a strategy requires wide and complex input. Whilst this can sometimes be time-consuming and costly, this can have a beneficial effect on managers' personal development and awareness.

44 C COMPANY (NOV 08 EXAM)

Key answer tips

This requires a discussion on the viewpoints of two particular senior managers within C Company, regarding spending time and money on social and environmental objectives. The Chief Executive is keen to be more socially and environmentally responsible, while the Finance Director argues against this in terms of cost and the impact on shareholder value. Ensure that you present a balanced argument from both viewpoints.

Tutorial note

There are opposing views with regard to social and environmental responsibility. The view in favour is the **stakeholder view**, which suggests that organisations are members of society and that all members of society should obey their responsibilities to other members of society.

The opposing view is the **shareholder wealth view**. This suggests that the responsibility of a business is to maximise the wealth of its shareholders.

(a)   Increased public awareness of the social impact of large organisations has broadened the range of objectives which businesses must aim to achieve. New factors to be considered include pollution control, conservation of natural resources and avoidance of environmental damage.

A conflict between the Chief Executive (CE) and the Finance Director (FD) implies a position of managers pulling in opposite directions. The CE is trying to meet criteria of social responsibility, and the FD is concerned about financial performance and shareholder wealth.

The ideal solution is to agree on a balance between these conflicting objectives, and to settle on a strategy which satisfies both sets of objectives, to the extent that they can be reconciled.

Part of the difficulty in pursing aspirations towards social responsibility lies in the relative novelty of the concept and that while costs may be easy to quantify, benefits are not. The FD who is used to a culture of profit maximisation may find it hard to appreciate the importance of social responsibility, and to adapt accordingly.

The Chief Executive (CE) believes that the firm's image will be strengthened and is motivated by the media attention as well as his own personal beliefs. He needs to stress to the FD the importance of social responsibility. C Company will benefit from the media attention, is more likely to win government contracts, and it may prove easier to raise finance when needed.

The FD is concerned with the cost involved and a potential negative impact on performance and shareholder value. However, the CE needs to stress that the strategies will lead to more stakeholder groups being satisfied and therefore better relations with these groups.

The employees of C Company will be more motivated and product quality will improve, which will lead to reduced costs. More socially aware customers will be attracted to C Company's products leading to increased revenue. The overall effect is that the business will become more financially sound. *and long term sustainability will be obtained.*

The FD is concerned about the increased costs involved in reducing emissions and using more eco-friendly methods. The main concern is usually that the social and environmental objectives may distract management thus leading to reduced financial performance and diversion of funds from the shareholders.

However, Friedman argued that pursuing profit would result in increased employment, generate growth, stimulate innovation and generally raise living standards.

It may well be a short-term shareholder sacrifice for the greater good of the company.

To 'operationalise' social responsibility with C Company involves making the FD aware of the need for it. This may be achieved by:

- Appropriate training

- Dissemination of targets and measures related to social objectives

- Formal incorporation of social objectives into the decision-making process

- Collaboration with other organisations to launch a common approach

- Appointment of external consultants to assess existing performance in this area and to recommend improvements

- Monitoring achievement by logging and publishing of performance indicators

- Appointment of a committee to review and implement social and ethical policies.

We have removed part b of the question as it no longer applies to E2.

45   GCU COMPANY (NOV 09 EXAM)   *Walk in the footsteps of a top tutor*

Key answer tips

Parts (a) and (b) of the question both cover the <u>positioning view</u> and the <u>resource based</u> view. It is important to plan your answer to this question to ensure that you answer both parts as required.

(a)   This part of the question focuses on competitive advantage, there are two parts to (a): explain competitive advantage **and** distinguish between the two approaches. The second part must discuss GCU.

(b)   This part of the question focuses on the <u>strategic models</u> and frameworks which can be used to analyse information for both approaches. You will be expected to know the models and be able to discuss them.

Tutor's top tips – part (a)

With narrative questions, it can often be difficult to ensure that you have made enough points to pass the question. Planning your answer will help you ensure that you have and will give your answer more structure. It is clear from this question that you are going to use the information given in the scenario. Theoretical knowledge is not sufficient to pass E2; application of knowledge is the key.

Tutor's top tips – part (a)

Start by carefully reading the requirements, this way you will have a better idea of what to look for when reading the scenario. The requirement for part (a) can be broken down to three distinct parts:

–   The concept of competitive advantage

–   The positioning view

–   The resource-based view

Tutor's top tips – part (a)

Next, look at the marks on offer for the question and the verbs used in the question; this will help you to assess how many points you have to make in your answer. Part (a) is worth ten marks and the verbs used are level two verbs (explain and distinguish). This suggests that you will have to make around ten points in your answer.

Break the question requirement up into its component parts and decide how many marks you think each part is worth. This way you will ensure that you provide a full answer and that you have addressed all of the requirements. You can amend this during the planning of your answer as long as you ensure you provide ten marks worth in your answer.

A reasonable split here would be three for the concept of competitive advantage and three to four for each of the views.

Tutor's top tips – part (a)

When explaining competitive advantage, start with a broad description of what competitive advantage is, then go on to explain the ways in which companies can obtain competitive advantage. Porter's generic strategies can be used here: cost leadership, differentiation and focus.

(a)   Competitive advantage refers to the advantages one company has over its competitors. There are several ways in which companies can achieve competitive advantage, one may be to be able to provide goods and services at the cheapest price, and another would be to differentiate the products of one company from those of other companies. Whichever way a company chooses to try to gain competitive advantage, it must find ways to set itself apart from other companies in a way which would attract customers. As GCU operate in the luxury goods market, it seems that their way of obtaining competitive advantage would be through differentiation.

Tutor's top tips – part (a)

Now go on to the views on strategy formulation. You are looking for around three or four marks for each of these so ensure you discuss them fully.

There are two opposing views on strategy formulation that consider how the organisation attempts to gain competitive advantage. **The positioning view** sees competitive advantage stemming from the organisation's position in relation to its competitors, customers and stakeholders. It is referred to as an 'outside-in' view as it is concerned with adapting the organisation to fit its environment.

The **resource-based view** sees competitive advantage stemming from some unique asset or competence possessed by the organisation. It is often referred to as an 'inside-out' view as the focus is on what the organisation has (its resources) and what it is good at (its competences). In order to gain competitive advantage, the resources should be **unique** and difficult for competitors to gain, and the competencies should be **core** and difficult for competitors to imitate.

Barney identified four criteria for unique resources: valuable, rare, imperfectly imitable and difficult to substitute. Prahalad and Hamel identified three characteristics of core competencies: provides potential access to a wide variety of markets, increases perceived customer benefits and hard for competitors to imitate.

Ensure you apply your answer to the scenario as much as possible.

The positioning view of strategy is more of an outside view where competitive advantage comes from the company's position in the marketplace relative to competitors. It is known as the "outside-in" approach.

The resource-based view is known as the "inside-out" approach. With this approach, competitive advantage is derived from the resources and competencies which a company possesses. For competitive advantage to be present, the company's resources must be unique and its competencies need to be core, that is their resources and competencies need to be difficult for others to copy.

For GCU, the positioning view would see them achieving success from their high market share relative to competitors. With this approach, the company has to be very aware of its environment and of the other companies operating in that environment and must exploit its position as market leader. Any changes in the external environment must be identified and the company must respond quickly to these changes in order to maintain its position.

With the resource-based view, GCU will have to identify those resources which it possesses that others do not have. Resources include financial, human, physical, intellectual and intangible resources. The resources which offer the most in terms of uniqueness are often the intangible resources such as brand name. Competencies also have to be considered and companies must identify those competencies which they are good at and which other companies find difficult to copy. From the question, it is not clear which core competencies GCU possess.

Tutor's top tips – part (b)

Go through the same process for part (b). Look at the requirements carefully and plan how many points you will have to make for each.

You are asked for models or frameworks which can be used in connection with the positioning and resource-based views.

Tutor's top tips – part (b)

Part (i) looks at the positioning view. This is the view which considers the outside environment; therefore you need to discuss the models which are used for external analysis. The main models are PEST and Porter's five forces. You should be familiar with both of these models and be able to discuss how they would help GCU Company.

(b)   (i)   The positioning view focuses on the external environment, therefore the models used in this approach are those which would help assess and understand the external environment. Two main models could be used in this approach and these are PEST(LE) and Porter's five forces. PEST(LE) forces the company to consider certain aspects of the environment, namely political, economic social, legal and environmental issues. These are important issue to consider when assessing the environment, especially when a company is considering moving into a new market or a new country. Given GCU's current situation, they may have to consider looking at moving into new markets.

These aspects can all change over time, for example a change in the political party leading the country can influence polices which can affect the companies operating in that country. It is important that companies continually review these aspects for any changes which may reveal new opportunities or threats.

The second model which is useful for external analysis is Porter's five forces where companies can assess the profitability of a market by considering five aspects. These aspects are; the power of buyers and sellers, the competitive rivalry, the barriers to entry and the availability of substitutes, This model is useful when considering entering a new market and also useful for reassessing the market in which the company currently operates. GCU have experienced changes in their market from increased competition.

Tutor's top tips – part (b)

Part (ii) looks at the resource-based view. This is the view which considers the internal capabilities of the company; therefore you need to discuss the models which are used for internal analysis. The main models are the resources audit and Porter's value chain. Again, you should be familiar with both of these models and be able to discuss how they would help GCU Company.

(ii)   The resources based view focuses on the internal capability of the company. There are two main approaches which assist in the analysis of the company in this approach and these are a resources audit and Porter's value chain,

A resources audit comprises an evaluation of the resources and competencies within the company. The company must identify all resources and categorise them as basic resources, which all competitors will also have, or unique which are only held by the company. The audit would also consider the competencies within the organisation, or what the company is good at.

Again these can be categorised into 2, either threshold competences, which are a minimum level which all companies will possess, and core competencies which set companies apart and which others find difficult to copy. It is these unique resources and core competencies which give a company competitive advantage.

The second model which can be used in the resources view is Porter's value chain which looks at the activities within a company and divides them between primary and support. Primary activities are those associated with the main objective of the business and the support activities assist the primary activities. In viewing the activities carried out within the company, they can consider which add value. They can also focus on which areas need improving. It is never enough to just focus on one activity and be good at that one alone, the value chain must be balanced and all aspects must add value.

46   S COMPANY (NOV 10 EXAM)

Key answer tips

(a)   requires a detailed explanation of Porter's Diamond model. There are 15 marks available for this part, so your answer will have to have enough depth to achieve a good mark. Ensure to explain how the aspects of the model contribute to competitive advantage.

(b)   asks for the information required to assess the external environment of NN Country where S Company are considering setting up as a new market. The framework suggested in this question is PEST.

Tutorial Note

Porter's Diamond was developed to explain why some nations tend to produce firms with sustained competitive advantage in some industry more than others. The model identifies four factors which determine national competitive advantage:

–   Factor conditions, such as the availability of raw materials or infrastructure

–   Demand conditions. This is the home demand for the good or service, which must be present as a starting point for international success.

–   Related and supporting industries. Competitive success in one industry can lead to success in other associated industries.

–   Firm, strategy, structure and rivalry. Competition in the home market can lead to all the companies in the industry becoming stronger in the world market place.

Examiner's comments – part (a)

Overall strong performance with candidates evidencing a good knowledge of Porter's Diamond.

Common errors

Weaker answers tended to know the dimensions of Porter's Diamond but were not then able to develop their answers to explain the various dimensions in the context of the scenario. A few candidates used Porter's five forces as the basis for their answers, hence did not score any marks. Other candidates did not read the question or scenario sufficiently carefully and referred to companies in the wrong country.

(a)   The theory of competitive advantage of nations, proposed by Michael Porter, examines why organisations may achieve competitive advantage over their rivals by virtue of being based in a particular country. It tries to isolate the national attributes that further the competitive advantage of an industry.

Often referred to as Porter's Diamond, the theory helps to explain why some nations tend to produce firms with sustained competitive advantage in particular industries using specific sources of advantage that can be substantial and hard to imitate. In essence it seeks to explain:

- Why do certain nations house so many successful international firms

- How do these firms sustain superior performance in a global market

Porter concluded that it is specific industries within nations that seem to be able to use their national backgrounds and conditions to lever world-class competitive advantage, rather than the entire nation having a particular competitive advantage. In the case of the new entrants in D Country it would appear that PP Country has achieved national competitive advantage in the consumer electronics industry.

To explain how this can be achieved, Porter suggests a diamond of four interacting determinants within a nation that assist the country to be more competitive in international markets. These are factor conditions, home demand conditions, related and supporting industries, firm strategy structure and rivalry.

Taking each determinant in turn:

- Factor conditions refer to the factors of production that go into making a product or services. Different nations have different stocks of factors which can be categorised as human resources; physical resources; knowledge; capital; infrastructure. It is not sufficient to have an abundance of the factors; rather it is the efficiency with which they are deployed that is important.

    Porter also distinguishes between basic factors, which he claims are unsustainable as a source of competitive advantage, and advanced factors. The latter are likely to be those creating advantage in the electronics industry in PP country, based on well-developed knowledge and expertise in R &D and technology design.

- Home demand conditions refer to the nature of the domestic customer becoming a source of competitive advantage. Dealing with sophisticated and demanding customers with high expectations in an organisation's home market will help drive innovation and quality, which in turn will help train an organisation to be effective in other countries. Although economies of scale are relevant, it is not necessarily about the quantity of home demand but the information that the home market gives organisations and the pressure to innovate. If the customer needs are expressed in the home market earlier than in the world market, the firms benefit from the experience. This may be the case for the consumer electronics companies from PP Country

- Related and supporting industries mean that local clusters of related and mutually supportive industries can be a source of competitive advantage. In other words, competitive success in one industry is linked to success in related industries. Having a domestic supplier industry can be preferable to a good foreign supplier as proximity to managerial and technical people along with cultural similarity can facilitate free and open information flows. Clusters of industries offering expertise and world class service can be vital. In the case of new entrants, it is likely that they enjoy the support of producers of component and related products and accumulated expertise in consumer electronics.

- Porter proposes that a nation's competitive industries are clustered, where a cluster is a linking of industries through relationships which are either vertical (buyer-supplier) or horizontal (common customers, technology, skills). Internationally, competitive suppliers and related industries represent a critical resource for international success.

- Firm strategy, industry structure and rivalry are related to the fact that nations are likely to secure competitive advantage in industries that are more culturally suited to their normal management practices and industrial structures. For example, industries in different countries have different time horizons, funding needs, infrastructures. Fierce domestic rivalry and competition will drive innovation, force down costs and develop new methods for competing. This can enhance global competitive advantage. If there is little domestic rivalry, organisations may be happy to just rely on home markets, as is probably the case for S Company, whereas tough domestic rivalry teaches an organisation about competitive success.

The value of Porter's Diamond is that it can be used to identify the extent to which the organisation can build on home based advantages to create competitive advantage in relation to others on a global front.

(b)

Examiner's comments – part (b)

Some high marks achieved.

Common errors

Some candidates based their answers on Porter's five forces model and, whilst gaining some marks, did not fully address the requirement, focusing on competitive environment rather than the wider external environment.

In order to assist in the decision on whether to pursue a market development strategy in NN Country, the team could use the PEST framework to assess the external factors in NN country. This would involve undertaking an analysis of the political/legal, economic, social-cultural and technological factors which could be used to help determine potential opportunities but also threats for selling consumer electronic products in NN country.

Taking each element of the PEST framework in turn:

- It will be important to assess the nature of the political environment in NN country to establish, for example, the government's policies and attitudes towards competition. In addition, information should be collected on the political stability of NN country. If there is political instability and unrest then this could pose a threat rather than an opportunity for a market entry strategy.

- Information should also be collected on the nature of the economic climate such as the rate of economic growth, level of tax rates, interest rates, exchange rates, levels of consumer disposable income and the percentage of household income spent on consumer electronic products. All of these factors could impact on the demand for S Company's products.

- The assessment should investigate whether the social factors are encouraging for S Company, for instance in terms of the customer attitudes, values and beliefs of people in NN country and the extent to which they would be likely to buy electronic products from a foreign company. This links to issues related to the branding and whether the design and functionality of the products would need to be adapted in any way to meet local market and customer needs.

  Information on social factors would also help in determining the cultural context of NN country, for example, to gain an understanding of any potential cultural differences in the buyer behaviour of customers.

- Technological factors would need to be explored relating to the communications infrastructure and any technological issues that might impact on the way the consumer electronic products are sold and associated distribution issues. This also links to a point made under the previous heading, but related to technology advancement in NN country, which could have consequences for the design and functionality of electronic products.

PROJECT MANAGEMENT

47   X (NOV 07 EXAM)

Key answer tips

In part (a) ensure you explain the project manager's responsibilities in sufficient detail rather than simply listing them. Using Fayol's heading of Organising, Planning and Controlling will give your answer structure.

Part (b)(i) is a four-mark question on the purpose of project control. Consider the problems a project would face without adequate control and this should help to highlight the purpose of project control.

Part (b)(ii) is trickier but linking controls into project stages and the control process will ensure that you do not limit the scope of your answer. Ensure you link your answer back to the scenario.

(a)   As the project manager, X is a key stakeholder in the project. His ultimate responsibility is to ensure the successful delivery of the project objectives to the satisfaction of the final customer. "Successful delivery" in this context means achieving the project on time, within budget and to an acceptable level of quality.

This will be by providing leadership to the project team who carry out the project tasks in order to achieve the project objectives.

Specific project manager responsibilities can be categorised using Fayol's headings of organising, planning and controlling as follows:

Organising

- The project manager is responsible for ensuring that adequate resources are made available to undertake the project. This will involve deciding which tasks should be carried out internally, which externally and then managing them.

- For internal tasks the project manager will select, build and motivate the project team. This will involve assigning roles to specific teams and individuals and delegating authority to them. This seems to be a major problem for Y Company as the project team are complaining that they do not know what is expected of them.

- Where tasks are subcontracted, the project manager will be involved with selecting and managing subcontractors. There is no information given in the question to suggest that sub-contractors are involved in Y Company

Planning

- The project manager is a key stakeholder within the planning stage of a project and has the primary responsibility of ensuring that the project objectives are clearly defined with the customer.

- This then needs to be communicated to the rest of the project team so everyone understands what constitutes a successful project outcome.

- Within the planning phase the project manager should seek to gain participation of team members in the planning, to ensure greater motivation and ownership. For Y Company some team members do not appear to have bought into the project as shown by their reluctance to provide information necessary for a successful outcome.

- The project manager often sets up project information reporting systems at this stage but at stated above, this is an area of weakness for Y Company.

Controlling

- After planning phase, the project manager is responsible for monitoring and controlling the project to achieve a successful outcome.

- For example, once tasks have been delegated to them, project team members are accountable to the project manager to complete tasks on time and within budget. This is not happening within Y Company, suggesting a lack of "hands-on" control.

- The project manager should ensure that he has the required information to assess whether or not the project is on schedule in terms of scope, time, cost and quality.

- When problems are identified, the project manager must decide what corrective action is necessary, taking advice from the project team. The main problem for X is that the project is behind schedule and deciding on appropriate action will involve analysis of the implications for time, cost and quality. The project sponsor is pushing for short cuts but if theses compromise the functionality of the final system, then they should be resisted.

(b) (i) The purpose of project control is to

- Monitor the progress of the project by producing the required products/ outcomes meeting the required quality

- Ensure that the work on the project is carried out within budget and by the required deadline

- Maintain project viability against the business case for the project, although the latter may be subject to change. In some cases it may be decided that the project is no longer worth continuing.

By monitoring actual progress against plans and standards, corrective action can be taken to ensure the above.

(ii)

Tutorial note

The stages of the project lifecycle are:

Initiation

Planning

Execution

Controlling

Completion

Discuss the controls at each of these stages.

A basic control system has the following steps:

— Set a standard or target

— Measure the actual result

— Compare the actual result to the target

— Feedback/feedforward can be used to take action required

Any control system effectively involves the following steps

1 Deciding upon targets and standards,

2 Measuring actual progress

3 Comparing actual progress against targets and then

4 Taking corrective action.

Within this framework X should set up the following controls to help manage the customer information database project:

Initiation stage

- The main control aspect of the initiation stage is to define the business need. This should be developed in the project initiation document (PID) which clearly sets out the purpose of the project, its scope, key deliverables, overall cost and time estimates and key objectives and milestones.

- Ultimately the success of the project will be assessed against this "project charter". This would also have made X's discussions with the project sponsor clearer when discussing the potential compromises of taking short cuts.

- For example, Y Company should have involved detailed discussions with end users – the different business areas – to determine exactly what functionality they wanted from the new system and why, highlighting which features here considered essential and which merely desirable.

Planning stage

- During the planning stage the overall objectives and estimates are translated into greater detail and the production of budgets, gates and milestones. This can involve tools such as work breakdown structure, cost breakdown structure, critical path analysis, Gantt charts and resource histograms.

- Had X carried out all of this, then the project team would have had a very clear idea of their responsibilities.

Implementing and controlling stages

- During implementation and controlling stages actual progress is measured and compared against budget.

- Key controls here can include regular meetings with staff, the production of budget and progress reports, detailed cost analyses and formal feedback and reporting mechanisms.

- The above tools such as Gantt charts and resource histograms can be adapted to show both actual and budget to help identify where performance has diverged from plan.

- At the very least, X should have set up a clear programme of daily/weekly/monthly meetings where team members understood that they would be discussing their performance against key targets and milestones.

Completing stage

- The completing stage has three elements. Firstly As part of completion a post-completion audit should be carried out to ensure that all of the benefits promised at the initiation stage have been realised. This will involve getting the feedback of the different business areas regarding whether they, as end-users, are satisfied with the outcome.

- A post implementation review is also useful to revisit the project history, analyse cost variances, schedules and so on, to ensure that lessons are learnt to facilitate better controls of future projects.

48   S COMPANY (MAY 05 EXAM)

Key answer tips

Part (a) asks for an explanation of the activities undertaken at the planning stage of a project.

When considering part (a), remember initial planning starts at the initiation stage, where the feasibility study and risk assessments are carried out. At the planning stage itself, the more detailed plans are drawn up. By the end of the planning stage there must be a comprehensive plan containing details of the timing, cost, quality and resource requirements of the project. Consider the activities which have to take place in order to achieve this detailed plan. It would be worth mentioning the project management tools that could be used at this stage.

Part (b) is a straightforward question that tests candidate's knowledge on the roles of a project manager and sponsor. Avoid simply listing the roles of each; ensure you clearly highlight the similarities and differences in the roles.

(a)   **Planning**

Introduction

To ensure that the proposed move is a success, it is vital that the planning phase is carried out effectively. The move is a complex process and could be broken down in a number of separate sub-projects such as upgrading the IT, the relocation itself and setting up a customer support team. Together with her project team, D should look at the following activities.

Establish project objectives

D should start by establishing the project's aims and objectives. For S Company these would include the following:

- the move is completed on time
- the move is completed within budget
- the new customer service team will be ready to start work from day one
- the new IT systems are installed and operational from day one
- staff disruption is kept to a minimum
- disruption to customers is kept to a minimum
- any outstanding problems with the building work are identified and resolved before the move takes place.

Define the scope of the project

D should next define the scope of the project, based on the project objectives already established. This involves clarifying:

- which deliverables are within the project and which are not
- time limits for the project
- cost limits for the project
- quality specifications, for example for the new IT facilities
- a more detailed analysis of the objectives.

Perform risk assessments

D should next examine the key risks to the project being a success. This would involve:

- examining any assumptions made to date about the project to see if they need revising

- identifying possible areas where time delays are more likely, for example, installing new phone systems

- identifying possible areas where cost overruns are more likely, for example, installing the new IT systems

- identifying possible areas where quality problems are more likely, for example, ensuring that the new customer service team is adequately trained.

The above activities are started at the initiation stage of the project and details of the project objectives and scope should be contained in the project initiation document. At the planning stage these activities will be considered in more detail.

Producing detailed plans

D and her project team can now produce detailed plans for each aspect of the project. At this stage new members may be brought into the team to manage particular tasks or because they have expertise in certain areas. Authority and responsibility for different aspects of the project will need to be clarified at this stage. Producing detailed activity plans will involve the following:

- examining each activity to see the resource requirements

- deciding whether to do activities in house or subcontract. The installation of the IT system and the move itself will probably involve using contractors but training the customer services team may be done in house

- clarifying who needs to authorise expenditure

- clarifying what quality issues are involved and how they should be measured.

In addition to these detailed plans there should be an overall time plan and a cost plan.

A time plan will be necessary to ensure the project is completed on time. To develop this, the team would need to consider the different activities, their interdependencies and how long they should take. These need to be translated into detailed targets, milestones and check points. To help with this analysis the team could use any of the following tools:

- Work Breakdown Structure software

- Gantt charts

- Network analysis to identify the critical path.

An overall cost plan will help ensure that the budget is achieved and involves consolidating the individual activity plans. The bigger picture this affords should allow the detailed plans to be challenged and changed where necessary. For example, deciding which contractors to use if there are differences in cost and deliverable timescales. This is particularly true for activities identified as critical it may be worth spending more to reduce the overall duration of the project.

(b)

Tutorial note

The project sponsor and project manager are both key players in any project. The role of the project manager is more widely known. The sponsor makes the final yes/no decisions about the project and provides the resources to complete the project. They are responsible for ensuring the project is successful at a business level. They often chair the steering committee to which the project manger reports.

Project managers and sponsors

The similarities and differences between a project sponsor, P, and a project manager, D, are detailed below.

Similarities

- Both are committed to making the project a success.
- Both will ultimately be assessed on whether or not the project is a success.
- Both will have input into choosing the project team.

Differences

Project sponsor	*Project manager*
• Initiates the project • Acts as agent of the organisation to ensure that the project achieves the objectives set by the organisation (such as cost, quality and time) • Is the source of the project manager's authority and will usually appoint the manager • Agrees project outcomes • Authorises definition of project • Makes resources available to the manager • Oversees the financial aspects of the project • Promotes project at high level meetings and in turn provides senior management support to the project manager • Owns project risks and resolves major problems • Is responsible for reporting progress to the organisation and supporting the project manager • Does not get involved with operational aspects but will watch the manager's progress	• The person who takes ultimate responsibility for ensuring the desired result is achieved on time and within budget • Co-ordinates a project from initiation to completion, using project management and general management techniques • Gets very involved in managing the operational aspects of the project such as cost control, monitoring quality and problem solving • Is responsible for leading and motivating the project team • Chooses and manages sub-contractors • Reports progress to the sponsor and other stakeholders, particularly alerting the sponsor to potential problems

49   A2D ENGINEERING (NOV 09 EXAM)

Key answer tips

(a)   This is a straightforward question on leadership skills and why they are important for a project manager. Do not simply list the skills, but explain in the context of the scenario why Q needs to consider them.

(b)   You are required to use leadership models in this part of the answer. There are a number to choose from with which you should be familiar. Make sure you describe Q's current style, and explain different styles to be used at different project stages.

(c)   This is a straightforward question on mentoring; ensure you explain how Q could benefit from it.

(a)   Q is correct in that as project manager he is responsible for the delivery of the project. However, he has to use the project team to achieve delivery and in this aspect he has to employ effective leadership skills if he is to get the most from the project team.

He clearly has the technical skills required for the project, but he will not be able to deliver the project on his own.

In order to get the most from the project team, they must be motivated and feel valued. It is clear from the scenario that the team are not feeling motivated and are unhappy as many of them are asking to leave the project team. This may come down to the style of leadership that Q has been adopting. He is very task driven and has clearly stated that he favours an autocratic approach. Many theories of leadership suggest that a more participative style of management is more effective. Teams with effective leadership, which includes effective delegation, are usually more cohesive, more motivated and more productive.

Tutorial Note

There are a number of leadership style theories, which could be used to answer part (b), the main ones, are:

–   Lewin's leadership styles

–   Likert's four systems of management

–   Tannenbaum and Schmidt's continuum of leadership styles

–   Blake and Mouton's managerial grid

All of these models have a number of styles of leadership within them. Any of them would be useful in this answer.

(b)   During a project the requirements change. It is important that the project manager is willing to vary style depending on the situation. Most leadership theories offer differing styles of leadership within them and managers should be able to change between the different styles as the situation dictates.

Currently Q is adopting an autocratic style of management. Under this approach the manager closely monitors his staff and has a higher concern for getting the task done rather than concern for the individual. Using the Tannenbaum and Schmidt model, Q would be at the "tells" end of the continuum. This is characterised by little communication with staff except for directing them, and little freedom for the subordinates. Other models also have extremes which would fit with Q's style: on the Blake and Mouton grid, Q shows more concern for task than for people, so he would be at the (9,1) point on the grid, or he appears to favour McGregor's theory X where the manager believes that the staff need controlled or they would not work.

This style may be necessary during periods of crisis or where tight deadlines are pressing. In these situations, a more autocratic, task orientated style may be the most suitable.

Also, during the initial stages of the project, where there is conflict among team members as roles and responsibilities are not yet clear, it can be important for the project manger to show strong, decisive leadership.

At other stages during the project however it may be important for the project manager to spend more time showing concern for the needs of the individual members of the team. By adopting a more participative style of leadership, the members of Q's project team will feel more appreciated and this should lead to increased productivity.

Lewin's model showed that the democratic approach to leadership was the most productive and gave the most satisfaction to the workers.

It would seem from the scenario that during the implementation stage of the project, a more participative approach would be more suitable in order to get the team members to increase their enthusiasm for the project. It may also be important to allow the members more say in how the project is being run, although the ultimate decision regarding the project will rest with the project manager.

(c)   Mentoring could help Q adapt to his current situation. A mentor would be appointed from within the organisation, but preferably from outside Q's line management. In this way the mentor would not be party to decisions affecting Q, but they would be independent and can therefore offer objective advice to Q.

The mentor could help Q with issues such as his leadership style and could help him see the improvements which could make to improve his current situation.

Mentors should be available for advice and could be useful for Q if he wanted to consider a new approach. He could talk through his proposals with the mentor before implementing them.

Mentors can also help the development of the individual by helping to identify training needs which should be addressed.

Overall Q's performance could be enhanced by introducing a mentoring scheme for him.

50   C HOSPITAL (MAY 06 EXAM)

Key answer tips

The main danger in part (a) is that you interpret the concept of 'project' too narrowly and run out of things to discuss. Application to C Hospital is key.

Part (b) is easier; use any project lifecycle with which you are familiar. Again, application to the scenario is vital.

(a)   A project is a unique undertaking to achieve a specific objective. Even if a project subsequently affects the ongoing business of the organisation, it can be distinguished from 'business as usual' on the following grounds:

- It is unique, rather than a repetitive action.

- It is temporary, having a defined start and end time.

- It has a clearly defined lifecycle of problem identification, solution development, implementation and completion (Gido and Clements).

- It has clearly defined aims regarding scope, quality and cost.

These aspects can be applied to the proposed project at C Hospital as follows:

Repetition

Once the new pay and reward system is set up, it will be used on an ongoing basis. However, the design and implementation of the new system should be a one-off exercise.

Start and end time

C Hospital needs to implement the new system in time to meet the government target of May 2007, giving a clear end-time for the project. All tasks must be scheduled to be completed by this date.

Lifecycle

The different lifecycle stages are discussed in more detail in part (b) below.

Clearly defined aims

The hospital has already stated clearly defined aims for the project:

- design and implement a new pay and rewards system.

- The quality aspect of the project is that the new system must achieve the aims of:

- harmonisation of payment systems for all different categories of workers resulting in one pay scale

- rewarding people for their contribution to hospital targets

- assisting in recruitment and retention

- greater flexibility

The scope of the project will need to be clearly defined. For example, does it only include financial reward or could it be linked to staff appraisals and the possibility of promotion?

Cost objectives will be established through setting budgets and a project sponsor will need to be appointed to provide the necessary resources. In this case, the sponsor will be the Executive Board.

Tutorial note

All projects can be split into stages; this is known as the project lifecycle. There are a number of models showing the stages in the project lifecycle. It will not matter which model you use in your answer as long as you explain what happens at each stage. Gido and Clements identified four phases in a large project:

Need/ Solution/ Implementation/ Completion

Alternatively, the Project Management Institute uses a five-stage model:

Initiation/ Planning/ Execution/ Controlling/ Completion

(b) The project will involve the following stages:

Initiation

The initial phase is to identify the need or problem that must be resolved.

In this case, C Hospital must respond to Government demands and implement a new pay and rewards system.

During this phase, the following must take place:

- Key project deliverables will be established, as outlined in part (a) above.

- Key individuals will be brought together to form the project team. This will include members of the HR, IT and Finance teams, together with representatives from other affected groups such as nurses, physiotherapists, technicians and support staff. Given that pay is likely to be affected in the longer term, it is vital that the new system is seen to be fair, so participation from interested groups is essential.

- The project budget will be set.

- Timescales will be set – in this case working back from May 2007 as the final key finish time.

Normally this phase would also include a feasibility study to see if the project is worth undertaking by considering costs and benefits. However, in this case C Hospital has no choice but to try to comply with Government targets.

Planning

Planning involves defining the resource requirements to execute and complete the project. In particular, it looks at how the project team will achieve the objectives to the required quality in the required time and within budget with the resources available.

During this phase, the project team will need to schedule the different activities involved.

For example, to migrate every employee onto one pay scale, the hospital will need a points system (or similar) to assess the worth of each job. If such a rating system exists then one activity will be to correlate the existing points to the new salary grades. If not, then the project scope must be expanded to include designing a job ranking system.

During this phase, the project team will make use of techniques and tools such as:

- Work Breakdown Structure

- Gannt charts

- Network analysis.

Identifying key milestones and setting targets is also performed during planning.

Execution

This stage will involve actually designing and implementing the new pay system.

The project manager will need to ensure that the team remains motivated and focused, particularly if staff are expected to perform their normal routine tasks as well as being part of the project team.

It is also likely that key deliverables are challenged during this phase.

Controlling

Controls are necessary to ensure that the project achieves its stated deliverables on time and within budget. By monitoring whether key milestones and other targets are being met, the project leader can determine whether the plans are realistic, whether corrective action is required and even whether key deliverables need to be revised.

In this case, the implementation of a new pay scale is non-negotiable but there may be scope for asking for more resources if timing becomes a problem, for example.

Completion and closure

The completion stage involves ensuring that all key objectives and customer specifications have been met.

In this case, this will involve relatively straightforward aspects:

- Was the new system up and running by May 2007?

- Is there one pay scale that applies to all staff without excessive numbers of different grades?

- Others may be more difficult to evaluate:

- Is the new system more flexible?

Closure also involves integrating the project results into the ongoing running of the business. In this case, this might involve a handover of the system to the HR department, training for staff and communication of the new scheme to all employees.

51   T (MAY 08 EXAM)

Key answer tips

Part (a) requires candidates to know the Tuckman model which outlines the stages of forming an effective team (Forming, Storming, Norming and Performing). The question is looking for a description and application of these stages to the scenario given.

Part (b) is looking for issues that may hinder effective team working within T's team. Think generally what causes problems in the effectiveness of project teams and whether these could be applied to the scenario. For each problem identified, suggest a solution to overcome it.

Tutorial note

The level of group performance is affected by the manner in which teams come together. According to Tuckman, teams typically pass through four stages of development before they become able to perform effectively. The stages are:

–   Forming – where the team members are brought together, no one is clear as to their roles and responsibilities

–   Storming – this is a stage of conflict where all members struggle to fit into the team

–   Norming – this stage establishes the norms under which the team will operate and team relationships become settled

–   Performing – once this stage is reached (and not all teams reach this stage), the team is capable of operating at full potential.

There is a fifth stage called Dorming which is applied to teams which have been together for a long time and have started to operate on automatic pilot. When teams reach this stage, it can be beneficial to disband the team or change some members of the team around to reinvigorate it and allow it to perform efficiently again.

(a)   One of the most important criteria for a successful project is choosing an effective project team.

T's project team will be people who have never worked together before from a variety of different areas within J Company. T needs to allow the team to develop, as they do not always work effectively together.

To build an effective project team we could apply Tuckman's model, which suggests that team's progress through a number of stages in order to achieve the objective.

The stages are:

1   Forming

The team comes together (formed), finding out about each other's experiences, characters and ideas. Individual roles, relationships and codes of conduct will be established from the project scope and objectives set.

T is bringing together people from different parts of the organisation who have not worked together before and are from a variety of different business functions, so it important she undertakes a range of team building exercises to promote cohesion and buy-in.

2   Storming

As members of the team begin to work together and get to know each other, the team will have different views as to how the project objectives may be achieved and who should do what. Resolving this conflict is critical to the team's success.

T is bringing together people with financial, production, IT, sales and marketing backgrounds, with various qualifications, experiences and roles. They will probably have very different views on what is important in product design (for example, cost control, image, functionality, ease of manufacture) and what constitutes a good educational toy. Hence, conflict may emerge!

3   Norming

At this stage, team members need to reach an agreement and conflicts should be resolved. Team cohesion develops and standards of behaviour are set.

At this stage, T will agree procedures and standards of performance with the team members and emphasise the importance of working as a team.

4   Performing

By this stage, the team will hopefully be working effectively together as a project team. They will now be able to concentrate all their energies on completing the project objectives, rather than conflicts within the group.

T will use a variety of team building techniques to shorten the four stages listed above and project management tools and techniques to help motivate and control the team.

(b)   The project manager T needs to get every team member effectively working together.

There are a number of difficulties that can occur in trying to manage a project team and the project manger must find ways of overcoming these problems as they arise.

Project difficulties that may arise	Overcoming the problems
Project slippages may occur due to unclear objectives being set by T at the beginning of the project. Team members start working towards their own objectives by mistake.	T must brief the project team on the overall objectives and regularly reinforce these throughout the project.

Project difficulties that may arise	Overcoming the problems
Group conflict may arise due to team members have different experiences and views as to the way in which the project work should be done. There may be biased views due to the functions that they work in, or personality issues due to a lack of respect or trust.	T needs to be aware of these potential problems and have an action plan. She must us team building activities to encourage them to work together whilst respecting each other's views and opinions. The team must be frequently reminded of the importance of the overall objective.
Lack of clarification in team members roles. The team members may be unclear as to the level of their responsibility and how they are contributing to the overall project objectives. This may lead to a lack of communication and co-operation within the team.	Team roles and responsibilities must be communicated at the start of the project and T must make it clear how their specific role is part of the overall Toys project.
Poor leadership and communication from T can also lead to a lack of commitment from the other members.	T needs to be involved, setting targets and ensuring that everyone has the resources to do their job. She should give feedback on how the team is performing against the project deliverables.
Lack of conformity in the group. Members of the group are persuaded by others to agree with a decision which they know is wrong. This could have disastrous consequences on the overall project.	T could encourage certain team members to participate and encourage a carefully planned decision process.
Risky decisions being taken by a group than those an individual may take. This could lead to project delays or even failure.	T needs to encourage the group to look at all decisions and think about the level of risk and whether that level is acceptable or not.
Too much time spent in unproductive project meetings and reading complex project communications.	T must plan her meetings, giving agenda's showing the purpose of the meeting and how each team member needs to contribute. Minutes from the meeting should be distributed showing who is responsible for any action to be taken and a relevant timescale.

52   N (MAY 09 EXAM)

Key answer tips

In part (a) you should focus on the types of risks, the likelihood and impact of these and suggest corresponding control measures.

Part (b) looks at the "kinds of negotiations", focus on the different stakeholders the project manager would deal with, their needs and what kind of discussion is likely to take place.

Tutorial Note

Risk and uncertainty are always present in projects. It is important to assess the risks in a project and manage the risks appropriately, as this will have an impact on the likelihood of success of the project.

The risk management process has four main stages:

–   Risk identification, where a list of potential risks should be drawn up

–   Risk analysis, where the potential probability (likelihood) and impact (magnitude) of each risk is assessed and from this the risks can be prioritised

–   Risk planning, where the management of each risk is considered. The management methods are often summarised as TARA – transfer, avoid, reduce, accept

–   Risk monitoring, where the progress of managing the risks is tracked. It is important to continually reassess risks as new risks could have emerged, or existing risks could have changed in their likelihood or potential magnitude.

(a)   The best way for N to manage the risks and uncertainties of the project is to follow a formal process of risk management. The key steps for such a process are outlined below. An initial Risk Log should be prepared at the Initiation stage of the project and should be updated on a regular basis throughout the project. Assuming that the project manager has managed similar projects previously, he/she ought to be aware of some of the risks that could occur for this project. There is also likely to be information in the public domain from lessons learned on similar projects such as the construction of the new Wembley stadium (mentioned below):

- Identify risk – project is complex and there are likely to be many diverse risks to consider

- Analyse the risk by considering the potential impact and likelihood

- Impact – attempt to quantify the magnitude of the impact if the risk occurs

- Likelihood of this happening – attempt to assess the probability of the risk materialising

- Prioritise / rank risks

- Select and implement strategy to deal with risks identified, depending on the likelihood and impact. The following grid can be useful.

LIKELIHOOD

	Low	High
High	**Transfer**	**Avoid**
Low	**Accept**	**Reduce**

(IMPACT is shown on the vertical axis)

Accept (low likelihood/low impact). Risks which fall into this category can be accepted as a normal part of business. It is anticipated that the risk is unlikely to occur and even if it does the consequences can be coped with. In saying that, it is essential that the risk continues to be monitored to ensure the assessment of the risk has not changed.

Transfer (low likelihood/high impact). In this case, the risk should be shared in some way by either being passed to someone else, for example another contractor or insurer.

Reduce (high likelihood/low impact). In this case, N needs to consider ways to reduce the risk. This is normally done by putting controls or procedures in place; although the cost of the controls should not outweigh the impact of the risk should it occur. In this case, this could include having contingency plans in place should the risk actually occur. Such a plan might involve having an existing stadium put on standby to hold the event should the new stadium not be ready in time, just as the Millennium Stadium in Cardiff was used to host events during the delays to the construction of the new Wembley stadium in London

Avoid (high likelihood/high impact). Where a risk falls into this category, N must consider avoiding the activity altogether. This may involve cancelling a contract.

- Monitor and review

- Maintain record of risks and actions taken to deal with them

Risk management is a continuous process throughout the project and N must have regular reviews of the risks documented in the risk register. It is important that N also considers uncertainty within the project through contingency planning detailing plans of action dependent on the possible risks that may be identified or even PERT techniques, which can help in the planning phase with uncertainty.

(b)   Negotiating is an activity that seeks to reach agreement between two or more starting positions.

The skills of a negotiator can be summarised under three main headings:

- Interpersonal skills – communication, power, influence and negotiation

- Analytical skills – analyse information, diagnose problems and interpret results.

- Technical skills – attention to detail and thorough case preparation.

- Examples of negotiations N might need to undertake:

- on his/her own behalf e.g. when agreeing the terms of his contract for the project. He should have already done this prior to starting the project but, as it is likely to be a lengthy project, he may need to revisit this at some stage, if conditions were put into his contract.

- on behalf of a department or functional area e.g. with members of the project team regarding budgets and deadlines. Perhaps a delay in one department causes a problem for another department.

- with the external environment on behalf of the organisation e.g. with outside contractors involved in the building work on quality, costs or time schedules.

Negotiation is when persuasion and compromise is necessary to conclude an acceptable agreement for all interested parties. N the project manager must recognise the stakeholders involved in the project will have differing and sometimes potentially conflicting interests. These stakeholders' interests should be taken into account during the project in developing the project plan and any changes that may need to be made during the project life. N must try to develop solutions which genuinely benefit all parties.

This major construction project is dependent upon meeting a completion date for the Rugby World Cup final. The company that employs N as a project manager will receive its stage payments upon completion to time and quality standards of the various stages of completion.

In order to secure commitment and genuine co-operation from the outside contractors, N should pursue an integrative approach to negotiation, aiming to work constructively towards mutually acceptable solutions. A 'win win' solution committed to by both parties.

A non-negotiatory approach with the contractors, such as coercion or persuasion, may at best result in compliance and at worst turn into a costly and damaging delay to the project. E.g. bargaining that is aimed at resolving pure conflicts of interest on substantive issues such as hours of work and rates of pay.

53   T HOSPITAL (NOV 09 EXAM)

Key answer tips

(a)   This part requires you to discuss the benefits of a project management methodology. PRINCE2 is suggested in the question, but students could use another methodology such as PMBoK to develop their answer.

(b)   This is a reasonably straightforward question about the effectiveness of meetings. Ensure you relate your answer to the scenario given.

Tutorial Note

The major component parts of the PRINCE2 methodology address the following issues:

−   Organisation – PRINCE2 suggests using an organisation chart for the project so that there is a clear structure of authority and responsibility

−   Plans – to ensure successful control, plans/standards are set for all deliverables

−   Controls – regular and formal monitoring of actual progress against plan is essential

−   Products – PRINCE2 includes a number of tools associated with the control of projects

−   Quality – quality plans should set the standards required

−   Risk management – risks must be carefully managed so that plans can be made to avoid or reduce them

−   Control of change management – all changes to the project must be subject to appropriate approval and authorisation

(a)   Case to support a project management methodology

A project management methodology is a structured approach to undertaking projects. There are a number of methodologies available including PRINCE2. PRINCE2 stands for PRojects IN Controlled Environments and was developed by the UK government. It provides a project framework, tools and standards which can be adapted for use in most projects. The use of a structured methodology such as PRINCE2 would ensure that all stages of the project were clearly defined, undertaken and documented.

Another benefit of using PRINCE2 is that is encourages control throughout the project and this is an area which has been lacking in the patient management system project so far. The project is over budget and behind schedule. These are aspects which would be tightly controlled using a methodology. Tools within the methodology would provide detailed schedules for the project and would allow better control over the deadlines by use of various diagrammatic tools and checkpoints. With PRINCE2, stage plans are used which specify the deliverables of each stage of the project and the project is not able to proceed to the next stage until all stages have been completed.

The financial budget would also be better controlled if a methodology was used. The budget would be drawn up and the actual spend would be measured and compared against the budget throughout the project. Regular reports would be produced to advise of progress of the project and this can be used to alert the project manager of any potential overspends in the project, or any areas where changes need to be made to the project plan.

Regular reporting is a feature of PRINCE2 and this would be of great benefit to this project as there has so far been a problem with lack of updates as to project performance.

Another criticism of the project is that the quality of the development is not as expected. PRINCE2 ensures that the quality standards required by the project are clearly defined at the outset of the project and that progress is measured against these quality standards throughout the project.

PRINCE2 or other methodologies would give this project many benefits in terms of planning, controlling and reporting on the project. In addition, one of the strongest features of PRINCE2 is that it defines the structure of the project. It covers who should be involved in the project, their roles and the reporting lines. It appears that members of the project team are unclear as to their roles in the hospital project. PRINCE2 would provide a clear reporting structure so that all team members were aware of the organisation and reporting structure for the project and communication lines would be specified to ensure that all relevant parties were kept up to date of all developments as required.

(b)   It appears that team meetings have not been effective in the project. This is highlighted by the fact that there was lack of attendance at the project meeting and that there was a lot of negativity at the meeting as many felt that the meetings were a waste of time. Meetings can take up a lot of time during a project so it is crucial to ensure that they are productive. The project meeting should be the best way to ensure that all parties are all kept up to date with the progress of the project and these meetings allow discussions of problems so that any problems can be dealt with as soon as possible so they do not harm to progress of the project.

Preparation is the most important stage in meetings and, as project manager, J must ensure that she has prepared for each meeting. In terms of preparation, J must be clear what the purpose of the meeting is and should ensure that all attendees are also clear as to this purpose. An agenda needs to be drawn up and should be sent to all attendees prior to the meeting. This will allow all attendees to prepare for the meeting which will make the meeting itself more productive.

The list of attendees must be carefully drawn up to ensure that the right people are invited to attend the meeting. A meeting with too many attendees can be just as ineffective as a meeting with too few attendees. When the list of appropriate attendees has been drawn up, a suitable time and location must be selected for the meeting. It can often be the case that attendees are geographically dispersed and this must be taken into account when the timing and location is agreed.

At the actual meeting itself, J must act as chair and control the meeting effectively. The role of the chair is to ensure that all aspects on the agenda are fully discussed, that all attendees are given the opportunity to contribute during the meeting and that the meeting stays focused. Often during meetings, disagreements can flare up and conflict can occur which can greatly reduce the productivity of the meeting. The chair must be strong in managing any such disruption.

A secretary should be appointed to take notes during the meeting and these should be read back at the end of the meeting to ensure their accuracy. Minutes of the meeting should be circulated as soon as possible after the meeting. Action points agreed at the meeting should be discussed at the following meeting so that all attendees realise that anything agreed to in the meeting will be followed up.

As project meeting should be regular, the dates of the next few meetings should be agreed in advance which should help to achieve maximum attendance.

54 COL (MAY 10 EXAM)

Key answer tips

(a)   This part asks for an outline plan for the project. Consider all the headings which you would include in an outline plan and give a little bit of detail about each of the headings. Ensure you relate your answer to the scenario.

(b)   Project manager skills is a common exam question. In this one you should not simply write out a list of all the project manager skills, but you should specifically look at the skills required in managing the team and keeping customers confident.

Tutorial Note

There is no definitive list for the contents of a project plan, but most will include some of the following sections:

−   Overview or summary of the project, including outline estimates of time and cost

−   Objectives of the project

−   Scope of the project

−   Methodology to be used in running the project

−   Assumptions

−   Communication plan

−   Resources

−   Stakeholders

−   Risk management

−   Change management

(a)   **Outline plan for upgrade to COL's online system**

Outline of the project

This project will upgrade the computer system of COL.

1 Objectives

The new system will allow faster processing of information, which will enhance the delivery of online course material. This will allow COL to compete more effectively with other service providers such as private and public colleges.

2 Stakeholders

The sponsor of the project is COL's board of director. The development will be carried out by SYS, assisted by staff of COL, and the project will be managed by D.

3 Resources

The project team will be made up of design staff from SYS and a number of staff from COL including IT experts and users. The project tem will be managed by the project manager, D.

4 Communication

The communication between SYS and COL will be managed by D. D will also have overall responsibility for the communication of the project's progress to COL's senior IT manager. Regular progress meetings will be set up, as will regular reporting of the progress of the project.

5 Risk

A risk assessment of the project has been undertaken and the main risk of the project had been highlighted as security over candidate's details. Risk will continue to be monitored throughout the project.

6 Cost

The budget for the project is $3million. Any additional cost above this level will be borne by SYS. A detailed budget will be drawn up and regular variance reports will be produced to ensure adherence to the budget.

7 Deadline

The timescales agreed for the development of the system is 12 months. This deadline is fixed and cannot be moved. Various planning tools, such as critical path analysis and Gantt charts will be use to create project schedules.

8 Change Management

A process for change management will have to be agreed. All changes must be co-ordinated by D and approved by the management of COL.

(b)   In terms of leading the project team, D will require the following skills:

- Leadership. The project manager's role is to deliver the project, using the project team. He must motivate and encourage the team members to ensure that they are as productive as possible and that they are committed to achieving project success.

- Delegation. This is a key management skill and ensures that all members of the team have adequate and challenging work.

- Communication. This is one of the main roles of project manager. He is responsible for all communication throughout the project. In terms of the team, he must ensure that all team members are kept up to date with all development and changes to the project requirements. This will normally be done via regular team meetings or reports.

- Planning. D must ensure that all work to be carried out by the team is planned and organised to ensure the best use of staff members and to ensure efficient scheduling of activities.

In terms of creating customer confidence, D must possess the following skills:

- Technical knowledge. The project manager must have technical knowledge so that he can make decisions in the best interest of the project.

- Financial knowledge. Customers will feel confident knowing that the project manager has the skills to manage the budget and to understand the financial implications of the decisions he makes during the project.

- Communication. The project manager must keep all stakeholders informed at all stages of the project.

55   V REGIONAL AUTHORITY (NOV 10 EXAM)

Key answer tips

(a)   This is a relatively straightforward question which requires candidates to apply their knowledge of project management software to the scenario information. The project lifecycle could be used and application of project management software at each stage could be discussed, or a more general approach could be taken where the benefits of using software during various project activities is discussed.

(b)   This question requires the candidate to firstly identify the main stakeholders then, secondly, make recommendations as to how the project manager should manage the different expectations of these stakeholders. Use of the Mendelow matrix to identify the levels of power and interest of the stakeholders would be a useful approach in identifying appropriate strategies to manage the stakeholders. Other strategies for managing stakeholders, e.g. Scholes could also be used.

Examiner's comments – part (a)

A mixed response with a few very good answers but many weak ones.

Common errors

Many candidates did not do well on this part of the question because they described general aspects of project management tools and techniques, rather than explaining how project management software could help during the life of the project.

(a)   Many of the tools and techniques needed to manage large and complex projects can be effectively carried out using project management software. Most PC based packages contain facilities which assist in planning activities, work scheduling facilities, the ability to view relationships between tasks, resource management and progress monitoring and control.

Project management software could assist the project manager of the new sporting facility in a number of ways:

- **Budgeting and cost control**. This is critically important for V, as a regional authority as public funds are being spent on this project and therefore costs must be managed to ensure that spending is kept within budget. PM software will allow the project manager to continually compare actual costs against budget for individual resources and activities and for the whole project.

- **Multiple project handling**. It is likely that this project will need to be broken down into smaller projects to make them more manageable. This project is complex, with a number of sports facilities being constructed by specialist contractors. Therefore, it would be useful to break the project down into separate sub-projects that can be planned and monitored separately.

- **Planning**. PM software will allow the PM to define the activities that need to be performed. It will maintain detailed task lists and create critical path analyses. It will allow the project manager to plan several thousand activities, allocating resources, setting start and completion dates and calculating expected times to complete.

- **Scheduling**. PM software will build Gantt charts and network diagrams based on the task and resource lists and associated information. Any changes to the lists will automatically recreate a new schedule for the project.

- **Resource planning**. A critical issue in project planning is resource planning, that is, ensuring the project has the correct level of manpower, equipment and material at the right place at the right time. Again, in a complex project such as the sporting facility this will be critical as a vast amount of material and manpower will be required on the different individual projects going on at the same time.

- **Resource histograms**. These give the project manager a visual display of the usage and availability of the resources needed during the life of the project. This demonstrates clearly to the project manager where there may be resource shortages and will allow reallocation to take place or will indicate to the project manager where additional resources may need to be obtained to ensure critical activities are achieved.

- **Reporting**. The project manager will have to regularly report to the various stakeholders on the progress of the project. PM software allows the project manager to generate progress reports, budget reports, resource reports, work breakdown structure reports and financial reports. These can be presented in a variety of formats to suit the needs of the different stakeholder groups.

(b)

Examiner's comments – part (b)

Some high scores were achieved in this part of the question.

Common errors

Weaker answers identified stakeholders, but did not develop their answers to recommend appropriate strategies to manage the different stakeholder expectations.

Tutorial Note

It is important that companies recognise the objectives of each group of stakeholders. These vary and can conflict with each other making the task of managing stakeholders more difficult. The Mendelow matrix provides a process for assessing and managing stakeholders.

–   Identify stakeholders and determine each group's objectives

–   Analyse the level of interest and power each group possesses

–   Place each stakeholder group in the appropriate quadrant of the matrix

–   Use the matrix to determine the appropriate management strategy for each group

		Level of interest	
		Low	High
Level of power	Low	**MINIMAL EFFORT**	**KEEP INFORMED**
	High	**KEEP SATISFIED**	**KEY PLAYERS**

The main stakeholders of the project are:

- The Board of V (as the project sponsors)
- The local residents
- The three local businesses investing in the project
- The staff
- The contractors and equipment suppliers
- The end customers and users of the sporting facility (such as residents of the town and local school children)

All of the stakeholders identified will have different expectations from the project and the project manager must understand these differences and attempt to manage them. The project manager needs to understand the different levels of power and interest of the different groups as this will determine the most appropriate strategy for managing each stakeholder group.

Strategies for managing stakeholder expectations

The Board of V

These are likely to be 'key players' according to the Mendelow matrix, as they will have a high level of interest in the outcome and success of the project and they will also have a high degree of power, particularly in allocation of financial resources. The project manager must ensure that the Board of V is kept regularly updated on project progress, particularly in the area of project budgeting. Weekly progress reports should be presented to the Board of V, detailing progress on a number of key project activities and resources

Local residents

The residents who have expressed a concern about the location of the new sporting facility clearly have a high level of interest in the project as they have already clearly expressed their concern to the local newspaper. Their level of power is likely to be limited unless they are able to create wider publicity and hostility to the facility in the town. Therefore, the project manager must communicate effectively with this group of residents in order to allay their fears. The project manager needs to present the positive sides of the project to the residents and offer positive support and reassurance to their concerns. Regular communication through local meetings should be carried out or a local resident representative could be assigned to the project committee.

Local businesses investing in the project

These investors are likely to have a high level of interest in the project, as they will want to know that their money is being invested wisely and it will also be a positive boost to their local standing. Their level of power is likely to be limited to the amount of funds they are committing to the project. Again, the project manager must ensure that the local businesses are informed regularly of project progress and budget progress to ensure that a continual and good working relationship is maintained with these funding organisations. The project manager must make sure that these funding organisations maintain their commitment to the project throughout its life.

Staff

The staff who will have to relocate to the new facility are likely to have a high level of interest in the project as it is going to affect the nature and location of their working lives. However, their level of power will be limited as they are likely to be few in number and will have little influence in the decision. The project manager must communicate with the staff members and identify the benefits to them of the relocation of the facility. The project manager must consider how to make staff positive towards the new facility as their negative attitude may affect the attitude of users in the future, so it is important to ensure that staff have a positive attitude towards the facility.

Contractors and equipment suppliers

These stakeholders are likely to have a high level of power in the project as it is largely down to their level of work and commitment to the project as to whether it will be a success or not. They are likely to have a limited interest in the project itself, other than the assurance that they will be paid regularly for the work that they complete. Therefore, the project manager must keep the contractors satisfied by ensuring that they are provided with regular and accurate work schedules and plans to ensure that work is carried out efficiently and on time and to the project plan. The contractors and suppliers must be involved at the early stages of the project life cycle in determining the project schedule and resource planning and must be involved in the continual and on-going revisions to schedule where necessary.

End customers and users of the facility

The end customer who will eventually use the facility once it is in operation is likely to have a low level of power and interest in the project itself. The project manager must always bear in mind that the end facility should be designed with the users in mind and must correspond to their needs, but during the project itself the project manager will need to present little information to this group, other than limited local bulletins and progress reports through local newspapers or the regional authority web site.

56 E (MAR 11 EXAM)

Key answer tips

(a) The suggested approach would be to work through the various problems that could be encountered in the hotel project without good project planning. Ensure you make reference to the project described in the scenario to illustrate the problems.

(b) The answer should identify the different project management tools and techniques and explain how they could help P in the planning of the hotel project. There are a number of tools and techniques which can be used in your answer. Ensure you explain their contribution rather than just describing them. There are 15 marks available for part (b); therefore, you should be looking to include four or five different tools and techniques in your answer.

Tutorial Note

When considering part (a), do not simply consider the activities at the planning stage, but all aspects of planning. Remember initial planning starts at the initiation stage, where the feasibility study and risk assessments are carried out. At the planning stage itself, the more detailed plans are drawn up.

Take all the activities undertaken as part of planning a project and consider what problems could arise if these activities had not been undertaken.

Examiner's comments – part (a)

This question was generally well answered.

Common errors

There was a tendency for some candidates to concentrate on the process of planning rather than the 'potential problems the hotel project could face', with the consequent loss of a few marks.

(a) A key part of the planning stage of the project management process involves defining clear objectives and setting realistic estimates in terms of budget and time and resources needed. Without this, it is unlikely that an estimation of the baseline budget and project schedule can be constructed to present a realistic assessment of the time and funding required, and the resources needed for the successful execution of the hotel project. The outcome could be that the project ends up with unrealistic timescales and the different activities may not be sequenced logically, to make the most effective and efficient use of resources. This could also result in budget overspend and delays in various stages of the project. Ultimately, the hotel project may fail to be completed on time.

At the initial planning stage, feasibility studies should be undertaken, along with an assessment of the risks associated with the hotel project. If these critical dimensions are not understood, the project manager will not have the opportunity to identify potential problems and determine the actions needed to deal with them nor develop contingency plans.

Given the nature of the project, not undertaking social and environment feasibility studies could lead to future problems and disruptions once construction starts for the hotel. For example, the impact on the local environment where the proposed hotel is to be built may not have been considered, and potential social issues in terms of whether the local community might object to the plans due to the disturbances during the building work.

If the project objectives are not clearly defined and scoped, this can make it more vulnerable to changing client specification. Whilst it is not unusual for client requirements to change during the life of a project, if the project is to come in on time and within budget then E needs to be aware of what is feasible. When the objectives are changed during the life of a project, there is usually a significant impact on project success and it is important that E is made aware of the consequences.

It is at the early stages within the project that roles and responsibilities are defined for the project team. If they are not clearly defined this could lead to duplication of activities or activities missed. The result might be that members of the project team do not work effectively together, along with poor communications between the various stakeholders in the project.

Finally, it is at the planning stage that various control mechanisms would normally be put in place. Without developing an appropriate control system there is the strong possibility of poor cost control and overspend.

Effective planning can minimise the potential problems outlined above. In summary, E is putting the smooth running of the project at risk by wanting to cut out this stage.

Examiner's comments – part (b)

This question was generally well answered.

Common errors

There was a tendency for some candidates to confuse 'tools and techniques' with 'methodologies' and so lose marks by concentrating on the latter at the expense of the former.

(b)   There is a range of different tools and techniques that P could use to assist him in planning the hotel project. For example:

- *Work Breakdown Structure*. This technique is a critical part of project planning involving an analysis of the work required to complete the hotel project. The activities in the project are broken down into manageable components, referred to as work packages. The process defines the activities that must be carried out for each work package. Each work package will have defined responsibilities and deliverables for the hotel project.

  The analysis of activities for the hotel project can be undertaken at a number of levels, for example starting with the major phases then breaking them down into more detailed sub activities. P would be able to develop a task list from the work breakdown structure to assist in planning, control and monitoring the various stages of the project. The work breakdown structure can, therefore, assist in identifying the people responsible for each activity or work package.

- Another widely used project planning tool is the *Gantt chart*. This provides a visual way of illustrating the sequence of activities in a project. Complex project activities are converted into constituent tasks and a graphical and understandable picture is provided. Although it does not show dependencies and internal relationships, it is a helpful framework in the planning of construction projects, such as the hotel build. It will show the time taken for each activity and the resources required, hence can be used to monitor progress against the plan and assist project scheduling by planning the timescales for the project. It can also be used by P to communicate the responsibilities for tasks to the project team.

- A variation of the Gantt chart is the *resource histogram*, which shows the resource requirement usage and availability against a timescale. This will help P in the scheduling and rescheduling of resources for the hotel project.

- *Network analysis*, sometimes referred to as *critical path analysis*, is an important technique in project planning, providing a diagram showing the sequence and dependencies between activities or deliverables on a project. Using a work breakdown structure, network analysis arranges each work package/task into a logical sequence, and estimates the time to complete each. The outputs from the work breakdown structure analysis will help the identification of which tasks are dependent on others. Dependencies are critical to project planning. Simplistically, this involves determining the sequence, i.e. if activity B can only begin when activity A is completed there is a dependency. For example, planning permission must be sought for the hotel before construction work can commence. This is a crucial activity in project planning and the allocation of resources.

  Having identified dependencies it is then possible to calculate the critical path, which is the longest sequence of consecutive activities. It identifies those activities which, if delayed beyond the allotted time, would delay the completion of the hotel project and how much float time there is on other tasks. In other words, by how much certain activities could slip before there is an impact on the expected time completion for the hotel project. This then enables the minimum possible time to be determined, and can be helpful in identifying where there is some slack time available within the project plan for any unforeseen circumstances.

- Another project technique is PERT (project evaluation and review technique). This is a development on network analysis that P might find helpful in project planning. The technique is designed to account for uncertainty in the project lifecycle. For each activity in the project PERT uses three time estimates:

  - the optimistic time based on the duration the Hotel project would take if conditions were ideal

  - the most likely/probable duration if conditions were normal or as expected

  and

  - the pessimistic estimates which is the duration it would take if a number of things went wrong.

  These estimates are then converted into a mean time and standard deviation which means it is then possible to establish the duration of the Hotel project using the expected times, but also to calculate a contingency time allowance.

57   P COMPANY (MAY 11 EXAM)

Key answer tips

(a)   is a straightforward question which requires candidates to demonstrate their knowledge of the characteristics of projects. A good answer would identify a range of relevant characteristics of a project and explain why these are different to characteristics of 'business as usual'.

(b)   should be straightforward, requiring the candidate to explain to G the roles and responsibilities of a project manager. G has no experience of project management and therefore the candidate must explain a range of roles and responsibilities in order to clearly establish the importance of the role of the project manager of the website development project. There are 15 marks on offer here, so you must ensure that your answer is sufficiently detailed.

Tutorial Note

A project has a number of features which distinguishes it from business as usual. These include:

–   it is unique

–   it has a specific objective

–   it has a defined start and end date

–   it has resources allocated to it (including staff and funding)

–   it has a clear lifecycle

Once complete, the project should become incorporated into business as usual.

Examiner's comments – part (a)

The overall result was one in which too many candidates misread the question and ended up with low marks.

Common errors

Too many candidates produced answers which discussed the difference between an online store and a retail store, rather than the differences between the characteristics of the website project and 'business as usual' work

(a)   The website development project will have a number of characteristics or attributes that distinguish it from 'business as usual' work:

•   A project is usually undertaken to meet two sets of objectives: one relating to the accomplishment of the customer requirements of scope (i.e. the deliverables), quantity, quality and cost, and the other relating to the achievement of the organisation's objectives of profitability and reputation etc.

- The project will have a clearly defined start and end time and will usually be determined in terms of the scope, schedule and cost. In this case, the objective of the project is to develop a new website. The project will be focussed on the tasks needed to design and implement the new website within the stated time period. All tasks must be scheduled to meet this pre-determined end date.

- The project will also have stakeholders, i.e. all those who are interested in the progress and final outcome of the website. For example, the project will have a project sponsor, that is, the individual or group who will provide the funds for the project and who may also chair the project steering committee (or project board) to which the project manager reports. Other project stakeholders will be the project customer/end users and the project owner.

- The project will have a lifecycle, in that it will pass through a number of phases, starting with the identification of need, followed by the development of the product, implementation and completion. The project is also finite as it has a fixed timescale.

- The website development project will have a budget allocated to deliver its objectives. The project manager must plan the project activities within this budget for costs and resources needed.

- A key feature of a project is that it is unique, in other words it is a non-repetitive activity and does not usually involve routine work. Development of the new website will be a one-off activity. Each project is unlikely to have occurred in the organisation before and each project will differ in some way or other from other projects, even if they have similar outcomes and deliverables.

- A project will inevitably have some degree of uncertainty as the uniqueness of it will lead to some degree of risk in the deliverables and the activities to achieve the deliverables.

Examiner's comments – part (b)

A mixed response overall with some very good answers but also a lot of average to poor answers.

Common errors

There was a tendency for some candidates to lose focus and to stray into a discussion of project management skills and the detail of project management tools rather than sticking with the requirement of explaining the role and responsibilities of the project manager of the website development.

(b)   G, as the project manager, will play a key role in the success or failure of the website development project. She will be the person ultimately responsible for ensuring that the final desired website is achieved on time and within budget to the satisfaction of the project stakeholders (i.e. P Company's customers, the internal department users and the Board of Directors as the project sponsors. As the project team is multi-disciplinary, she will have a complex role in co-ordinating, managing, controlling and communicating the project tasks.

A key role of the project manager is the management of the team members, so G must take responsibility for the whole project team which is carrying out the various project tasks in order to achieve the project objectives. G will be responsible for planning, team building, communication and co-ordinating the various project activities, monitoring and controlling, problem resolution and quality control.

G will also have responsibilities, as the project manager, to the project sponsor (i.e. the Board of Directors) in ensuring that resources are used efficiently. G will need to keep the project steering committee informed and up to date with timely and accurate project communication. G will also need to co-ordinate the communication process between the various project stakeholders.

G will also be responsible for co-ordinating the project from initiation to completion, by making use of a wide variety of project management tools and techniques so that activities are performed on time, within budget and to the quality standards set out in the project plan.

G will also have responsibility for taking the lead in the planning and organisation of work for the project team throughout the project. She will be responsible for ensuring that the necessary resources (people, finance, information, materials, time, etc.) required for performing the project tasks are available. She will also be responsible for assigning particular tasks to the project team members to carry out. She will need to delegate responsibility for performing certain project tasks to team members who will then be accountable to her for the accomplishment of those tasks.

G will be responsible for building a cohesive and productive project team and also for supervising the activities of individual team members throughout every stage of the project. She will need to provide advice or make appropriate decisions in the case of technical difficulties or problems, and must be able to respond and take appropriate action to keep the website development project on target for successful completion.

G is responsible for monitoring and controlling the progress of the project towards its successful completion. She must take corrective action and solve any problems as they arise in the project and communicate the implications of any changes to planned activities.

From the above, it is clear that in view of the various responsibilities of the project manager's role, G cannot rely solely on her technical skills in website development, but rather needs a wide range of skills. For example, G needs strong leadership and team building skills, communication, negotiation, good interpersonal skills and also problem solving skills. These may be lacking from her previous experience in other organisations.

58   DG COMPANY (SEPT 11 EXAM)

Key answer tips

(a)   should first explain what is meant by the term PRINCE2 and then develop to explain the specific features of PRINCE2 that could help in the management of the client management IT systems project, minimising problems. Good answers will make reference to specific benefits of PRINCE2 in the context of the project. Weak answers will simply describe features of PRINCE2.

(b)   should start with an explanation of the role of the project sponsor and then go on to distinguish the role of the project manager by articulating what the project manager does. A weak answer will only explain the role of the project sponsor or project manager. A good answer will provide a range of examples to distinguish between the two roles.

Tutorial Note

PRINCE2 has six process areas:

–   Starting up a project. This stage involves designing and appointing the project management team, creating the initial plan and ensuring that all information required is available.

–   Initiation. This stage establishes whether or not there is the justification to proceed with the project.

–   Managing stage boundaries. The primary objective at this stage is to ensure that all planned deliverables are completed as required.

–   Controlling a stage. Monitoring and control activities are carried out by the project manager at each stage of the project.

–   Managing project delivery. This includes effective allocation of work packages and ensuring that the work is carried out to the required quality standard.

–   Project closure. This stage brings the project to a formal and controlled close.

While all good project management should include these elements, PRINCE2 requires a more detailed level of structure and documentation. This helps in providing controls within the project and forces the identification of potential problems.

Examiner's comments – part (a)

Many responses to this first part of the question consisted of an elaboration of Prince 2 methodology rather than that of applying the methodology to the problems contained in the question scenario.

Common errors

The main weakness of many answers was the lack of explicit reference to the problems that have occurred in the client management IT system project. Many candidates seemed to assume that by indicating that a project management methodology could overcome such problems in general that this was all that was needed. This was not the case; for a good mark, candidates were required to pick out the particular problems noted in the scenario and to state explicitly how a particular part of the project methodology such as the control system could have prevented problems like overruns on time and budget.

(a)   PRINCE2 is an acronym for Projects In Controlled Environments and is a structured approach to project management. Essentially it provides a project framework with a set of project tools, guidelines and standards. It includes bureaucratic controls on the planning and execution so that any potential problems that may arise are identified and can be resolved early in the process. Whilst it could be argued that aspects of PRINCE2 could be considered to be just good project management, the difference is in the level of structure and documentation required.

The key processes of PRINCE2 methodology offer a number of features that would help the client management IT system project, including:

- A defined management structure of roles and responsibilities

- A system of plans

- A set of control procedures

- A focus on product based planning

The key processes and documentation of PRINCE2 would provide the project team with a clear structure of authority and responsibility between members in the project team, so that each party has clear objectives. As part of this, the control responsibilities of the various members of the project team would be determined.

The methodology can help in the future planning of the project, which R will need to do to get the project back on track. The PRINCE2 hierarchy of plans include:

- The overall project plan.

- Individual work plans for each project team member.

- Stage plans – which involves preparing plans for each stage. This assists in managing stage boundaries in terms of ensuring that all deliverables planned in a current stage have been completed as defined before authorising the next stage.

- The exception plan which is used when there are signs that the project is slipping behind schedule or deviating from budget or quality targets. If the project is going to exceed its tolerance, for example variances in time, cost or quality, this would be reported to the project board including B, the project sponsor. The implications on the whole project deliverables would then be discussed and plans amended to reflect any changes needed to ensure the project delivers its objectives.

PRINCE2 has a set of progressive documents for a project and control is achieved through the authorisation of work packages. These include controls on quality, time and costs and identify reports and handover requirements, all of which appear to be problems with regard to the client management IT system project.

The methodology also includes a series of 'management products', for example, project initiation documents, project budget, quality plan and various checkpoint and progress reports which would improve controls for the project.

PRINCE2 would divide the project into:

- *Technical products*, which are the things the project has been set up to provide to users.

- *Quality products*, which define the quality standards the technical product must achieve.

- *Management products*, which include project management structure planning documentation and reports.

Examiner's comments – part (b)

The differences in the role of project sponsor and project manager were generally well distinguished and often enabled candidates to gain a pass for the question as a whole.

(b)   B, as the project sponsor, is the person who will initiate the project and appoint the project manager. She will make the resources available for the project and would be responsible for approving the project plan. B will also expect to receive status reports as the project progresses to see that key milestones have been reached. If any changes are made to the plan during the project lifecycle, then the project sponsor will need to be informed.

The project sponsor will primarily take the role of watching over the project, she will not get involved in the day-to-day operational aspects of project management. However, she will provide support and senior management commitment to the project, acting when appropriate as a champion for the project. B will also be responsible for overseeing the financial aspects of the project, and may need to approve any capital expenditure if it is over a certain budget.

In contrast, R, as the project manager, will take responsibility for planning the various activities of the project. He will want to ensure the success of the project in terms of delivering its objectives on time and within budget. He will need to secure stakeholder approval, inform key stakeholders of progress and manage the different expectations of the various stakeholders including, for instance, the project sponsor and the project customer.

R's role will involve co-ordinating, controlling and communicating project activities on a day-to-day basis. This will involve securing and allocating project resources, monitoring project progress and controlling costs. He will need to keep B, the project sponsor, informed of progress and alert her to any serious problems which could impact on achieving the project objectives, should they occur.

As project manager, R will be responsible for leading and motivating the project team and fostering a collaborative working environment. He may need to manage any conflicts within the project team.

However well planned a project is, if problems do occur it will be the responsibility of the project manager to be the negotiator and to resolve problems.

MANAGEMENT OF RELATIONSHIPS

59   X COMPANY (NOV 04 EXAM)

Key answer tips

Part (a) is a relatively straightforward question on the issues that may occur with X Company due to them having a reward system, which discriminates in favour of one particular group.

Part (b) requires you to think about how X Company can ensure fair treatment of all employees and prevent discrimination.

Tutorial Note

In the UK, The Equality Act (2010) is the most significant piece of equality legislation to be introduced for many years. It brings to together a number of existing pieces of legislation, has added to them, and strengthened them. It has extended the protected characteristics to encompass:

– Age

– Disability

– Gender reassignment

– Marriage and civil partnership

– Pregnancy and maternity

– Race

– Religion and belief

– Sex

– Sexual orientation

(a)   The implications for the performance of X Company of having a promotion system that discriminates in favour of any one particular gender/ethnic group is likely to be as follows:

Litigation

Any form of discrimination may result in costly litigation, depending on the local legislation in place.

In the UK, for example, the firm could be prosecuted under The Equality Act (2010). This act brings together, adds to and strengthens a number of previous pieces of legislation, including race, sex, age and disability discrimination.

Reputation

Even if the firm's activities are not illegal in the country concerned, they are certainly unethical. This could damage the reputation of X Company in the eyes of both potential employees and customers, resulting in a loss of both.

Lost skills and experience

The current approach fails to take advantage of all the potential talents, knowledge and skills of the workforce by only focusing on a limited group. Ability is not restricted to any particular group in society. Talented individuals exist in all groups, whether identified by gender, race, ethnicity, physical ability or sexual orientation.

The efficiency of X Company will suffer as a result.

Teamwork

Discrimination prevents the kind of social integration needed for good team working.

Motivation and staff turnover

Talented staff outside the preferred group will feel that the system is unfair and will become demotivated as a result. This may result in higher staff turnover and increased difficulties recruiting good staff.

Competitive advantage

Taken together, the above factors may result in increased costs and reduced quality, seriously eroding the firm's core competences and its competitive advantage.

(b) (i) The company can ensure fair treatment of employees by a mixture of the following methods.

Compliance with legislation

X Company should ensure that all legislation regarding the treatment of employees is adhered to. A compliance officer could be appointed to monitor legislation and champion the changes needed to follow it.

Equal opportunities

While some protection is afforded to employees by employment legislation, X Company should also adopt best practice regarding equal opportunities and implement appropriate policies accordingly.

'Equal opportunities' is a generic term describing the belief that there should be an equal chance for all workers to apply and be selected for jobs, to be trained and promoted in employment and to have that employment terminated fairly. Employers should only discriminate according to ability, experience and potential. All employment decisions should be based solely on a person's ability to do the job in question; no consideration should be taken of a person's sex, age, racial origin, disability or marital status.

Managing diversity

Diversity is a wider concept than 'equal opportunity' (as defined by law) because it recognises that individuals differ on a wider range of dimensions than the rather crude categories of sex, race, age and so on.

Managing diversity implies a pro-active response to the needs of a diverse and changing workforce, to produce an open, flexible and supportive environment that values the uniqueness of employees.

Failure to respect diversity should be made a disciplinary offence.

The award-winning diversity strategy of US multi-national Pitney-Bowes, for example, sets out five key goals for communication, education and training, career development, recruitment and work/life balance, in order to promote an understanding of individual differences ('including, but not limited to, age, gender, race, religion, ethnicity, disability, sexual orientation and family circumstances') and to create a culture and work environment supportive to all employees.

Target setting

Workforce diversity should be measured at all levels of the organisation and compared with the demographics of the local population. Targets should be set to rectify any differences and policies implemented to achieve those targets.

Positive action

Achieving new targets could involve positive action, for example, by targeting women and ethnic minorities. Focusing on selection, appraisal, development and coaching, this will provide individuals in such groups with necessary skills and competences and also encourage them to apply for senior posts.

Training

Awareness needs to be raised via a process of encouraging people to question their attitudes and preconceptions. A variety of workshops, conferences and training programmes can be used for this purpose. These should include senior management and trade unions.

Feedback mechanisms

It is important that feedback mechanisms are put in place to encourage employees to raise concerns over discrimination without fearing for their jobs.

(ii) Governments can play a role in ensuring fair treatment of employees by introducing legislation and by raising awareness of the problem.

Legislation

In some countries, such as the USA, legislation is already well established. Such legislation usually focuses on the following:

- preventing discrimination
- encouraging equal opportunities
- respecting diversity.

In some cases this is encapsulated within human rights legislation.

European Union (EU) legislation is moving to eliminate discrimination by emphasising the basic principle of respect for fundamental human rights. New laws will soon come into force to protect the right of everyone in the EU to be treated equally and fairly, no matter where they are from or where they live and work.

Existing laws (called directives) ban discrimination on grounds of racial or ethnic origin, religion or belief, disability, age and sexual orientation. The specific areas covered include:

- access to jobs
- conditions at work
- rates of pay
- the rights and benefits linked to a job
- access to education and training
- social security benefits and healthcare.

Governments in every EU country have to incorporate EU Directives into their own legislation.

Raising awareness

Changing legislation is not enough – a publicity campaign is often needed to inform both employers and employees of the law and to change attitudes.

60 J AND T (NOV 07 EXAM)

Key answer tips

In part (a) make sure you apply any leadership styles to the scenario. Simply explaining the models without application will not score well. There are a number of leadership models which could be used in this answer, although it is probably better not to mention Adair in part (a) as this is the focus of part (b).

Part (b) was very straightforward as long as you had learnt Adair's model. As with (a), you must ensure that you apply the model to the scenario.

Part (c) asked how a mentoring systems would help T. Briefly explain how a mentoring system works, then consider the benefits of such a system for T.

Tutorial Note

There are a number of leadership style theories, which could be used to answer this question, the main ones, are:

- McGregor theory X and theory Y
- Lewin's leadership styles
- Likert's four systems of management
- Tannenbaum and Schmidt's continuum of leadership styles
- Blake and Mouton's managerial grid

All of these models have a number of styles of leadership within them. Any of them would be useful in this answer as long as they were well applied to the scenario.

(a) The leadership approaches of J and T can be assessed using the following models and theories:

McGregor's theory X/Y

McGregor put forward two theories concerning managers' assumptions about their workforce and the implications of this for their leadership style.

J appears to have adopted McGregor's "Theory Y" approach to management as she clearly valued staff contributions and encouraged participation.

T's behaviour, in contrast, seems to fit better with McGregor's "Theory X" approach. He does not feel that staff have any valuable contribution to make to decisions and wants them to simply do as they are told.

While McGregor recognised that there may be some situations where a Theory X style would be preferred, he felt that too many managers were Theory X when a Theory Y approach would be more beneficial.

Likert's four systems of management

Likert identified four styles or systems of leadership on a spectrum ranging from "participative", through "consultative", then "benevolent-authoritative" and then to "exploitative-authoritative".

J would fit within the "participative" category as there appears to be a high degree of delegation, frequent communication, high degrees of trust and teamwork.

T is at the other extreme and appears to be using an "exploitative-authoritative" style. This is shown by the low value placed on staff who need support and the centralised decision-making.

Again, while recognising a contingency approach, Likert advocated a participative style, especially when introducing new work or systems.

Tannenbaum and Schmidt

Tannenbaum and Schmidt suggested a leadership continuum ranging from democratic to authoritarian.

J's style is nearer the democratic end of the continuum and manages by involving staff and delegating.

T, on the other hand, is nearer the authoritarian end and probably uses a "tells" or a "tells and sells" approach.

Blake and Mouton's managerial grid

Blake and Mouton designed the managerial grid, which charts people-orientated *versus* task-oriented styles.

J would probably score a (9,9) on the grid - the "team" style"- reflecting a concern both for people and production, as reflected in the high performance of the department.

T seems very concerned about the task but less so about employees. He would thus score nearer (9,1) – the "task-orientated" style

Tutorial note

Adair's Action- centred leadership model takes Blake and Mouton's managerial grid and adds a further dimension. While Blake and Mouton's grid looks at task and group needs, Adair's model looks at these plus individual needs.

The model stresses that it is important for the manager to balance the needs of these three dimensions.

(b) Adair's action-centred leadership model takes Blake and Mouton's ideas one step further, by suggesting that effective leadership regards not only task and group needs as important, but also those of the individual subordinates making up the group:

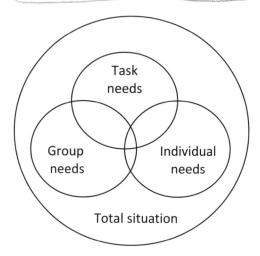

At present T seems to be focussed on the task needs, especially with regards to decision making. An understanding of Adair's model would force T to start to consider individual and team needs as well:

• T should be encouraged to respond to individual needs through goal setting, giving feedback, counselling, developing and motivating staff.

• Group maintenance roles will include communicating, team building, disciplining, encouraging, peacekeeping and standard seeking.

Tutorial Note

Mentoring is viewed as a useful technique for helping people develop. Mentoring is a relationship where one person helps another to improve their knowledge, work or thinking. It can be a very valuable development tool for both the mentor and the mentee.

A mentor should stimulate, guide, council, support, tutor and nurture learning.

(c)   Mentoring is a relationship where one person helps another to improve their knowledge, work or thinking. It is a very valuable development tool for both the person seeking support (the mentee) and the person giving the support (the mentor).

Mentoring could help T in the following ways:

- T will find a safe environment where he can admit gaps in his knowledge and skills, raise queries and discuss specific scenarios in more detail to consider alternative courses of action.

- In particular, T should gain an alternative and dispassionate view of his leadership style and be able to make a more rational assessment of his priorities

- Having a sounding board for discussion should give T more self-confidence and raise his morale. This will hopefully result in a more relaxed management style.

- The combination of the above is that T should learn to adapt his leadership style and become a better manager. In turn this will improve his career prospects and standing in the firm.

61   B LOCAL COUNCIL (MAY 07 EXAM)   *Walk in the footsteps of a top tutor*

Key answer tips

(a)   Herzberg's two-factor theory is the obvious framework to bring in to your answer to part (a) but do not restrict your answer to this. There are also marks for discussing cultural issues (Handy's cultural types could be used here) and leadership issues (there are a number of leadership models which could be used in this answer). Ensure that you make recommendations as well as discussing the problems.

(b)   This part of the question asks for the key issues in designing and implementing a staff performance system. Make sure you relate your comments to B Local Council where possible.

Tutor's top tips – part (a)

With narrative questions, it can often be difficult to ensure that you have made enough points to pass the question. Planning your answer will help you ensure that you have and will give your answer more structure. It is clear from this question that you are going to use the information given in the scenario. Theoretical knowledge is not sufficient to pass E2; application of knowledge is the key.

Tutor's top tips – part (a)

Start by carefully reading the requirements, this way you will have a better idea of what to look for when reading the scenario. There are three things to take from the requirements:

- The problems in B Local Council
- Recommendations to improve performance
- Reference to appropriate theories

The examiner will allow you to select the appropriate theory for your answer. It is therefore important that you have a good knowledge of various theories and that you can recognise which theories will work best given the scenario.

Tutor's top tips – part (a)

Next, look at the marks on offer for the question and the verbs used in the question; this will help you to assess how many points you have to make in your answer. There are 13 marks available for this part of the question, so you have to ensure that your answer makes enough points to pick up the marks available. The verbs used are 'analyse' and 'discuss' which are both level four verbs. With level 4 verbs, the examiner will expect a more in depth answer, so make fewer points but make sure you discuss each of them fully.

Tutor's top tips – part (a)

The first part of the requirement asks you to analyse the problems, so pick out the problems from the scenario. Given the 13 marks on offer, look for three or four main problems. By discussing these fully, then making recommendations and applying theory you should be able to gain four or five marks for each problem. The answer given has selected three main problems: the culture, the leadership style and the lack of motivation amongst the staff.

(a)   The main problems at B Local Council are the bureaucratic culture of the organisation, the attitude and leadership style of managers and poor motivation of staff. The new Chief Executive will have to overcome all of these if he is to be successful in improving the performance of the council.

Tutor's top tips – part (a)

When analysing the problems, make use of relevant theory.

Culture problem – Handy's cultural types is the most relevant theory to use here.

Culture

B Local Council has what Handy describes as a role culture, where job descriptions determine "the way we do things around here". While in some organisations this can give greater efficiency, here the resulting bureaucracy has stifled motivation and cooperation.

Tutor's top tips – part (a)

Leadership style problem – there are a number of leadership style theories, which could be used to answer this question, the main ones, are:

— McGregor theory X and theory Y

— Lewin's leadership styles

— Likert's four systems of management

— Tannenbaum and Schmidt's continuum of leadership styles

— Blake and Mouton's managerial grid

All of these models have a number of styles of leadership within them. Any of them would be useful in this answer as long as they were well applied to the scenario.

Leadership styles

Managers are adopting a very narrow, authoritarian approach to leadership consistent with McGregor's Theory X. It is likely that managers will need to adapt their leadership style to a more democratic "Theory Y" approach.

Tutor's top tips – part (a)

Motivation problem – the obvious theory to use for this problem is Herzberg. You can see from the scenario that the staff lack motivation despite enjoying benefits such as sport facilities, free car parking and competitive salaries. This suggests that these motivating factors are not working because some hygiene factors are lacking.

Motivation

Herzberg's two-factor theory is a useful framework to analyse the motivation problems at the council. Herzberg suggests that work factors can be divided into two types. Hygiene factors are unlikely to motivate staff but, if they are not right, can result in dissatisfaction and de-motivation. Motivators, on the other hand, can motivate individuals to superior effort and performance.

Hygiene factors include extrinsic factors surrounding the job such as pay, working conditions, company policy, supervision and interpersonal relationships. Whilst B Local Council offers competitive salaries, excellent working conditions, free car parking, a subsidised canteen and sports facilities, there are still some hygiene factors that could result in dissatisfaction. In particular the close supervision and poor relationships caused by the "them and us" culture need to be addressed.

A key element of a performance culture is high motivation, so the Chief Executive needs to ensure that motivators are present as well, once hygiene factors have been addressed. Motivators tend to be intrinsic to the job itself and include recognition, challenging work, responsibility and advancement. At present, it appears that all of these are lacking as employees say that they have no opportunities for advancement, are only allowed to do what is in their job description and get no feedback on their performance.

Tutor's top tips – part (a)

Now the problems have been well discussed, you should make recommendations to improve the performance of B Local Council. Use the problems you have highlighted above and consider what actions would reduce or remove each problem.

Recommendations

Cultures can become embedded and resistant to change so it is important for the Chief Executive to appreciate that such significant changes cannot be achieved overnight. A long-term approach is needed where core values are changed. For example, the Chief Executive needs to ensure that each member of staff understands the overriding objectives of the local council: that is providing services to local residents as efficiently and effectively as possible. A switch to a task culture (Handy) with this in mind, with greater customer focus is required. Training programmes for staff could help in customer service to help change attitudes and behaviours as well as improving skills.

To strengthen the forces for change there will need to be some incentive for individuals to change their behaviour and improve performance. The Chief Executive could thus consider the introduction of recognition schemes since recognition is a motivator. This could involve any of the following:

- encouraging managers to give staff more feedback and thanks for their contribution, acknowledging extra effort and performance.

- formal recognition schemes could be introduced such as employee of the month.

- financial reward systems linked to performance targets could be introduced

- the proposed staff performance appraisal system (see below) could also be used to provide feedback and recognition.

The Chief Executive should also consider redesigning job roles to widen the scope of jobs, providing more interesting and challenging work for staff. Newly empowered employees would gain new skills and be more responsibility. This would require a more participative leadership style with greater delegation. Less senior staff should be given greater responsibility for their own areas of work and participation in decision-making.

Prospects for career development could be improved by providing opportunities for lateral moves, such as job rotation, to enable staff to gain new experiences and competencies.

(b)

Tutorial note

Performance appraisal can help improve the effectiveness and efficiency of an organisation. A staff appraisal system can be used to review, change, inform, monitor, examine and evaluate employees. In order to implement an effective appraisal system, the following must be considered:

– the systems must be fair and consistent

– it must have the commitment and support of senior management

– it should have serious intent

– it must be set up so that it relates to the main objectives of the organisation

– its purpose should be clearly understood by all parties

– it must be cost effective

The key issues that need to be considered by B Local Council in designing and implementing an effective staff performance system include the following:

• Performance appraisal systems can have many objectives including assessing employees' performance, potential and development needs and linking performance with pay. It is thus important that the primary purpose of the system be determined and communicated. For B Local Council the system should focus on performance, though in the longer term it could be developed to link performance to rewards.

• The purpose of the appraisal must be clearly expressed and understood by both appraisers and the appraisees. Particularly within B Local Council there is a danger that it is seen as yet another bureaucratic form filling activity. Greater effectiveness will result if all stakeholders (staff, managers, etc) are clear about what the system is for and how it integrates with other organisational activities. Ideally, any performance measures should link to the key strategic objectives of B Local Council.

• To ensure widespread commitment to the new system it would be worth including staff from different backgrounds in the Local Council to contribute to the design of the system. The greater the extent of appraisee participation in the development of the system, the greater the chance of ownership.

• It is important that measures used to assess performance are seen to be relevant, fair and objective, rather than subjective. This is to reduce the potential for biased managers or personality differences to distort assessments. Furthermore, there should be a consistent approach across the different areas of the Local Council with criteria standardised where possible.

• Senior managers in B Local Council must be fully committed to the new appraisal system. Otherwise it will be viewed as something that the Chief Executive has imposed upon them. Regular meetings with managers to discuss the scheme are advised.

- Both those undertaking appraisals and those being appraised will need to be trained in areas such as interviewing and assessment techniques. In particular, feedback should be communicated in a balanced way to avoid compounding current poor morale.

- The developmental aspect of appraisal systems must be followed through to avoid cynicism. Action plans need to be agreed by both the appraiser and appraisee and monitored to make sure that they do take place. For example if training needs are identified, and the member of staff does not actually receive the training, this failure to follow up may lead to the system losing credibility.

- Appraisals should be frequent and sufficient time given so both parties can make a constructive contribution. However, they should be viewed as part of a continuous process of performance management, and not just as an annual event.

62   T4M (MAY 10 EXAM)

Key answer tips

(a) Part (a) asks you to consider the advantages and disadvantages of outsourcing some finance functions. It is important to use the scenario in your answer.

(b) Part (b) looks at negotiation. There are two negotiations to consider in this question. The first is between T4M and G20 and the second is between T4M and the trade unions. With 13 marks available, you will have to discuss both.

Tutorial note

Outsourcing elements of the finance function to an external party is known as Business Process Outsourcing (BPO). This has a number of advantages:

- Cost reduction. Outsourced partners can perform these functions more cheaply and efficiently due to economies of scale.

- Access to capabilities. The outsourcing partner will be a specialist provider in that field and will bring best practice expertise to the role.

- Release of capacity. The retained finance staff are able to concentrate on value added activities.

There are however disadvantages of this approach:

- Loss of control. Business areas may not be able to dictate what information they need and when they need it.

- Over-reliance on external providers.

- Confidentiality and risk to intellectual property.

- Risk of unsatisfactory quality. The information required may not be as required for decision-making purposes.

(a) T4M are considering outsourcing some activities undertaken by the Finance Department to a specialist company based in a different country.

Advantages of outsourcing

- Cost saving. One of the main advantages to be gained from the outsourcing proposal would be cost saving. The main saving for T4M would be in staff costs, they are estimating that around 300 staff will be lost if the proposal goes ahead. This will amount to a large cost saving as the saving would not only be a saving in salary cost, but also in associated benefit and human resources costs. Obviously, the saving within T4M will have to be balanced against the cost to be paid to G20 for provision of the services and the costs of setting up and controlling the outsourced provision.

- Head count reduction. For many companies operating with lower headcount is a benefit. Less staff means less in terms of pension payments, benefits and facility costs.

- Specialist services. G20 are a company specialising in providing this sort of service. It is likely that they have gained considerable knowledge and experience in providing similar services for other companies. This expertise could result in the task being performed more efficiently and overall costing less than T4M could provide the service themselves.

- Focus on core activities. In outsourcing these types of services , which can equally as well be provided by a third party, T4M will free up the Finance Department and allow them to focus on the activities which they undertake which add value to the business.

Drawbacks of outsourcing

- Quality standards. When companies outsource activities, they are contracting another company to carry out work on their behalf. In this case, T4M are looking at outsourcing functions such as customer bill payment and some areas of customer service. These are customer-facing activities and T4M must ensure that the outsourcing partner carries out the activities to the same standard that T4M would themselves carry them out. If they go ahead with the proposal, T4M will no longer control these activities and could find that if quality standards slip to below acceptable levels, they will lose customers.

- T4M also face a fight with the trade unions over the proposed redundancies and it seems likely that the unions will fight the company over this issue. T4M run the risk that other members of staff who are also union members may be asked to take industrial action to protest against the cuts. Any industrial action would affect T4M and their ability to provide a service to their customers.

- Bad publicity. The outsourcing proposal may damage the reputation of T4M. Some customers may be unhappy at the idea of their bills being processed in another country and having to deal with customer advisors who are not employed by T4M. They may have concerns about the security of their information and may be unhappy with T4M as a company for making people redundant to move the jobs to another country. The bad press from the trade unions may further add to the potential reputation damage which T4M could face as a result of the outsourcing decision.

(b)   Negotiation is required when two or more parties are trying to reach an agreement on an issue where they both want to benefit as much as they can from the outcome. In terms of the outsourcing, T4M must take the negotiation with G20 seriously to ensure that they get the agreement they need in terms of cost and in terms of quality standards and control. Each of these issues will have to be discussed at length by both parties until agreement is reached.

T4M will also have internal negotiations to carry out in terms of the job losses. They will have to ensure that this is done fairly and within the law. There will be negotiations with the trade unions on this matter where F will have to persuade the unions that some redundancies are necessary for the company to remain competitive in a very difficult market.

Negotiations often start with both parties stating their objective and considering any areas for movement. The ideal outcome is a win-win where both parties come out happy with what they have achieved. In other cases the outcome is a win-lose where one party gets what they wanted, but the other feels like they have lost out.

In the negotiation with G20, T4m would hopefully manage to obtain a win-win solution. Both companies want to reach an acceptable agreement and both will benefit from the contract being taken forward. They are both hoping to enter into a long-term business relationship with each other and this should be borne in mind during the negotiations as a good working relationship will be important if the contract goes ahead.

With the negotiations with the unions, a win-win solution is less likely as the starting positions are so opposed. T4M want to cut headcount and the union wants to protect the jobs. There is not a solution to this where both parties will feel like they have one, it is likely that one will win and the other will lose. This depends largely on the strength of the unions.

The normal process to follow in negotiations is as follows:

- Preparation
- Opening
- Bargaining
- Closing

During the preparation stage, both parties gather their information. This will include having a good understanding of the position of both parties. Each party should go into the negotiation knowing what they want out of it, what the other party is likely to want and how much they are willing to compromise their position. This preparation is carried out before the negotiation meeting.

At the meeting, the first stage is the opening where both parties present their point of view and state their position and what they are looking for. At this stage, the two positions are likely to be far apart.

The bulk of the meeting is taken up with the bargaining stage where both parties try to narrow the gap between the opening positions and look for areas of compromise. It is likely at this stage that both parties give some things away. Hopefully at the end of this phase, a working agreement can be reached.

Finally the closing part of the meeting where the outcomes are formally agreed. It is normal at this stage to involve lawyers to draw up a contract between the two parties to formalise what has been agreed. Both parties will then have the opportunity to study the documents produced at this stage and ensure that everyone understands and agrees with the outcome.

63   S CITY POLICE FORCE (MAY 09 EXAM)

Key answer tips

Part (a) is a straightforward definition question worth three marks. Ensure that you know the difference between vision and mission.

Part (b) asks about the benefits of developing a mission. Apply your knowledge of the benefits of developing mission statements to the scenario given and remember that the organisation in question is a police force.

In part (c) you have to select a framework that will give you a better understanding of what culture is within S City Police. There are a number of models which can be used to discuss culture. Handy's cultural types could be used, as could Schein's levels of culture, McKinsey seven S's model, the cultural iceberg or Johnson's cultural web framework. Note that the examiner is not looking for one specific model, more how you relate the model you have selected to the scenario in your answer.

(a)   A mission statement concerns what an organisation is all about. The statement answers three key questions:

- What do we do?
- For whom do we do it?
- What is the benefit?

A mission statement gives the overall purpose of S City Police, while a vision statement describes a picture of the "preferred future." A mission statement explains what S City Police do, for whom and the benefit. A vision statement, on the other hand, describes how the future will look if S City Police achieves its mission.

(b)   P has realised that the S City Police Force has no clear direction and that her colleagues have no clear direction. They have different opinions and this has led to inconsistencies in objective setting within the police force.

It is important that P convinces her colleagues of the need for developing a mission and the benefits of this in place. Reducing the cynicism that exists with regards to a not for profit organisation, such as S City Police force having a mission.

During the events, P needs to demonstrate the need for and the benefits of a mission, to the various stakeholders.

The mission will consider ALL stakeholders' views and act as a yardstick (benchmark) against which progress can be measured and from this identify its strengths and weaknesses.

It describes what the S City police force is about, giving purpose and a guiding philosophy to the S City police force. Defining and communicating the actions and goals that will help the police force achieve their vision whilst allowing the police force to evaluate its values.

It is important for P to stress that missions are not just for profit-making organisations and it would add credibility if she can provide examples of mission statements from other, similar organisations. It would be especially useful if she could find an organisation that is prepared to offer an endorsement of where they have benefitted from introducing a mission statement in their organisation.

Tutorial note

According to Schein, culture exists at three different levels:

1   Artefacts and creations. These are the things that can be seen, heard and observed. It includes dress code, office layout, branding etc.

2   Values. These can be identified from the stories and opinions of those within the organisation. It includes language, behaviour and how people justify what they do.

3   Basic assumptions. These are beliefs which are so deeply embedded in a culture that members are no longer consciously aware of them. These include beliefs on environmental issues, or about how people should be treated.

(c)   First and foremost, a culture defines identity. It communicates a corporate and professional membership to employees within S City Police Force and to outsiders. It creates boundaries as to 'This is the way we do things here, not everywhere else'.

Organisational culture is an important concept since it has a widespread influence on the behaviours and actions of employees. It represents a powerful force on S City Police Force strategies, structures and systems, the way it responds to change and ultimately, how well it performs. This can be either positive or negative, depending upon the nature of the culture and how well people relate to it and embrace it.

S City Police Force, like other organisations, will have evolved over time into a system of beliefs, values, norms of behaviour, symbols, myths and practices that are shared by members of the police force and these are all elements of organisational culture

Shared values or dominant beliefs – these underlie the culture by specifying what is important and need to be shared by everyone in the organisation so that they are reinforced and widely accepted.

Norms – which guide people's behaviour, suggesting what is, or is not, appropriate. The commitment to shared values must be strong enough to develop norms of behaviour or informal rules, which influence the decisions and actions throughout the organisation.

Symbols or symbolic actions – there are many examples of persistent, consistent and visible symbols and symbolic actions that make up an organisation's culture. These include role models, activities and the organisation's unique roots established by the personal style and experience of the founder and the original mission.

Within an organisation, managers can do more than simply understand the culture and work within it. They have the power to alter it. **Handy:** 'corporate cultures' describe the way the organisation is managed, not the set of values shared by employees.

Power culture

Here, there is one major source of power and influence. This is most likely to be the owner(s) of the organisation, who strive to maintain absolute control over employees. There are few procedures and rules of a formal kind. An example might be that of an entrepreneur such as Richard Branson, who initially managed a power culture within his organisation.

Role culture

In this version of culture, people describe their job by its duties, not by its purpose. It is a bureaucratic organisation, where the structure determines the authority and responsibility of individuals and there is a strong emphasis on hierarchy and status. For example, the Civil Service or the Armed Forces continue to operate a role culture, although less rigidly than in the past.

Person culture

This is characterised by the fact that it exists to satisfy the requirements of the particular individual(s) involved in the organisation. The person culture is to be found in a small, highly participatory organisation where individuals undertake all the duties themselves, for example, a barrister in chambers or those in professions within small partnerships.

Task culture

This is a 'can-do' attitude, often created by project teams or matrix structures in an organic manner, receptive to change.

It is important to recognise that, just as culture comes about over time, it should not be expected that it can be changed overnight. Rather, there needs to be an understanding that this will take time if a new culture is to become embedded and working successfully within the organisation.

64 ZEZ COMPANY (MAR 11 EXAM)

Key answer tips

(a) asks for a discussion of the conflict handing strategies which could be applied to the scenario. One approach would be to use Thomas's conflict handling framework (Thomas-Kilmann Conflict Mode Instrument (TKI)). The answer should start by providing a brief explanation of the framework, then work through the different conflict handling strategies. Ensure the answer makes reference to the scenario to illustrate the appropriateness of the different strategies for the managing of the conflict situation facing ZEZ Company.

(b) asks for the stages of effective negotiation. The answer should start by providing a brief explanation of negotiation. It could develop to comment on the specific factors on how negotiation should be approached to be effective. The different stages involved in negotiation should then be discussed. Good answers will explain the range of tactics associated with effective negotiation along with the stages that effective negotiation should go through, making links to the scenario context.

Tutorial Note

A useful framework for classifying different ways of handling conflict is the Thomas's typology (TKI). This is based on two conflict-management dimensions. These are the degree of assertiveness in pursuit of one's interest and the level of co-operation in attempting to satisfy others' interest. The strength of each of these in a particular situation can suggest the ways conflict may be resolved:

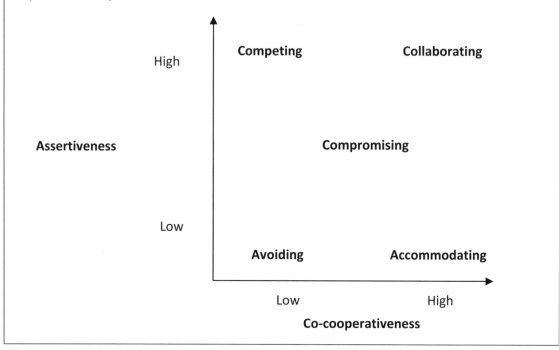

Examiner's comments – part (a)

Candidates familiar with Thomas's typology were able to answer this question very well.

Common errors

A significant number of candidates appeared to have no knowledge of conflict handling strategies and therefore scored very few marks for this question.

(a)   There are a number of different ways of handling conflict. A useful way of explaining the alternative approaches has been developed by Thomas who identified five conflict-handling strategies based on two conflict management dimensions. These consist of the degree of assertiveness in pursuit of one's interests and the level of cooperation in attempting to satisfy others' interests. The strengths of each of these in a particular situation can be regarded as lying along two continuums respectively:

The five identified strategies are:

Avoidance: This is where one or more parties in conflict may seek to avoid, suppress or ignore the conflict. This would not be recommended in the case of ZEZ Company since it does not end up resolving the conflict and could therefore impact negatively on the future survival of the company if the industrial unrest is not resolved.

Accommodation: This involves one party putting the other's interests first and suppressing its own interest in order to preserve some form of stability. Again, in the case of ZEZ Company this is not recommended given that the nature of the conflict is endemic and the accommodation strategy will not resolve the differences of the management and employees satisfactorily. ZEZ is fighting for survival and unless costs are reduced there may be nothing left to negotiate on.

Compromise: This is often viewed as an optimum strategy.   Each party gives something up and a deal somewhere between the two is accepted. For ZEZ Company this approach might be used between management and the trade unions to determine the number of redundancies, the criteria for redundancy, the redundancy package and changes to terms and conditions.

Competition: This is a state where both or all parties do not cooperate. Instead, they seek to maximise their own interests and goals. It ends up creating winners and losers. This approach is not recommended for ZEZ Company since it can prove damaging both to the organisation and to individuals, rather than working to resolve the conflict.

Collaboration: This is where differences are confronted and jointly resolved, with a win-win outcome achieved. Whilst this is also viewed as a favourable approach to managing conflict, it is not always possible. In the case of ZEZ Company, where some harsh decisions and actions will need to be taken, collaborating with the unions to work out solutions will only work if they accept that there will be a need to make some redundancies and changes to contracts, but can benefit from collaborating on 'the how'.

Examiner's comments – part (b)

This was a generally well answered question with most candidates showing evidence of good preparation.

Common errors

Several candidates could have improved their performance by elaborating on the respective phases of negotiation.

(b)   Negotiation involves argument and persuasion in order to strengthen one's own case by undermining the opposition. It occurs when there is no established set of rules for resolving the conflict and parties are committed to search for an agreement rather than fighting openly. Negotiation is often necessary within organisations to resolve conflicts of interest between two or more parties which have arisen because the parties have different objectives and is a useful and civilised way of settling disputes.

In the case of ZEZ Company, conflicts have arisen as a result of the need to make changes to terms and conditions of contracts and also the redundancies. These conflicts may be resolved through negotiation between management and the unions who are representing employees. The process of negotiation between employers and trade unions is often referred to as 'collective bargaining'. Without any negotiation the result could be that the union calls for industrial or strike action which could have a detrimental impact on the ZEZ Company's future survival.

Approaches to the negotiation process can be through focussing initially on each side's primary objectives, rather than becoming distracted by minor negotiating points at an early stage. It is necessary to maintain some flexibility within the negotiation process and for both parties to be prepared to settle for what is 'fair'. It is important to listen to what the other side wants and to make an effort to compromise so that both sides can attain their goals. However, this is often where negotiation can fail because of the tensions between the different objectives that can never coincide. This could occur for ZEZ Company since the union's main objective will be to keep jobs, whilst the organisation may see no alternative to its long-term survival without the job cuts and changes to terms and conditions.

It is likely that in the first stages of negotiation that the union will reject the proposals as unacceptable and will prepare their negotiation strategy. Whilst the union will not want to agree to job losses, it might recognise that they are inevitable and concentrate instead on persuading management to provide generous severance pay above the legal minimum and compensation for staff who are being asked to relocate. ZEZ Company management will have anticipated such a reaction and should have their negotiation strategy worked out.

The ideal will be to achieve a win-win outcome where both sides achieve enough of their objectives to be satisfied with the end result, trading-off wins and losses so that each side get something in return for everything they concede on. Win-lose or lose-lose outcomes are in no one's best long-term interest.

Important tactics for negotiation are to use questions effectively so as to control the situation, also the use of persuasion, and not to weaken your case inadvertently.

It is suggested that effective negotiation between ZEZ Company and the trade union should go through the following four stages:

- *Preparation*, which involves both parties gathering information and insight to the problems in order to understand the constraints acting on the negotiating parties. At this stage, who is involved in the negotiation, what the concerns of each party are and what the goal of the negotiation is will need to be determined. Another key feature at this stage is the establishment of the time for negotiation.

- The *opening* phase of negotiation involves both sides presenting their starting positions to one another. It is at this stage that the greatest opportunity is present to influence the other side.

- The *bargaining* phase is where both parties will aim to narrow the gap between the two initial positions to persuade the other party that its case is so strong that the other must accept less than it had planned. This might, in the case of ZEZ Company, be on the total number of job losses, the financial arrangements for redundancy or in relation to specific aspects of terms and conditions. The union will want the best for its members, whereas the management may be constrained by the financial position of the company.

- The *closing* phase of negotiation represents the opportunity to capitalise on the work that has been done at the earlier steps. It is at this stage that agreement is reached. The outcomes from the agreement should be publicised and implemented.

During the negotiation process, particularly in the case of negotiations surrounding the changes in ZEZ Company which are formal in nature, it is important from time to time to test that both sides understand clearly what is being proposed and at what stage the negotiations

65   FPC COMPANY (MAY 11 EXAM)

Key answer tips

(a)   asks what should be covered in the training sessions to help improve the communication skills within the Finance Department. The answer could start with an explanation of the importance of effective communication as a management competence in building relationships. It could then refer to the scenario to highlight some of the existing barriers to communications. It should then develop to discuss what the training should focus on to help finance staff develop their communication skills, referring to the communication process.

(b)   asks how implementing a staff appraisal system could improve the performance of the department. The answer should start with an explanation of the role of an appraisal system. It should then develop to explain how the various aspects of a staff appraisal system could help the Finance Department staff improve performance. It is important to use the scenario and to focus on how performance will be improved.

Tutorial Note

The communication process can be defined as a process that is used to impart a message or information from a sender to a receiver by using the medium of communication. The stages in the process are:

—   Sender – the entity sending the message

—   Message – this is what is being transmitted

—   Encoding – the process through which the message is symbolised

—   Channel – the medium through which the message is being sent

—   Receiver – the entity receiving the message

—   Decoding – the process in which the message is translated and meaning is generated out of it

—   Feedback – the process through which the receiver sends his/her response

Examiner's comments – part (a)

A mixed response with some very good answers from those who read the question carefully.

Common errors

Too many candidates lost focus after reading the scenario and tended to discuss the problems of conflict between the departments rather than tackling the question to do with the improvement of communication skills for members of the Finance Department.

(a) If the finance staff are to play a fuller role in FPC Company they will require a broader understanding of business. They will need to be trained not just to furnish and assemble financial information but draw insights and to communicate these effectively to support other functions in the company in decision-making. To achieve this, developing effective communication skills will be crucial.

The training on communication could start by getting the Finance Department staff to explore the barriers that currently exist in their communications with other members of the company. For example, helping them to appreciate that the messages they currently send are often too complex and are not fully understood by the other members of staff because of the technical jargon used. Also, that the receivers feel that they are overloaded with emails from the Finance Department and it can be difficult to find relevant information on the spreadsheets they receive. Hence, they may not be picking up the most important elements of the message to inform decisions.

The training could refer to the communication process model (see diagram below) as a framework to help the finance team understand the different elements in the communication process which could help them improve their skills.

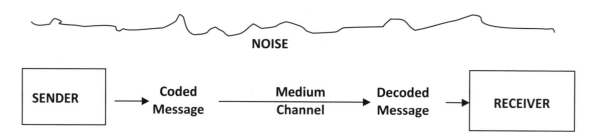

The training should provide an explanation of the things the sender needs to do to be effective in communication. This would include ensuring that the sender of the message is clear on its purpose with the receiver in mind. The sender of the message should have a clear objective in terms of what he/she wants to achieve from the communication. For example, is the communication aimed at providing information, or does it require specific actions to be taken. This needs to be coded into messages in a way that is understood by its audience. To make communication effective the sender of the message should plan the communication. For example, the sender needs to think about what is to be communicated, to whom it is to be communicated and the best medium to use for the message. For instance, should the message be communicated verbally or written, formal or informal etc?

The training could also cover issues associated with the medium used. It is important to select the most appropriate language and medium for the message thinking about the situation that the receiver will be in when the message is received. When creating a message, care needs to be taken so as not to cause confusion in the communication process through the overuse of jargon or lack of fluency in the message to ensure that communications are not being made unnecessarily complex.

Moving through the process of the communication to the receiver, the training should help the finance staff to understand the need to anticipate possible reactions by the receivers to the message and cater for these through the message or choice of medium. For example, if the message from the Finance Department relates to bad news about the financial position or budgets then this could upset the recipient and it would therefore be appropriate to use face-to-face communications.

Finance staff should also be made aware of the concepts of individual bias and selectivity and the implications of this for the receiver, i.e. people often hear and see what they want to. To help minimise this problem they should view communication as a two way process, encouraging feedback from the receiver. Feedback is often a neglected part of the communication process, but provides a crucial check for the finance staff to ascertain if their messages have been correctly understood and interpreted.

The training should highlight the concept of 'noise' that can occur in the communication process. This refers to any distractions or interference in the environment in which the communication is taking place and which can impede the transmission of the message. It happens when the message becomes distorted by extraneous factors between the sender and the receiver of the message such as distractions in the environment, information overload, such as the overuse of emails for complex messages. People can feel weighed down by the high volumes of information that are being transmitted, and hence ignore the communication.

The training should also cover non-verbal communication. For instance, it is important that any non-verbal communication reinforces verbal messages and does not undermine them. If the medium channel selected involves personal presentations, such as finance briefings, then it is important to ensure that all elements of communication, for instance, words used, tone and non-verbal signals (gestures, facial expressions, and posture) all fit with each other rather than contradict, so as not to confuse the receiver.

The overriding aim in terms of improving the communication skills of staff in the Finance Department should be to improve relationships enabling them to make a greater contribution taking on a partnership role in decision-making, rather than simply a provider of information.

Examiner's comments – part (b)

Some very good answers to this question.

Common errors

A surprising number of candidates failed to make good use of their knowledge of performance appraisal when applying it to the scenario for this particular question. Some candidates simply described the stages involved in staff appraisal rather than developing the answer to explain how it could help improve staff performance.

(b)   A staff performance appraisal system can be viewed as a method of internal control which can be used to assess employees' performance, potential and development needs. It could be used in the Finance Department of FPC Company to help influence the behaviour of staff in order to improve effectiveness and performance in the drive to achieve the department's objectives.

An appraisal system consists of a number of elements, which together will help improve performance of staff in the following ways:

Clearly Defined Performance Standards

Appraisals are designed to measure an individual's contribution to the organisation in as objective a way as possible. The process involves setting criteria for assessment and the agreement of objectives with members of staff. Therefore, staff in the Finance Department should be clearer on their key deliverables with greater clarity on what they are trying to achieve.

The performance measures should link an individual's objectives with those of not only the Finance Department but also with key strategic objectives and priorities of FPC Company. This would help individuals in having a better understanding of their responsibilities and how their contribution fits with the strategic business objectives of the company, to provide a unifying framework.

Effective monitoring system

As an example of an internal control system, staff appraisal would provide a system whereby their performance is measured against objectives. Through the appraisal process individual performance can be compared against the objectives set. Performance appraisal should therefore help staff in the Finance Department to be aware of how they are progressing in relation to the agreed targets set and can be used to ensure any problems are identified. Where there are gaps, the reasons can be discussed to help staff understand the areas they need to focus on to improve their performance, to correct problems and encourage better future performance.

Regular Discussions on Performance

Research has shown that individuals have a strong need to know how they are doing, but to date this does not appear to have been happening in the Finance Department. The appraisal process should provide the opportunity for open communications between staff and the manager. If carried out properly, it should be motivational since it is an opportunity for staff to reflect on their performance, reviewing past performance, receiving feedback from their manager with discussions on how to improve. In addition, a good appraisal system should be a continual process with regular discussions and feedback. This should provide for a positive experience for all staff, strengthening management/subordinate relations and raising the self-esteem of staff, through helping them to improve performance and develop.

Development of Appropriate Action Plans

An effective performance appraisal system should be viewed as a problem solving, participative and developmental activity rather than just a management tool of internal control. The appraisal process should provide the opportunity to recognise and agree individual training and development needs and discuss future career aspirations necessary to achieve future goals. Appraisal will therefore help identify potential and inform decisions on promotion, and help employees in think about their career development. This can be instrumental in keeping employees motivated through recognition, which should increase staff satisfaction

To derive the benefits it is important that there are jointly agreed outcomes from the appraisal process and there is good follow up. Actions need to be agreed by both the appraiser and appraisee and monitored to make sure they do take place. For example, if training needs are identified, and the member of staff in the Finance Department does not actually receive the training, this failure to follow up may lead to cynicism on the part of staff.

An appraisal system can have a profound effect on the levels of employee satisfaction and motivation through management recognition and interest in individual performance.

If the appraisal system is properly used then it should help improve the motivation and performance of individuals and enhance the effectiveness of the Finance Department.

66   Z COMPANY (SEPT 11 EXAM)

Key answer tips

(a)   asks for the sources of conflict between the groups on Z Company. The answer should start by providing a brief explanation of the concept of conflict. It should then develop to explain the different sources of conflict with reference to the question scenario.

(b)   asks for the various things that the Finance Director should do to ensure meetings are effective. Good answers will develop in the chronological order of planning and running effective meetings, with specific reference to the scenario context. Weak answers will be a list of points without reference to the scenario.

Examiner's comments – part (a)

This part of the question was often poorly answered in that many candidates repeated the points of the scenario rather than specified the underlying reasons for conflict as required.

Common errors

Neglecting to specify sources of the conflict such as those listed in the marking guide above.

(a)   Organisational conflict can occur on a number of different levels and can have a detrimental impact on the business. The conflict in Z Company is best characterised as horizontal conflict. This is where conflict occurs between groups or departments at the same level in the hierarchy. A number of factors play a part in creating the conflict:

Goal incompatibility is often the main cause, where the goals of one area block the achievement by other areas. In Z Company, the functional structure of the organisation could encourage employee loyalty to particular departments with employees wanting to concentrate on their own goals. The goals of different departments are often seen as mutually exclusive. This can result in conflict and lack of cooperation between different departments during the New Product Development (NPD) process.

Goals of innovation often can cause more conflict than other goals since the NPD process requires departments to co-operate. However, where there is an increase in task interdependence between different departments, then the potential for conflict increases. This is because the greater interdependence means that departments may exert pressure for fast response because the work in one department has to wait on other departments. Employees will need to spend time sharing information and communicating. As a result, differences in goals and attitudes can emerge leading to conflict. There appears to be a lack of understanding and appreciation of the pressures and needs of other departments during the NPD process.

For example whilst the Research & Development (R & D) Department wants to come up with the best possible product range from a technical perspective, in doing so it may not take account of the cost aspect, nor of the implications for the production of the new products, which will be of concern for the Production Department.

The marketing sales staff will want a new product range ready for the sales team. The Finance Department is viewed very much as a controller and an obstacle to the NPD process. The marketers and R&D staff may see finance as only taking a short-term view rather than investing for the future of the company.

Another source that can lead to horizontal conflict is the differences in the personalities, attitudes and experience of managers in different functional departments. This is often apparent between the different values of those working in marketing, finance and R &D. This stems from the different skills, qualifications and time horizons of the people working in these different areas.

Examiner's comments – part (b)

This part of the question allowed many candidates who did badly on part (a) of the question to make up ground and secure a pass. Many of them were able to draw on their general knowledge of how to run a good meeting to make the essential points and apply them to the case in question.

Common errors

A number of candidates did not read the question sufficiently thoroughly and as a result produced an answer explaining how conflict could be avoided in future meetings rather than what the FD could do to make future meetings effective.

Tutorial Note

Meetings can be an effective communication method for the manager. In order to ensure that the meeting is effective and useful it is important to adopt the following steps:

- Determine the purpose of the meeting

- Establish who needs to attend

- Determine the agenda in advance

- Make suitable arrangements for location and time

- Facilitate discussion

- Manage the plan of action

- Summarise the discussions

- Publish results/minutes

It is useful to remember that for a meeting to be successful, it requires 80% preparation and 20% execution.

(b)   Meetings can take up a significant amount of time and should, ideally, be seen to benefit those who attend. However, as in the scenario, people often leave meetings feeling frustrated at the time spent without any useful outcomes for them.

As a first step, the Finance Director should prepare for the meeting, set clear objectives on the purpose of the meeting, and establish who from the project team needs to attend. This should ensure that the time is not wasted for people who do not need to be there and to ensure the objectives of the meeting can be achieved. A practical aspect is to make arrangements in terms of the location and time of the meeting to encourage attendance.

An agenda should be drawn up by the Finance Director in advance and circulated to those attending. The agenda should provide a focus for the discussion and allow people to prepare before coming to the meeting, ensuring that they have relevant information with them. In the scenario, it is likely this had not been done since the necessary information from finance was not brought along to the meeting.

Other common problems that can occur during the meeting stem from having an ineffective chairperson, which can then result in the domination of discussion by a few people, conflict between attendees and the agenda items being unrealistic or badly structured. These problems can be addressed by the Finance Director acting as an effective chairperson. Ideally, there will also be a secretary or administrator who will be responsible for taking the minutes at the meetings.

The Finance Director should impose some order on the meeting and ask participants to contribute in accordance with meeting protocols, such as time constraints. His role is to facilitate discussion at the meeting. The Finance Director should also be able to manage conflict should it arise in a meeting and control any disruptive elements. Whilst encouraging constructive debate the skill is in limiting the scope of the discussion to agenda items.

Throughout the meeting the Finance Director should summarise and clarify key points made, explaining any jargon used and check understanding by all attending the meeting. He should note the actions that need to be taken, by whom and when, so that it is clear who is responsible for what. At the end of the meeting, a summary of the results should be gone through so that all participants are clear on the action points and their commitment is gained.

The Finance Director needs to bear in mind that the level of attention of participants diminishes towards the end of a meeting, particularly when it goes on too long. People may agree to anything towards the end of the meeting simply to get away.

After the meeting, the main problem is that actions are not always carried out. Therefore, minutes should be distributed to the attendees and other interested parties so that the outcomes are not lost, and team members are reminded of their responsibilities, priorities and action points. This should be kept as brief as possible to improve the chances of the minutes being read and action points acted upon. The minutes should form the basis of the next meeting so that failure to carry out actions is identified.

Section 5

SPECIMEN PAPER QUESTIONS

QUESTION 1

CN Company is a manufacturer of confectionary products with a well established position and brand recognition in Country P. The potential for future growth in Country P is, however, limited, with the market reaching saturation. A proposal put forward is that to achieve growth CN Company should move into new markets in other countries, offering its existing product range. One possible method of achieving market entry that has been identified is through a joint venture with a company that is already established in Country K.

The business development team are undertaking a feasibility study to explore the viability of the proposed strategy to sell CN Company's confectionary product range in Country K. As part of the feasibility study there will need to be some assessment of industry competition and the attractiveness of the market in Country K.

Required:

Explain how Porter's Five Forces model could be used by the business management team to assess the confectionery industry competition in Country K.

(Total: 10 marks)

QUESTION 2

Required:

Explain how the work breakdown structure (WBS) technique and Gantt charts can assist in the project management process.

(Total: 10 marks)

QUESTION 3

OD Company is in the business of designing, manufacturing and retailing outdoor equipment including hiking boots, rucksacks, tents and other associated products. The company's headquarters, including its manufacturing function, is in LM town where it is one of the major employers. It also has a chain of 25 retail shops in Country A.

The company is still owned by its founder J, who has been hugely successful in building up the OD brand, which now has global recognition. J has recently received a takeover bid from ZZ Company, which is based in another country. ZZ Company is particularly interested in buying the brand and design capability of OD Company. If the bid was accepted, then ZZ Company would close down the manufacturing activity in LM town and would outsource this to other parts of the world where production and labour costs are significantly lower. This would mean the loss of over 800 jobs in LM town, and the trade union has already stated it will fight any job cuts.

J is contemplating whether or not he should accept the bid.

Required:

Discuss the power and interests of the different stakeholder groups who are likely to be affected by the takeover bid.

(Total: 10 marks)

QUESTION 4

MT is the entrepreneurial owner of S Software Development Company which he set up five years ago with his business partner ZF, who provided the financial backing. Since that time the company has grown. Despite MT not having any clear view on what should happen, strategies have tended to emerge without any formal approach. ZF feels that, whilst still a small business, the company has come to a point in its lifecycle where perhaps a more formal approach to establishing its future strategic direction would be beneficial. However, MT has a different view and argues that the company has been a success to date. He feels that ZF's suggestion to adopt a formal rational approach to strategy development would have more disadvantages than advantages.

Required:

Describe the potential advantages and disadvantages of the formal rational approach to strategy development for S Software Development Company.

(Total: 10 marks)

QUESTION 5

E is Chairman and Managing Director of SP Company which he started 10 years ago, specialising in the manufacture of kitchen cabinets. The company has been very successful and through a series of acquisitions has diversified into the manufacturing of a range of household furniture and currently employs around 2,000 people. SP is now a public quoted listed company, and whilst E is no longer the majority shareholder, he remains a major force in the company. He still acts as if he is the owner manager and his management style is very autocratic, illustrated by his unwillingness to involve other Board members in decisions concerning the future strategic direction of the company.

F, the Finance Director, has become increasingly concerned about the decisions being made by E and the fact that he has put pressure on her to participate in some illegal accounting practices. This included covering up the substantial remuneration package which E has awarded to himself. F is also aware that E has accepted bribes from foreign suppliers and of insider dealing relating to a number of the acquisitions.

F has discussed her concerns with other members of the Board including the Marketing Director, Production Director and HR Director. However, they seem willing to overlook the wrongdoings of E and never challenge the decisions made by him. The opportunity to do so is limited since the Board meets on an irregular and infrequent basis with no external representatives.

Required:

Discuss the corporate governance issues facing SP Company.

(Total: 10 marks)

QUESTION 6

P is the project manager responsible for the implementation of a new customer information database in G Company. This is the first time he has taken on the role of project manager and was selected for the position on the basis of his strong technical skills. His project team is made up of representatives from different parts of the company, including the Customer Services Department, Finance Department and IT Department.

The project represents an important development and financial investment for G Company. A number of different business areas in the company have strong interests in the success of the project and are dependent on the new customer information database going live. It is business critical that the project is delivered on time, which is in six months time.

Unfortunately, the project is not going well. P feels that he lacks the support of his project team, who keep complaining that they do not know what they are supposed to be doing. It would appear that some members of the project team are not completing tasks on time and are not providing the information needed to progress with the database development. However, members of the project team feel that P is the cause of the problems. They have criticised P for getting too involved in the detailed technical aspects of the design of the customer information database and, as a result, is ignoring his wider responsibilities as project manager.

Required:

(a) **Distinguish the attributes of the project work in G Company from 'business as usual' work.** **(8 marks)**

(b) **Explain to P what his role and responsibilities should be as project manager for the customer information database project.** **(17 marks)**

(Total: 25 marks)

QUESTION 7

F is the Chief Executive of RM Company, a manufacturer of readymade meals. The company is facing difficult business conditions as a result of strong competition from supermarket own brand products and consumer demand for variety and new products.

F appreciates that the company needs to improve its performance in bringing new products to market. However, she is aware of the problems the company currently faces in its approach to new product development (NPD). Whilst collaboration is essential to successful NPD, in the past the NPD process in the company has resulted in disagreements and arguments between the various departments.

The marketers complain that the Research and Development (R&D) Department is very slow in responding to their proposals for new recipes and the whole process of R&D takes too long. The Production Department complains that R&D does not consider the implications for the production process when coming up with new recipes and product packaging. The sales team is frustrated with the length of time the whole NPD process takes. It says that the lack of new products puts it at a disadvantage when negotiating with retailers to sell RM Company's products.

The Finance Department is concerned that the investment in NPD does not provide adequate returns, and both the Marketing and R&D Departments are always over budget. However, the other departments see Finance as controlling and sanctioning spend rather than supporting new product development.

F knows that to remain competitive NPD is essential but that changes need to be made to the NPD process in the company. She has decided to establish a cross functional team to work on a new range of luxury readymade meals designed to appeal to the sophisticated end of the market. She has appointed T as head of NPD and given him the particular remit of leading and managing the NPD team.

Required:

(a)   **Identify the nature and sources of conflict between the different departments in RM Company.**   **(10 marks)**

(b)   **Discuss what T should do to be effective in leading and managing the NPD team.**
                                                                          (15 marks)

                                                                      (Total: 25 marks)

Section 6

SPECIMEN PAPER ANSWERS

QUESTION 1

Porter's five forces model is a useful framework that the business development team of CN Company could use to help it assess the competitive forces at work in the confectionary industry in Country K. It can be used to help management of CN decide whether the industry is an attractive one to enter.

Porter's model brings together the following five competitive forces:

- Threat of new entrants/barriers to entry
- Bargaining power of suppliers
- Bargaining power of buyers
- Threat of substitute products/services
- Competitive rivalry

It is the collective strength of these forces that will determine the profit potential of the confectionary industry in Country K. Essentially, it would only be a sensible strategic decision for CN Company to enter Country K if the forces are relatively weak and the potential returns are high. The information from the analysis would also help in identifying the factors driving profitability and inform the competitive strategy needed.

Taking each force in turn:

CN Company will be a new entrant so it needs to assess the potential barriers to entering the confectionary industry in Country K. These might include issues associated with gaining access to appropriate distribution channels for its confectionary. However, the fact that it is seeking to enter the market in a joint venture with a company already established in K Country could help minimise this barrier.

Another possible barrier to entry is product differentiation. If there are already established firms in Country K with strong brands in the confectionary market it may be hard for a new entrant to rival these. CN Company will also have to assess government policy in Country K to determine whether there are any legal or bureaucratic factors to deter foreign businesses entering the marketplace. From this information, the business development team should be able to assess whether entry barriers are high, moderate or low.

Bargaining power of suppliers is primarily related to the power of suppliers to raise their prices to the industry. Power will increase where the supply is dominated by a few firms, or suppliers have propriety product differences. It is unlikely that the supply of raw materials and resources needed for the production of confectionary will be concentrated in the hands of a few suppliers; therefore supplier power is likely to be moderate to low.

The bargaining power of buyers is gained through their ability to either gain products/services at lower prices or get improved product quality. It also depends on the size and number of buyers. Power will be greater when buyer power is concentrated in a few hands and when products are undifferentiated. CN Company will need to determine who its buyers are but assuming these are the end consumers, as individual buyers they will have relatively little bargaining power. Buyer power is increased when there are low switching costs, in other words where moving to a different supplier involves little risk. This would be the case in terms of buying confectionary products, from the perspective of the end consumer, because they are relatively low value purchases.

The buyer could, however, be the distribution channels in which case buyer power may be high if there is a concentration of these buyers.

Pressure from substitutes is where there are other products that satisfy the same need. In the case of confectionary products, it is probable that there will be a high threat of substitutes in the industry since there are many alternatives such as light food snacks, savoury snacks, fruit and other healthier product options available in most markets.

In the confectionary industry, the rivalry amongst existing competitors will be influenced by the number of firms operating in the industry, and industry growth rates. If there are numerous organisations, particularly with strong brand images already operating in Country K, and there is low industry growth then this will not be an attractive market for CN Company. If however, in contrast, the rivals are relatively small domestic producers with a poor brand image, the market could prove to be attractive.

QUESTION 2

WBS is an abbreviation for work breakdown structure and is a systematic approach to ensure that all activities required to complete a project are included and carried out. It helps in setting out the logical sequence of project events through breaking down of the project work into smaller parts which are known as work packages. These work packages can be put into the project plan as a comprehensive list of tasks and activities that need to be undertaken during the lifecycle of the project. This provides a hierarchical tree of the way a project is structured and identifies the manageable work elements that need to be undertaken by the project team in order to deliver the project. It also helps in the sequencing of tasks and priorities.

WBS can be used to help calculate the total cost of the project by asking those responsible for each work package to estimate the time and resources needed to deliver the project objectives. Each work package will have defined deliverables which can then be allocated to the appropriate person in the project team so aiding communication of responsibilities amongst the project team and providing a framework for monitoring and control.

Gantt charts can use information from the WBS process to construct a graphical illustration of the activities of a project shown as a bar chart with start and finishing times clearly identified. They can provide a simple representation of a project in terms of presenting the planned time that each activity will take. This helps in showing the resources required for each activity at a point in time.

Gantt charts can be used as a reporting tool in the monitoring of actual progress of the project, for example on a week-by-week basis, or indeed a day-by-day basis. As part of project control they could be used to illustrate both the planned duration of an activity and the actual duration, so any variances are clearly identified. Gantt charts can assist in project coordination and are useful as a communication tool since they are easy to understand and provide an overview of responsibilities and the progress of the project. For instance a Gantt chart could be produced for each member of the project team to show their total workload.

QUESTION 3

In making his decision J will need to consider the potential influence of different stakeholder groups. Mendelow's matrix can be used to plot the power of interest of different stakeholder groups, which would help J in understanding the effect of his decision of those groups. The stakeholder groups who will be impacted by the takeover bid will include:

J, as owner of the OD Company will have significant power in deciding whether or not to accept the bid. His interest may be in terms of the money he will make from the takeover. However, assuming J is a good employer with an awareness of the social responsibilities of his company, he should also have an interest in how the takeover bid would impact on his employees and wider stakeholder groups.

Employees who work in the manufacturing function of OD Company will have a high level of interest in whether or not the takeover bid is accepted, since they will be most affected in terms of potentially losing their jobs. Whist as individuals they may have relatively little power, they could collectively lobby the local government of LM town in order to gain support, have demonstrations and take industrial action gaining media attention. These actions could damage the reputation and brand of OD Company.

Linked to the above point, the trade union will have high level of interest in how the takeover bid will impact on its members, and could use its power to coordinate industrial action and support its workers.

Employees in design function and retail stores will have a high level of interest in the takeover bid since, whilst they would hope to keep their jobs if the takeover bid is accepted, they would have a new owner, who may have a different style of management, and may want to make changes to the way they work. They would have relatively little power, although if any changes to their working conditions were proposed, the trade union could act on their behalf. They may feel that they are in a difficult position in terms of how they support their fellow workers in the manufacturing function.

The Board of ZZ Company making the takeover bid will have a high level of interest since it will want T to accept the bid to gain access to the brand and design capability. The power they have is linked to financial resources, for example, in terms of how much they are prepared to offer for OD Company.

Other stakeholders who will have an interest in the takeover, but perhaps have relatively little power are the existing domestic suppliers to OD Company. If OD Company is one of their major customers, the proposal to outsource manufacturing could result in them losing business. This could impact on their future viability, unless they can find new customers.

The community in LM town and families of those losing their jobs are also stakeholder groups who will have an interest in the takeover bid and J's response. They could support the workers through industrial action and lobbying of local government and politicians regarding the potential impact on the community and economy of LM town, particularly since OD Company is a major employer in the town.

QUESTION 4

The formal rational approach to strategic planning being proposed by ZF usually results in a consciously thought out or deliberately intended strategy. It assumes that strategy making is a rational process with strategies based on careful analysis of the opportunities and threats posed by the external environment, and consideration of the organisation's strengths and weaknesses, relative to other players in the industry. MT says that he prefers to let his strategy emerge. This approach arises from ad-hoc, unanticipated or uncontrollable circumstances. It is often referred to as developing from patterns of behaviour in response to unexpected events rather than a consciously thought out or a deliberately intended strategy.

Whilst there are a number of disadvantages to the formal rational approach, ZF's view is that there are a number of potential benefits / advantages. These might include:

The process could help S Software Development Company take a longer term view than a short term reactive approach to strategy development. It should help encourage both MT and ZF to actively monitor the business environment and conduct formal analysis of the company's strengths, weaknesses, opportunities and threats to help them in understanding how they can best stay ahead of the game. The outcomes should inform plans and decisions, helping identify future strategic issues and promote a more proactive approach.

A rational approach could also help the company in assessing the optimum way to allocate its resources more effectively. It can also assist in establishing standards against which the performance of the organisation is measured and controlled. This would provide a basis for strategic control so that there are targets and reports enabling review of the success of the strategy.

As an entrepreneur, it is possible that MT may get frustrated with the bureaucracies that often accompany organisational growth, and he may decide to move on and sell his stake in the business. A rational approach can avoid succession problems, since the strategy of the company should be articulated and understood by other employees.

However, the formal rational process may also have disadvantages for S Software Development Company, as suggested by MT.

The potential disadvantages include the following:

The rational approach can be very expensive, time consuming and complicated for a small business. The opportunity cost needs to be considered, in terms of the time MT would need to spend on planning, taking him away from his main interest in software design which has been the basis for the company's success in the past.

Rational planning may also be considered too static and a process that tends to be undertaken on an annual basis. In a rapidly changing environment, it could be argued that the outcomes on which formally planned strategies are based often become quickly outdated, with the result that the intended strategy fails.

MT may be concerned that such an approach will just end up as a bureaucratic process with systems and targets unhelpful to a small business. The rational approach could also get in the way of MT's interest and talent in software design, since it could be conceived as a rigid approach bound up in processes, undermining MT's core competencies.

One of the aims of formal strategic planning is to achieve goal congruence between different business areas and stakeholders. However, in the case of S Software Development Company the goals are likely to be inseparable from the goals of MT and ZF as the owners. In a small business it could be argued that the rational approach is not appropriate because the success is more dependent of the ideas of MT. Indeed MT may not have aspirations for growth.

As an entrepreneur MT may have a desire to maintain absolute control and may well be unwilling to share or delegate control to others, that may be required as a result of formal strategic planning.

QUESTION 5

Corporate governance concerns the ownership and control of profit making organisations and the relationship between owners and managers. A number of reports have been produced to address the risk and problems resulting from poor corporate governance. In the UK the most significant reports include the Cadbury, Hempel and Greenbury reports. The recommendations are merged into a Combined Code which comprises the purpose and principles of good corporate governance for listed companies.

There are a number of corporate governance issues facing SP Company.

Firstly, it is problematic for one person to hold both the role of Chairman and Managing Director since this can result in too much concentration of power being in the hands of one person, and the greater dangers of the misuse or abuse of power. E, through his dominance and associated behaviours, combining chairperson and chief executive roles contravenes much of the recent thinking on corporate governance. This advocates that the separation of the two roles is essential for good control. As illustrated in the scenario, the current arrangement makes it difficult for other directors to challenge E's decisions.

One of the core principles of the Combined Code is that listed companies should be led by effective Boards which meet regularly. Membership should be a balance of executive and non executive directors so that no individuals or small groups can dominate decision making. It is evident from the scenario that Board meetings of SP Company are ineffective; it would seem that they are held on an irregular and infrequent basis with E wielding his power over other directors. It would appear that E has forced through decisions that are in his own personal interest, and could be detrimental to the company. If SP Company does not have non executive directors on the Board, then it would be appropriate to make some appointments to provide independent judgements on decisions.

It also seems that there is a lack of adequate control, accountability and audit in SP Company. The Board should be responsible for presenting a balanced and understandable assessment of the company's financial position. It is responsible for maintaining a sound system for internal controls to safeguard the company's assets and shareholders' investment. To meet corporate governance recommendations, SR Company should establish an audit committee and introduce formal and transparent arrangements for considering how to apply the principles of financial reporting and internal control. The non executive directors appointed to the Board should satisfy themselves on the integrity of financial information and that controls are robust.

The scenario suggests that E has determined his own remuneration package, which he is keen to keep covered up. However, good corporate governance practice states that no director should be involved in determining his/her own remuneration. Non executive directors should be responsible for determining a policy on the remuneration of executive directors and specific remuneration packages for each director, a proportion of which should be linked to corporate and individual performance. It is good practice to include a report on the remuneration policy for directors in the annual accounts. The above points would help support the Finance Director who has been placed in an awkward situation regarding the illegal accounting practices and E's remuneration.

The Finance Director could be encouraged to 'whistle blow', a practice in which she could expose the misdeeds of E, preventing further wrongdoings. That said, because of the lack of legal protection, the Finance Director could risk losing her job. It is apparent from the scenario that she doesn't have the support of other colleagues on the Board.

QUESTION 6

(a)   The customer information database project will have a number of characteristics or attributes that differentiate it from 'business as usual' work. The project can be characterised as having a lifecycle, since it will tend to pass through a number of phases, starting with the identification of need, followed by the development of a solution, implementation and completion.

A project is usually undertaken for a specific purpose to accomplish an objective or goal through a set of interrelated tasks and as such is a temporary process. It will have a clearly defined start and end time and will usually be determined in terms of the scope, schedule and cost. In this case the objective of the project is to develop a new customer information database. The project will be focussed on the tasks needed to design and implement the new database which needs to be completed in the six month period. All tasks must be scheduled to meet this pre-determined end date.

The customer information database project will have a budget allocated to deliver its objectives. The project manager must plan the project activities within this budget for costs and resources needed.

It will also have stakeholders, i.e. all those who are interested in the progress and final outcome of the customer information database project. For example, the project will have a project sponsor, that is the individual or group who will provide the funds for the project and who may also chair the project steering committee (sometimes called project board) to whom the project manager reports. Other project stakeholders will be the project customer/end users and project owner.

A key feature of a project is that it is unique, in other words it is a non-repetitive activity and does not usually involve routine work. Development of the new customer information database will be a one off activity.

A project will often cut across organisational and functional lines, in this case it includes representatives from the customer services department, finance department and the IT department.

(b) P, as the project manager, should play a key role in determining the overall success or failure of the customer information database project. He is the person who will ultimately be responsible for ensuring that the desired result of the project is achieved on time and within budget to the satisfaction of the various project stakeholders. Since the project is interdisciplinary and crosses organisational reporting lines, he will have a complex task in managing, coordinating, controlling and communicating project tasks. The scenario suggests that he is not fulfilling these tasks very well. The role of project manager involves managing people, so P must take responsibility for the whole project team who are carrying out the various project tasks in order to achieve the project objectives. It also involves carrying out the process, i.e. the project work and tasks and producing the final deliverables, in this case the customer information database, on time.

P will be responsible for coordinating the project from initiation to completion, making use of project management tools and techniques so that activities are performed on time within budget and to the quality standards set out in the project plan. He is, therefore, responsible for planning, teambuilding, communication and coordinating the various project activities, monitoring and controlling, problem resolution and quality controlling.

In the early stages of the project P should work with the project sponsor and project customer to clearly define the project objectives, and then communicate these to the project team so that everyone is clear on what constitutes a successful project outcome.

P also has the responsibility for taking the lead in the planning and organisation of work for the project team throughout the project lifecycle. He is responsible for ensuring that the necessary resources required for performing the project tasks are available and for assigning particular project members to carry out the work. In addition, he should delegate responsibility for performing certain project tasks to team members, who will then be accountable to him for the accomplishment of those tasks. From the information in the scenario it would appear that P is not doing this, since project members have said they are uncertain about what they should be doing. He should make sure they know what is going on and that all the members of the project team are properly briefed.

P is not only responsible for building a cohesive project team but also for supervising the activities of individual team members. He must provide advice or make appropriate decisions in case of technical difficulties, taking action to keep the project on target for successful completion.

As project manager, P has responsibilities to the project sponsor in that he must ensure resources are used efficiently and should keep the project steering committee informed with timely and accurate communication. P must coordinate the intercommunications between the various project stakeholders, and linked to this must attempt to satisfy the objectives of both outcome and process stakeholders.

P should be responsible for monitoring and controlling the progress of the project towards its successful completion. He must take corrective action and solve any problems as they arise in the project and communicate the implications of any changes to planned activities.

From the above, it is clear that in view of the various responsibilities of the project manager role, P cannot rely solely on his technical skills but needs a range of skills. For example, P needs strong leadership and teambuilding skills, communication, negotiation, good inter-personal skills, and also problem solving skills.

QUESTION 7

(a)   Organisational conflict can occur on a number of different levels and can have a detrimental impact on the business, as in the case of RM Company. The problems mean that management time and effort is being wasted on addressing conflicts rather than concentrating on NPD. Collaboration between the different departments is not occurring. The conflict in RM Company is best characterised as horizontal conflict. This is where conflict occurs between groups or departments at the same level in the hierarchy.

A number of sources creating conflict can be discerned:

Goal incompatibility is often the main cause, where the goals of one area block the achievement of other areas. In RM Company the functional structure of the organisation could encourage employee loyalty to particular departments with employees wanting to concentrate on their own goals. The goals of different departments are often seen as mutually exclusive and it is this that is potentially resulting in conflict and lack of cooperation between the different departments in RM Company.

Goals of innovation can often cause more conflict than other goals since the NPD process requires departments to co-operate. However, as task interdependence between different departments increases, the potential for conflict is also likely to increase. The greater task interdependence means that some departments may exert pressure for fast response since their work has to wait or is reliant on the completion of work by other departments. Employees will need to spend time to share information and communicate across departments, but this can lead to differences in goals and attitudes resulting in conflict.

In RM Company there appears to be a lack of understanding and appreciation of the pressures and needs of other departments during the NPD process. For example, whilst the R&D Department will want to come up with the best possible menus for the new range of luxury readymade meals from a technical perspective, in doing so they may not take account of the cost aspect, nor of the implications for the mass production of a product, which will be an issue for the Production Department.

The sales staff focus will be on achieving their sales targets and they want the new product ready for market as quickly as possible. They are disinterested in the various activities involved in the NPD process, they just want results. The Finance Department is viewed very much as a controller and an obstacle to the NPD process. The marketers and R&D staff may see finance staff as only taking a short term view rather than investing for the future of the Company.

Another source that can lead to horizontal conflict is the differences in the cognitive and emotional orientations of managers in different functional departments. This is often apparent in the values of individuals, for example, it is probable that those working in marketing will have different values from R&D food scientists. This stems from the different skills, attitudes and time horizons of the people working in these areas.

(b)   There are a number of things that T must do if he is going to be effective in leading and managing the NPD team.

Firstly, when forming the NPD team, T should consider the team members in terms of their personalities and characteristics and their personal goals, since the NPD team will bring together individuals from different specialisms and functional departments to contribute to the process of NPD.

In establishing the NPD team, T should consider the suitability of members by assessing how members are likely to fit with the rest of the team and whether or not the team has a balanced portfolio of characteristics relative to the task, in this case the NPD process. To help him T could draw on the research by Belbin who suggests that an effective group should have a balance of team roles. Belbin provided managers with a tool to help guide the nature or mixture of people who will be required to undertake the NPD project. The classification of roles identified by Belbin included: the coordinator; the shaper; the monitor-evaluator; the resource investigator, the implementer; the team worker; the finisher; the specialist.

In addition, when first establishing the NPD team, T should consider the stages of team development and maturity which can affect the effectiveness of the team. Tuckman identifies four successive stages of group development: **forming** where the group come together and starts to establish the purpose of the group, structure and leadership; **storming**, where members get to know each other better. At this stage disagreements can occur over roles and behavioural expectations; this can lead to conflict and hostility; **norming** where the group will establish agreed guidelines and standards and develop their own norms of acceptable behaviour and performance; **performing** which occurs when the group has progressed through the earlier stages of development and created the structure to work effectively as a team.

T will need to ensure that team members understand their roles, responsibilities in the NPD process and the activities that the other team members are contributing. Therefore, it important that T establishes clear communication procedures holds regular team meetings and status reviews. If T can help individuals to understand each other's roles, rather than for which functional department individual comes from, this should have a positive impact on the interactions between team members.

As well as encouraging members to communicate and interact regularly it is important that T establishes a common task/goal that all team members are working towards. T should set out the objectives for NPD and set targets so that all members of the team are clear on what they need to work towards, and provide feedback on progress. He should encourage all members to participate in team meetings. It is important that T motivates all members of the team so that they are committed to achieving the NPD objectives, and feel accountable for their individual activities.

T should also think about the environment such as the physical surroundings at work and where team members are situated. If they are in close proximity then this is probably more conducive to encouraging team work and effective communication than where members are geographically separated from each other.

T also needs to consider the form of leadership style he adopts since this can influence the relationship between members of the team, and can have a major impact on team effectiveness. The team will be affected by the way in which the manager gives guidance and encouragement to the team, provides opportunities for participation and deals with any conflicts. Usually a participative or democratic style of leadership is most appropriate to encouraging high team performance.

Enterprise Pillar

Management Level

E2 – Enterprise Management

22 November 2011 - Tuesday Afternoon Session

Instructions to candidates

You are allowed three hours to answer this question paper.
You are allowed 20 minutes reading time **before the examination begins** during which you should read the question paper and, if you wish, highlight and/or make notes on the question paper. However, you are **not** allowed, **under any circumstances**, to open the answer book and start writing or use your calculator during this reading time.
You are strongly advised to carefully read all the question requirements before attempting the question concerned (that is all parts and/or sub-questions).
ALL answers must be written in the answer book. Answers or notes written on the question paper will **not** be submitted for marking.
ALL QUESTIONS ARE COMPULSORY.
Section A comprises 5 questions and is on pages 2 to 4.
Section B comprises 2 questions and is on pages 5 and 6.
The list of verbs as published in the syllabus is given for reference on page 7.
Write your candidate number, the paper number and the examination subject title in the spaces provided on the front of the examination answer book. Also write your contact ID and name in the space provided in the right hand margin and seal to close.
Tick the appropriate boxes on the front of the answer book to indicate which questions you have answered.

E2 – Enterprise Management

TURN OVER

© The Chartered Institute of Management Accountants 2011

Question One

TF Company is about to embark on a restructuring programme which will mean significant changes to the roles and responsibilities of staff in the Finance Department. It is anticipated that there will be some resistance to the proposed changes, so the Board of TF Company has asked KK, a senior manager in the department, to lead the changes. The Board has chosen KK because she is generally well liked and respected by her colleagues. She is also held in high regard for her expert knowledge and her interest in, and support she gives to, all those who work for her.

Required:

Describe the different sources of power KK possesses and which could help her to manage the changes in the Finance Department.

(Total for Question One = 10 marks)

Question Two

Project control processes cannot be overemphasised in their importance to the success of a project. The project manager must continually take a pro-active approach in controlling a project.

Required:

Discuss the actions the project manager should take as a project progresses to ensure effective project control.

(Total for Question Two = 10 marks)

Section A continues on the opposite page

Question Three

The Head of Insurance at JKL Bank has been considering how to make efficiencies in the operation of the Car Insurance Business Unit. One option under consideration is to outsource the Customer Contact Centre (CCC) for its car insurance business. The work of the CCC currently involves dealing with customer telephone enquiries on issues such as insurance claims, policy changes, renewals and premium/payment information.

To help him make a decision on whether or not to proceed, the Head of Insurance has asked for an evaluation of the proposed outsourcing of the CCC.

Required:

Explain how transaction cost theory could help the Head of Insurance on deciding whether or not to outsource the Car Insurance Business Unit's Customer Contact Centre.

(Total for Question Three = 10 marks)

Question Four

D is a CIMA member and financial controller for a local government authority. D has recently undertaken an analysis of expense claims for the local authority and believes that the Finance Director, also a CIMA member, has been claiming for non-business related expenses which the authority does not permit. D is unhappy about the situation and has approached the Finance Director with her concerns but has failed to get the answers needed from him.

The Finance Director has offered D a large personal bonus in exchange for her silence. As a member of CIMA, D knows that any action taken should be compliant with CIMA's code of professional ethics.

Required:

Discuss how the fundamental principles of the CIMA Code of Ethics for Professional Accountants might be compromised if both D accepts the bonus and the Finance Director is allowed to claim non-business related expenses.

Note: You should refer to both D and the Financial Director in your answer

(Total for Question Four = 10 marks)

Section A continues on the next page

Question Five

T, a member of the finance team, has been constantly arriving late to work and in recent months he has consistently made significant errors in his work. A number of colleagues have complained to P, their line manager, about T's aggressive behaviour towards them and V, a junior administrator, has suggested that T has bullied her.

P knows he must take action to deal with the situation.

Required:

Explain to P what is involved in the process of taking disciplinary action.

(Total for Question Five = 10 marks)

(Total for Section A = 50 marks)

End of Section A

Section B starts on the opposite page

[You are advised to spend no longer than 45 minutes on each question in this section]

ANSWER *BOTH* QUESTIONS FROM THIS SECTION – 25 MARKS EACH

Question Six

VRC is a family owned business which has been manufacturing racing cycles for over a century. Over the years, the company has been relatively successful, although its growth has tended to happen in what can only be described as an unplanned, ad hoc, and opportunistic way. To some extent the developments have been as a result of the personal interests of F, the owner and Managing Director, who was a former road racing cyclist.

Two years ago, R, who is F's son, joined the company. The plan is for him to succeed as Managing Director when his father retires. To date he has spent his time working in the various departments to familiarise himself with the operations of the company. More recently, R has taken on a more strategic role and, in particular, is trying to form a view on the longer term future strategic direction the company should take. He acknowledges the company has built up a strong brand but feels this could be used to expand into other product areas.

R has approached a Business Consultant for advice on strategic planning. In the first meeting, the Business Consultant has suggested that the company should adopt a more formal/rational approach to business planning and strategy development.

The Business Consultant has recommended that, as a first step, R should undertake a strategic analysis of the company in order to help R better understand its current position.

Required:

(a) **Distinguish** between the way strategy is currently developed in VRC Company and the approach the Business Consultant is recommending.

(12 marks)

(b) **Discuss** the strategic management models\frameworks that R could use in undertaking his analysis of the strategic position of VRC Company.

(13 marks)

(Total for Question Six = 25 marks)

Section B continues on the next page

TURN OVER

Question Seven

J Company is a retailer of fashion goods operating in a highly competitive market place. The Board of the company has given the go-ahead to redesign the company's website to make it more convenient for customers to use.

The project is currently at week 12 and there are problems with the functionality of the site and the fact that it is not easy to navigate. The Project Manager, CW, has expressed concern about the rising costs of the project and the time needed to improve the functionality. He estimates that the change to the functionality will delay the project by three weeks. CW understands that improved customer satisfaction (by making the website easy to use) is important. There will also be diminishing returns since the increased levels of customer satisfaction obtained by the change in functionality will be offset by the increased time and cost spent.

The Board has had feedback from the project team members who have complained that there has been a lack of visibility of CW. Team members have said that they were unaware of any deadlines as they had not been shown any plan or schedule of work and this had made it difficult to prioritise tasks and understand how they can contribute to the project.

The Board of J Company has called an emergency meeting with the Project Manager in order to come up with some immediate solutions which address the project slippage. It has been recommended that CW needs guidance on how to improve his management of project teams before he leads any future projects.

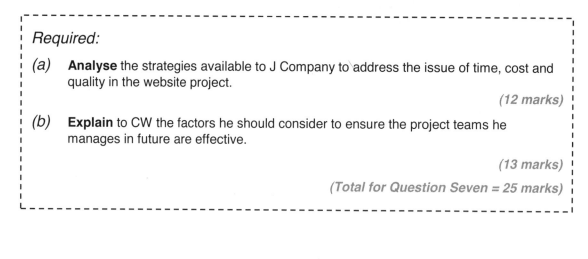

Required:

(a) **Analyse** the strategies available to J Company to address the issue of time, cost and quality in the website project.

(12 marks)

(b) **Explain** to CW the factors he should consider to ensure the project teams he manages in future are effective.

(13 marks)

(Total for Question Seven = 25 marks)

(Total for Section B = 50 marks)

End of Question Paper

LIST OF VERBS USED IN THE QUESTION REQUIREMENTS

A list of the learning objectives and verbs that appear in the syllabus and in the question requirements for each question in this paper.

It is important that you answer the question according to the definition of the verb.

LEARNING OBJECTIVE	VERBS USED	DEFINITION
Level 1- KNOWLEDGE What you are expected to know.	List State Define	Make a list of Express, fully or clearly, the details of/facts of Give the exact meaning of
Level 2 - COMPREHENSION What you are expected to understand.	Describe Distinguish Explain Identify Illustrate	Communicate the key features Highlight the differences between Make clear or intelligible/State the meaning or purpose of Recognise, establish or select after consideration Use an example to describe or explain something
Level 3 - APPLICATION How you are expected to apply your knowledge.	Apply Calculate Demonstrate Prepare Reconcile Solve Tabulate	Put to practical use Ascertain or reckon mathematically Prove with certainty or to exhibit by practical means Make or get ready for use Make or prove consistent/compatible Find an answer to Arrange in a table
Level 4 - ANALYSIS How you are expected to analyse the detail of what you have learned.	Analyse Categorise Compare and contrast Construct Discuss Interpret Prioritise Produce	Examine in detail the structure of Place into a defined class or division Show the similarities and/or differences between Build up or compile Examine in detail by argument Translate into intelligible or familiar terms Place in order of priority or sequence for action Create or bring into existence
Level 5 - EVALUATION How you are expected to use your learning to evaluate, make decisions or recommendations.	Advise Evaluate Recommend	Counsel, inform or notify Appraise or assess the value of Propose a course of action

Enterprise Pillar

Management Level Paper

E2 – Enterprise Management

November 2011

Tuesday Afternoon Session

The Examiner's Answers –
E2 - Enterprise Management

Some of the answers that follow in Sections A and B are fuller and more comprehensive than would be expected from a well-prepared candidate. They have been written in this way to aid teaching, study and revision for tutors and candidates alike.

Answer to Question One

Leaders have a number of sources of power that they can use to influence the behaviour and actions of others. A useful framework that can be used to describe the different sources of power that KK could use in managing the changes to the Finance Department is that proposed by French and Raven which includes referent, reward, coercive, expert and legitimate power.

- ***Referent power***, sometimes referred to as charismatic power, is found in a person who is respected, likable and worthy of emulation. The scenario mentions that KK is well liked and respected, and also highly regarded for the interest in and support she gives to those who work for her. It is, therefore, likely that she will have referent power which will help her in the change process, since people are often motivated to comply with requests made by a charismatic leader since they will want to please her and gain her approval.

- Another source of power is ***reward power***. This is where the leader is able to directly influence the intrinsic or extrinsic rewards available to followers. For example, this would include the ability to provide incentives for individuals who behave in a particular manner and the control over the organisation's resources such as salary, bonuses or promotion. This type of power is usually used in a positive manner. It is worth noting though that it can be used in a negative way through the threat or removal of rewards. As a senior manager, KK may have reward power that she could use to encourage people to adopt the changes in roles and responsibilities. As well as financial rewards, KK could use intrinsic rewards such as verbal praise and even, perhaps, recommendations for promotion.

- ***Coercive power***, as the term implies, is the ability to threaten, punish or deprive people of things that they value. This includes the use of penalties or sometimes physical punishments to enforce compliance. It is based on fears and the use of the 'stick' or sanction, making life unpleasant for people. It is doubtful that KK would want to resort to using this type of power, unless there is strong resistance to the changes, in which case she may have no choice. Whilst the immediate response might be compliance, it is unlikely to result in long term commitment by staff, but rather resentment, anger and possibly retaliation.

- ***Expert power*** is based on the followers' belief that the leader has certain expertise and knowledge relevant to a particular problem or issue. It will only work if staff acknowledge the expertise. The scenario suggests that KK is respected for her expert knowledge so this should assist her in introducing the new roles and responsibilities and should encourage respect from staff.

- **Legitimate power**, sometimes referred to as position power, is the power which is associated with a particular job and formal position in the organisational hierarchy which gives an individual authority to make decisions and command the action of others. It is when followers accept that the leader has the right to influence them in certain areas or aspects of behaviour. Since KK is a senior manager and leader of the change, she will be deemed to have legitimate power and hence the right to issue instructions to staff.

The list proposed of sources of power identified by French and Raven is not exhaustive and there are other sources of power, such as resource power, personal power and connection power, the latter resulting from personal and professional access to key people and information.

Answer to Question Two

As a project evolves it is important that the project is kept on track. A process of project control will ensure that performance is checked at regular times throughout the project process.

Project Planning

The early stages of the project must be spent carefully establishing a baseline plan that provides a clear definition of how the project scope will be accomplished on time, to budget and using available resources. The plan is establishing the targets that need to be controlled throughout the project.

The resource plan checks peaks and troughs of workload to ensure the plan is feasible and will list purchases to be bought. This enables the control of limited resources.

The time plan lists all of the activities, who will do what and how long each activity is planned to take. This includes the milestone finish dates of each stage of the project lifecycle and the estimated completion date of the whole project. This enables the control of critical activities.

The cost plan will include cost of products from the product breakdown structure, costs of purchases from the resource plan, plus any contingency in order to create a budget for the project. This enables the control of expenditure.

Calculate updated project timings, budget and resources

It is important for project control that all data is collected about the actual progress of the project. This should be collected on a regular timely basis. As the project evolves, it is important to monitor it continually in order to ensure that it is progressing towards the final objective.

This requires a continual measurement of actual activities, including monitoring activities started and completed, how long it has taken so far (and how long it is estimated to take up to completion), and how much money has been spent on each activity.

Analyse current status compared with plan.

When the update information has been collected a comparison needs to be made with the baseline budget and timings in order to determine whether any variances have occurred.

One of the most important aspects of project control is ensuring that monitoring progress is carried out on a regular basis. More complex projects are likely to require more frequent progress assessment.

Reports from the project manager to the project board should be made on a regular and frequent basis. Areas covered in the report would focus on progress in terms of cost, scope and time, with any variances from plan highlighted.

Identify corrective actions and incorporate into revised schedule.

The next part of the project control process would be to establish any corrective action required. If it is considered that the project is satisfactory and on target then no corrective action is required. If corrective action is required then how to revise the schedule or budget needs to be established. The project manager must report the deviation and, following authorisation if necessary, take corrective action to get the project back on target.

These control decisions may be very difficult as they will require a trade off of cost, time and scope. For example, getting the project back on time may require extra resources and therefore additional costs or a compromise on the original scope. Reducing excess expenditure may mean using fewer or lower quality resources which may again affect the overall scope and performance of the final project.

Once a decision is taken the changes must be incorporated into the schedule and budget. This project control process should be carried out continually throughout the duration of the project.

Ensure the revised schedule and budget is sent to all project stakeholders.
The updated schedule and budget need to be sent out, on a timely basis, to all project stakeholders. This control is important to ensure that all stakeholders are working with the correct updated version. The new version should be given a unique number so that everyone is clear about the items within the correct configuration. If any project stakeholder is working with an incorrect version of the plan this might take the stakeholder off in the wrong direction and result in a waste of time and effort.

Answer to Question Three

Transaction cost theory was originally proposed by Williamson and is concerned with the way in which resources are organised for producing a product or delivering a service. The foundation of the theory is based on how best an organisation can achieve economic efficiency.

The theory proposes that whilst asset specificity may drive vertical integration, outsourcing activities that are not viewed as core should be considered by the organisation. In the case of JKL Bank the key issue will be to determine whether or not the activities of the CCC are designated as a core business. It would also need to investigate whether the activities of the Car Insurance Customer Contact Centre (CCC) could be performed at a lower cost by external providers.

Transaction cost theory is essentially based on a more complex development of make or buy decisions. In other words, JKL Bank can choose between two mechanisms to control and carry out the activities of its customer contact service. The two mechanisms are hierarchy solutions, where the service is within the organisation using a hierarchical arrangement, or market solutions, where services are bought in, obtained through the market. Developing this further:

- *Hierarchy solutions* occur when management decides to own the assets or employ staff directly, in other words, internalise transactions. The policies and procedures of the Bank in this case would be used to control all resources and its performance. This is the way JKL Bank has operated to date.

- In contrast, *market solutions* are when the management of a company decides to buy in the uses of assets or staff capability from another organisation under the terms of a contract. This mechanism involves an increased reliance on the market and will result in the company incurring transaction costs.

The proposal to outsource the CCC would suggest that JKL Bank is looking to shift from a hierarchy solution to a market solution. Adopting this solution is based on the assumption that CCC activities can be provided at lower transaction costs by markets, and hence achieve the efficiency gains the Bank is requiring.

In making the decision on whether or not to outsource, JKL Bank needs to look beyond the fact the outsourced company can perform the activities of the CCC function more cheaply but must also consider the transaction costs. These will include those costs associated with performing a transaction with the organisation to which the CCC activities are being outsourced. The proposal will create reliance on an outside provider to provide the quality and reliability of service JKL Bank's car insurance customers expect. Therefore, the decision to use external providers will need to take into consideration the costs connected with managing the transactions and setting and monitoring service standards.

Other additional transaction costs JKL Bank will incur if it outsources are those associated with selecting a suitable partner, specifying what is required, writing and managing the contract, enforcing the contract, and communications with the partner organisation. A further consideration, given the nature of the outsourced activities, concerns the confidential nature of the information given to the external provider, such as bank account details.Therefore JKL Bank will need to put in place security measures as part of the contract to limit the risk of any breach in the use of confidential customer information.

Answer to Question Four

Like many other professional bodies, CIMA has adopted a professional code of ethics which is designed to regulate the conduct of its members and, in doing so, protect the individual client or employer and the public interests more generally. A number of fundamental principles are in danger of being breached by the actions of the Finance Director and D, if she accepts the bonus, as outlined in the scenario.

The Finance Director's claim for non-business related expenses does not observe the principle of **professional behaviour**. This states that a professional accountant should comply with relevant laws and regulations (in this case the regulations of the tax authorities). This could also be regarded as damaging public interests since in effect, as a local government authority, it is the public through payment of rates and taxes, who would ultimately be paying for the Finance Director's non-business related expenses. In condoning the behaviour of the Finance Director, D would also be taking action that could discredit the profession. In not informing the relevant authorities she is not carrying out her duties as a financial controller.

If D accepts the bonus from the Finance Director and remains silent, then the principle of **integrity** is compromised. D is not being honest in dealing with the non-business related expenses claims and is accepting a bonus to which she is not entitled. In making the claim in the first instance, the Finance Director is also in breach of the integrity principle because he has not acted in an honest way.

In addition, the principle of **professional competence and due care** is contravened since D is expected to deliver a competent behaviour towards her employer and act diligently in accordance with applicable technical and professional standards.

Whilst there is a principle of confidentiality with regard to the information acquired as a result of professional and business related relationships, in this particular case D would be expected to disclose the claim of non-business expenses to her employer, the local government authority. It is part of her professional duty to disclose to the local government authority the infringement of regulatory requirements by the Finance Director.

The principle of **objectivity** requires a professional accountant not to allow bias, conflict of interest or undue influence of others to override professional or business judgement. This could be compromised since D may feel she is under undue influence from the Finance Director. In accepting the bonus this could create a conflict of interest in that D may feel she needs to do whatever the Finance Director requests, because she may be worried that he might report her acceptance of the bonus at some point in the future.

In offering D a large personal bonus, the Finance Director could be guilty of the charge of bribery and attempting to corrupt a fellow employee if no action is taken. This could have the effect of damaging the standing of CIMA as a professional body.

Answer to Question Five

Disciplinary action requires a manager to use authority to deal with situations whereby an employee has made some offence. For example as in the scenario, T constantly arriving late for work, poor work performances, aggressive behaviour towards others and bullying. The main purpose of undertaking disciplinary action is to achieve a change in the behaviour of an employee so that future action is unnecessary. Whilst this should be viewed as a positive approach, in reality it is often seen as carrying out the threat of punishment rather than as remedial and corrective.

In advising P what is involved in the process of discipline, P must first check that T has been informed that certain behaviours could lead to disciplinary action, what constitutes misconduct and gross misconduct and what the consequences are. In large organisations this is usually covered in the employee handbook.

The starting point of the disciplinary process, in this case, would be for P, as T's line manager, to give T an informal warning. This would involve having an informal discussion to explore the issues and establish why T is behaving in an unacceptable manner and to try to determine how to resolve the problems. At this stage, it is important that P carries out a full investigation in order to be clear on what 'rules/regulations' have been broken, how frequently and the implications for other members of staff. T must be made aware of the complaints, and also provide his version of events. After the meeting a way forward should be agreed on and progress reviewed.

T should be advised that if, following the informal discussions, there is not an improvement in his behaviour, then it may be necessary to implement formal disciplinary proceedings. The HR Department should be involved and kept informed of what is happening.

If T's behaviour does not change P will need to move to the formal process, the first step will be to issue a formal verbal warning via an interview. This would highlight to T the seriousness of the situation and that he is on notice that his conduct will not be tolerated. At this stage it is important that T is asked if he wants to be represented or accompanied by a colleague. The purpose of this meeting should be to help T correct his behaviour and to prevent the need for future formal action. A written record should be kept, detailing why the action has been invoked and what level of improvement is required.

During the disciplinary interview P should explain its purpose and outline the charges regarding T's offences in an unambiguous manner, so the employee is clear on the reasons for the action. P should go on to explain the company's position with regard to the disciplinary issues involved. He should then explain the expectations on the individual with regard to future behaviour, for instance there must be no repetition of the offence, or performance must improve.

P should explain the reasons for the penalties, and explain that an entry of the formal warning will be made on T's personnel record. A record of the interview should be kept in T's staff file, for formal follow-up review, and in case of any future necessary action. There should be clear warning given about the consequences of T's failure to meet the improvement targets or continuation of inappropriate behaviours. The appeals procedure should then be explained.

The next step, if there is no improvement by T is a written warning, which is more formal in nature and will become a permanent part of the T's staff record. The nature of the offences will be stated and it should specify the future disciplinary action that will be taken if there is no improvement in T's behaviour. A copy of the written warning will be placed on T's staff record. The documentation is necessary in case of grievance procedures. As with the verbal warning, T has the full right of appeal.

If performance and behaviour problems continue it may be possible to demote T or to transfer him to another part of the organisation. The ultimate stage of disciplinary action is dismissal which could lead to T exiting the organisation.

In the UK, the Advisory Conciliation and Arbitration Service (ACAS) publishes booklets on internal disciplinary procedure, so P could also refer to this information to help him understand the process of discipline.

[*Note: Candidates may refer to practices governing disciplinary proceedings that are specific to their country*]

Answer to Question Six

Requirement (a)

The way strategy currently develops in VRC Company would seem to be characterised by the emergent approach to strategy development. This perspective was suggested by Mintzberg and is based on the notion that most of what organisations intend to happen, often does not happen. Indeed very few strategies followed by organisations are consciously planned but rather emerge.

Emergent strategies result from a number of ad-hoc choices or responses to circumstances. They can be described as developing out of patterns or behaviours that are realised despite, or in the absence of, specific intentions. This means that they just happen along the way with differing degrees of management intervention. The role of the manager is to craft a vision through moulding the organisation and its strategy.

Mintzberg argues that strategy formulation is a continually evolving process in which strategies emerge, as a result of the processes of negotiation, bargaining and compromise, rather than due to a deliberate planning process. He contends that intended strategies often becomes invalid and not implemented because the pace and unpredictability of developments in the business environment overtake it. The claim here is that strategy should not be considered a linear process, but rather an iterative process in which problems raised in implementation are fed back so that the strategy can be adjusted to take account of changing circumstances.

Mintzberg further maintains that the strategy development process is not so much about thinking and reasoning, as it is about involvement, a feeling of intimacy and harmony, developed through long experience and commitment. This is perhaps the case for F, who has adopted an opportunistic approach to strategy formulation which to some extent represents his own personal interests in the development of racing cycles.

In contrast, the formal/ rational approach that is being proposed by the Business Consultant, assumes a step by step organised approach to strategy development which requires a systematic analysis of competitors and markets. It involves the careful and deliberate formulation, evaluation and selection of strategies for the purpose of preparing a cohesive long term course of action to attain objectives. The three main stages are strategic analysis, strategic choice and strategic implementation.

The process is iterative and is often linked to an annual planning cycle. Strategic analysis helps in understanding the current position of VRC Company in terms of its internal and external environments in which the company operates. In other words, what its strengths and weaknesses are and what opportunities and threats exist. It also helps in formulating what the Company's mission and objectives should be which can then be communicated to employees.

The next stage in the linear process involves generating strategic options for VRC, exploring how it might develop in the future, given its current position. The different options would be evaluated in terms of whether each is feasible, suitable, and acceptable to VRC's key stakeholders.

The strategies selected need to be implemented, in other words strategy needs to be translated into action plans to make the strategies happen.

Requirement (b)

Analysing the strategic position of the VRC Company will involve an assessment of both its internal and external environment since the future strategy of VRC company needs to achieve a 'good fit' with its environment.

An external appraisal will involve scanning the external environment for factors relevant to the Company's current and future activities. A number of strategic management tools could be used to assist in this process. For instance the PESTEL framework could be used to analyse factors in the general environment for cycle manufacturing. This framework is used to categorise the environmental influences into headings, political, economic, social, technological, ecological and legal. This will assist in the assessment of the external factors that might impact on VRC's future strategic development and can help in identifying key trends and drivers for change in the industry for cycles.

As well as the general environment factors, part of the external analysis also requires an understanding of the competitive environment in order to establish what are likely to be the major competitive forces in the cycle industry in the future. A well established framework for analysis and understanding the nature of the competitive environment is Porter's Five Forces model. The basis of the model is that competition in an industry is determined by its basic underlying economic structure - the five competitive forces:

- Rivalry among existing firms
- Bargaining power of buyers
- Bargaining power of suppliers
- Threat of new entrants
- Threat of substitute products/services.

The results from the external and competitive environment analysis should help VRC gain a better understanding of the opportunities and threats it faces.

In understanding VRC's strategic position an assessment of the company's internal environment will also need to be conducted. This will involve appraising the company's internal resources and capabilities in manufacturing cycles, identifying the things which VRC is particularly good at in comparison to its competitors.

The analysis will involve undertaking a resource audit to evaluate the resources VRC has available and how it utilises those resources, for example financial resources, human skills, physical assets, technologies, brand and so on. It will help in assessing the company's strategic capability, which is to establish the adequacy and suitably of the resources and competences to survive and prosper in the bicycle industry.

The internal position of the company can be analysed by looking at how the various activities performed in manufacturing cycles by the company add value, in the view of the customer. To do this use could be made of the Value Chain model. The value chain of VRC can be divided into its primary activities and support activities. Each of these activities can be considered as adding value to the company's products or services.

The internal appraisal for VRC Company should highlight:

- **Strengths**, which are the particular skills or distinctive/core competences which the company possesses and which will give it an advantage over its competitors in the bicycle industry. These are the things the company should seek to exploit. In indentifying strengths it is important that it highlights not just what VRC Company is good at, but how it is better, relative to the competition, for instance brand.
- **Weaknesses**, which are the shortcomings in the company and which can hinder it in achieving its strategic aims. For example, lack of resources, expertise or skill.

Strengths and weaknesses should relate to industry key factors for success and help VRC Company to assess how capable it is in dealing with changes in its business environment.

Having undertaken an analysis of the external environment and internal capability that may be significant to VRC Company, the next step is to bring together the outcomes from the analysis. This is often referred to as a corporate appraisal or SWOT.

The outcomes from the analysis could then be used to determine VRC's current position in the bicycle industry and it will facilitate the identification and generation of possible future strategic options for VRC.

Answer to Question Seven

Requirement (a)

The successful accomplishment of the project objective is usually constrained by time, cost and quality factors. Time and cost tend to be positively correlated in projects (i.e. when time increases so does cost) as taking longer to complete a project generally means that human resources are needed for longer.

Project decisions on the strategies to implement are difficult as they will often require a trade off of cost, time and quality. For example getting the project back on time may require extra resources and therefore additional costs or a compromise on the original scope. Reducing excess expenditure may mean using fewer or lower quality resources which may again affect the overall scope and performance of the final project.

Time

If there is a degree of urgency in a project it may be possible to reduce the timescale to completion by adding additional resources. The timescale can also be reduced by scheduling overtime working. Both of these situations will increase cost while reducing time.

Resources could also be asked to work smarter, eliminating any distractions and focusing time on real output producing activities. The team should focus on activities that add real value to the website project for example the website functionality and eliminate any non-value adding activities.

Increasing the amount of resource will have an impact on profitability. The addition of resources will reduce the profit margin and indeed, in the extreme, may make the project itself unprofitable.

Although the deadline date is important to J Company, due to the revenues that might be generated by the website, it is unlikely to be crucial. It is unlikely that the customers will know that the website is being re-designed so will have no expectation of when the new site is due to come on-line. The deadline is not crucial in the wider scheme of things and there is no statutory requirement to deliver on time.

Quality

Project quality is usually about customer specification and requirement. Quality in terms of computer systems can be measured in terms of the number of errors, response times and fit-for-purpose, i.e. matches the business process it is intended to support.

For J Company, quality is linked to customer convenience and it will be important that the website is easy to use and navigate. A customer will want quick response times and a guarantee of secure transactions.

Fit for purpose is an important concept for a customer facing process. It is important that J Company has a clear understanding of the customer specification and requirements and that the project plan ensures that sufficient testing is included to ensure that quality requirements are fully met.

Costs

In order to manage the issue of costs, the website may have to have a slightly reduced scope in terms of its functionality. Any reduced scope might have an impact on how many customers use the site in the future. The importance of the customer perception has already been discussed. Any reduction in scope is likely to have a detrimental impact on the revenues generated by the website.

The Board J Company has recommended that CW needs guidance on how to improve his management of project teams. The following are some suggestions for CW:

Improve Leadership
As project manager, CW needs to dedicate time to a project and ensure they are visible to the key project stakeholders including the project team. He must continually encourage individuals and support progress. It will be difficult to achieve if he is not visible. CW must make himself more available when managing future project teams.

CW should create an environment in which members can feel free to contribute and provide feedback. He needs to determine the motivating factors important to each individual and should ensure that the project environment is a motivating one.

Increased Communication
Communication mechanisms should be set up by CW to ensure regular, multi-directional flow of information about plans, adjustments and progress of the project. CW could hold daily team review meetings with regular progress reports.

Clear Goals and Objectives
It is the responsibility of CW to explain the project objective to the team. The goals of the project need to be clear and the team needs to be focused on its achievement. CW must ensure that all team members understand their goals and the benefits of achieving them. Otherwise, they may work to their own objective rather than project objectives.

Team Building
CW needs to undertake team building throughout the life of the project. This will help with improving communications between team members and understanding project objectives. One way of helping with this would be to organise a social event outside the work environment, so the project team can get to know each other. CW could also periodically call team meetings (rather than project meetings).

Group Performance
CW needs to understand that effective group performance is affected by the manner in which groups come together. According to Tuckman's analysis, groups typically pass through four stages of development:

Forming is the first stage, in which members try to find out about each other and about how the group is going to work. CW needs to understand that this awareness stage is essential but not conducive to task effectiveness.

Storming is the second stage, this is more or less open conflict, but this may also be fruitful as more realistic targets are set and ideas are generated. CW needs to resolve the conflict so that the team can move forward to the next stage.

Norming is the next stage, team cohesion develops and the group establishes cooperation.

The final stage is **performing**, the team is now beginning to work smoothly and full productivity is achieved. It is only once this stage is reached that effective team performance is achieved.

Clear Team Roles
The team members need to be clear on how they can contribute to a project. CW must communicate the role and responsibilities of each team member and make sure each individual is clear on the specific role they are performing on the project. It is important that roles are not duplicated leading to a waste of time and effort. This would help the team to work smarter.

Mixed Balance of Individuals

Belbin suggests that an effective team is made up of people who, between them, fill nine roles. The model will help CW with team selection and management. Examples of team members would include the Plant who is a creative, imaginative individual who solves difficult problems. The Team Worker is cooperative, mild, and perceptive and who listens, builds, averts friction and calms the waters. If there is not the right balance of team roles, work will not be performed effectively.

Supervision of Team Activities

CW will be responsible for building a cohesive and productive team and also for supervising the activities of the team members throughout every stage of the project. He will need to respond to any difficulties and take appropriate action to keep a project on target for successful completion.